PRO
FOOTBALL
A TO Z

How does a blitz differ from a red dog? What is a hitch? A fill? A rouge? When did the Giants last win the National Football League championship? Who came up with the term "Super Bowl"? You'll find the answers to these questions and thousands more in *Pro Football A to Z*.

This a book on *all* of pro football—not just the NFL, but the Canadian League, the WFL, and all the associations, conferences, and leagues that preceded them—with concise historical information on every team from the Canton Bulldogs to the Philadelphia Bell. All the players are here, too: Thorpe, Grange, Hirsch, Nagurski, Baugh, Lombardi, Hornung, Unitas, Brown, Namath, Simpson, and dozens more. Every player of the year, every coach of the year, and every member of the Pro Football Hall of Fame is profiled in colorful detail. And each of these capsule biographies has been checked for accuracy by players, coaches, and team and league officials.

But pro football is a great deal more than just players and teams, and so is this book. *A to Z* is the first book to define all the words and phrases in pro football's specialized vocabulary. In addition, there are full discussions, accompanied by explicit diagrams, of all the important plays and formations. And extensive entries deal with point spreads, parlay cards, injuries, the player draft, the option clause, the Rozelle rule, and other such topics that conventional books avoid.

Sullivan's crisp, lively style makes the book a pleasure to read, whether you pick the

(continued on back flap)

(continued from front flap)

alphabetically arranged entries here and there or go from cover to cover. And it's all illustrated by more than 200 photographs and line drawings. For fans, spectators, sports writers, trivia freaks—anyone who follows football—*Pro Football A to Z* is a unique and useful guide, the most comprehensive reference available on the sport.

PRO FOOTBALL

A TO Z

A FULLY ILLUSTRATED GUIDE TO AMERICA'S FAVORITE SPORT · GEORGE SULLIVAN

WINCHESTER PRESS

Photographs were provided by the following: Pro Football Hall of Fame, pages 11, 12, 16, 33, 40, 43, 45, 66, 71, 74, 76, 82, 100, 103, 105, 110, 113, 119–124, 130, 133, 145, 150, 153, 161, 162, 168, 170, 172, 179, 190, 191, 195, 205, 209, 216, 218, 230, 262, 287, 302, 307, 310, 313, 316, 325, 330, 335; CBS-TV Sports, 25, 28, 94, 157, 282, 292, 298, 323; San Francisco 49ers, 23; Kansas City Chiefs, 59; New York Public Library, 73; Canadian Football League, 109; Buffalo Bills, 138; Detroit Lions, 220; Oakland Raiders, 280; Monsanto Chemical Corp., 294; National Football League, 327. All other photographs by George Sullivan.

Library of Congress Catalog Card Number: 75-9259
ISBN: 0-87691-202-1

Library of Congress Cataloging in Publication Data

Sullivan, George, 1927–
  Pro football A to Z.

  1. Football—Dictionaries.   2. Football—Biography.
I. Title.
GV951.S898   796.33′2′0922 [B]   75-9259
ISBN 0-87691-202-1

Published by Winchester Press
205 East 42nd Street
New York, N.Y. 10017

Printed in the United States of America

1881291

Introduction

The aim of this book is to provide the pro football fan with an intimate knowledge of the game and its participants. Words and expressions are defined; players and other individuals important to the sport are profiled.

In preparing a book of this type, one intended to increase the reader's knowledge but not bewilder him, the problem is often not what to include, but what to leave out. To set down the definition of every word and term common to pro football would result in a book unwieldy in size, and one which surely would add to the confusion that has already been generated.

Not to include the esoteric has thus been one objective. Simplistic terms—e.g., first down and shoestring tackle—have also been avoided.

In selecting the players and individuals profiled, several criteria were used. The book's listings for "Player of the Year" and "Coach of the Year" are based on the annual Associated Press selections in those categories. The "Most Valuable Player" in each Super Bowl contest is a *Sport* magazine selection. All members of Pro Football's Hall of Fame are included in the book.

Every team that has ever played in the National Football League (NFL) is listed, as are teams that were members of the American Professional Football Association (APFA), the various American Football Leagues (AFLs), the All-America Football Conference (AAFC), and the World Football League (WFL).

A book of this type necessarily relies on others to some extent. These have been helpful sources: *The Dictionary of Sports,* by Parke Cummings (A. S. Barnes); *The Language of Pro Football,* by Kyle Rote (Random House); *The Football Playbook,* by Sam DeLuca (Jonathan David); The New York *Times Guide to Spectator Sports,* by Leonard Koppett (Quadrangle); *Pro Football U.S.A.,* by Hal Higdon (G. P. Putnam's), and *The National Football League Digest of Rules* (National Football League).

Many individuals were especially helpful to the author. Special thanks are offered Don Weiss and Joe Browne of the National Football League; Murray Rose, sports editor, Associated Press; Don Smith, Pro Football's Hall of Fame; Bill Brendle, CBS Television; Lou Sahadi, *Pro Quarterback,* Gary Wagner, Wagner-International Photos; Frank Ramos and Jim Trecker, New York Jets; Ed Croke, New York Giants; and Pat Horne, New England Patriots.

AAFC

See All-America Football Conference.

action point

One of the innovations introduced by the World Football League in 1974, the action point refers to the method used in attempting to score an extra point following a touchdown. There is no placekick play. Instead, the ball is placed on the 2½-yard line for a run or pass attempt for the extra point.

AFC

See American Football Conference.

AFL

See American Football League.

A formation

An offensive formation developed by Steve Owen, coach of the New York Giants, in 1937. It came at a time when most teams were using the single wing (which *see*), with the line unbalanced to one side and the members of the backfield deployed on that side. The A formation had an unbalanced line, too, but the backfield was set to the other side. As in the single wing, the tailback received the ball on a direct snap from center.

The name "A formation" had nothing to do with the way in which the players were aligned. "Owen

A formation

1

had planned to use several different formations," according to Hank Soar, a backfield man for Owen for many years, "so he called this one the A formation, with the others to be B, C, and D. However, he ended up using this one almost exclusively."

During the early to mid-1940s most of the pro teams of the time switched to the T formation. Not the Giants; they stayed with the A until 1949.

Akron Pros

APFA team, 1920, 1921; won APFA championship, 1920. NFL team, 1922–1926.

All-America Football Conference

Founded in 1946, taking advantage of the postwar surge in the economy, the All-America Football Conference was an eight-team league with Eastern and Western Divisions. In its first year of operation the Eastern Division consisted of the Miami Seahawks, Buffalo Bisons, Brooklyn Dodgers, and New York Yankees. The teams in the Western Division included the Chicago Rockets, San Francisco 49ers, Los Angeles Dons, and Cleveland Browns.

The league was successful in luring more than 100 players away from the NFL, and quality football was often the result. The Cleveland Browns, coached by Paul Brown and quarterbacked by Otto Graham, became one of the most powerful football teams of all time. They won the league title in each one of the four years the AAFC operated.

A bidding war for playing talent, combined with sluggish gate receipts, were significant factors in the league's demise. After the 1949 season, the AAFC agreed to surrender to terms dictated by the NFL. The Cleveland Browns, San Francisco 49ers, and Baltimore Colts were taken into the NFL, but the remaining teams disbanded.

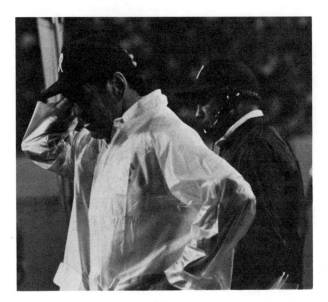

Allen

Allen, George

Coach of the Year, 1967, 1971.

The method used in assembling a championship team is well known. You build with the draft, selecting players carefully round by round. It takes years, of course, but that's the route that Don Shula, Chuck Noll, and Bud Grant followed.

The exception was George Allen, the *rare* exception. No one else operated the way he did. When he took command of the Washington Redskins in 1971, he embarked on a frantic trading program, bartering future draft choices for veteran players. The "Over the Hill Gang," the team called itself.

Once he had what he thought to be a winning team, Allen sought to motivate them. "Football games aren't necessarily won by the best players," he said often. "They're won by the team with the best attitude."

Thus, Allen sometimes sounded and acted like an evangelist, exhorting his men to give 100 percent and then a little bit more. THE DIFFERENCE

3

BETWEEN MEDIOCRITY AND GREATNESS IS EXTRA EFFORT, proclaimed a locker-room sign. When on the sidelines, Allen never stopped yelling and cheering.

Redskin fans were ecstatic about the way Allen did things. And why not? In his first four years with the 'Skins, he always managed to bring them to the playoffs, and in 1972 he took them all the way to the Super Bowl.

Allen used much the same philosophy in Los Angeles, where he coached from 1966–1970. And it worked there, too. He took a team that had had nothing but losing seasons for almost a decade and soon had the players winning division titles.

Before taking over as the Rams' head coach, Allen served for eight years as an assistant to the Bears' George Halas. Allen's college experience spanned nine seasons with Morningside College in Sioux City, Iowa, and Whittier College in Whittier, California.

During Allen's pro days, people kept making dismal predictions about his future teams because there were never any young players around. That never bothered Allen. He just kept winning.

All-Pro

A member of a team voted as the best in professional football. The most prestigious All-Pro teams are selected by the Professional Football Writers Association of America, the Associated Press, United Press International, and the Newspaper Enterprise Association.

American Football Conference

One of the two conferences of the National Football League, consisting of the Eastern, Central, and Western Divisions. The other is the National Football Conference. Conference champions meet each year in the Super Bowl.

American Football League

To most people, the name "American Football
League" refers to such teams as the Oakland
Raiders, New York Jets, and Buffalo Bills that
began operation in 1960 under the AFL banner.
The league merged with the NFL in 1966, although
it continued to play a separate schedule until 1970.

American Football League

But that was not the first attempt to establish an
American Football League; it was the fourth.

The premiere effort occurred in 1926. When Red
Grange, C. C. Pyle, his manager, and George
Halas, owner of the Chicago Bears, sat down to
negotiate Grange's contract for the 1926 season,
Pyle asked that his client be given a part ownership
in the Bears. His demand was based on Grange's
enormous box-office appeal the season before. But
Pyle might just as well have asked Halas to wrap
up the Tribune Tower and hand it over to him. He
had not the slightest intention of parting with any
of the Bears' stock.

Pyle's next gambit was to request an NFL franchise in New York City. Nineteen of the 20 teams
that made up the league were in favor of granting
his request. The 20th team, the New York Giants,
weren't, and Pyle was thus frustrated a second
time.

But not for long. He and Grange established the
first American Football League, and they granted
themselves the New York franchise, calling it the
Yankees.

Other teams included the Boston Bulldogs,
Brooklyn Horsemen, Chicago Bulls, Cleveland
Panthers, Rock Island Independents, Los Angeles
Wildcats, Newark Bears, and Philadelphia Quak-
ers. The Quakers, finishing the season with a 7–2
record, won the league title, then, in what might be
termed pro football's first Super Bowl, lost to the
NFL's Giants, 31–0.

Many of the AFL teams became so engulfed in
red ink that they were unable to finish the season.
Those that did manage to struggle through chose
not to resume operations the next year. Pyle was

5

not greatly saddened, for he was given permission to operate the Yanks as an NFL team, and that was all he wanted in the first place.

The next attempt to get an American Football League going occurred in 1936. It fielded such teams as the Boston Shamrocks, Brooklyn Tigers, Cleveland Rams, New York Yanks, Pittsburgh Americans, Rochester Tigers, and Los Angeles Bulldogs. Unable to withstand the competition from the more solidly entrenched National League, this AFL agreed to disband after the 1937 season.

A third AFL tried to get established just three years later, and offered such teams as the Boston Bears, Buffalo Indians, Cincinnati Bengals, Milwaukee Chiefs, New York Yanks, and the Columbus Bullies. The league remained active for just one season, the Bullies winning the championship.

The most successful of the American Leagues was organized in 1959 and began competition the following year. Lamar Hunt, son of the wealthy Texas oilman, H. L. Hunt, played a dominant role in its founding. Hunt had tried to purchase an NFL team and switch it to Dallas. When his efforts were thwarted, he decided he would start a league of his own.

In its first season the league consisted of the Dallas Texans, Los Angeles Chargers, Oakland Raiders, Denver Broncos, Houston Oilers, New York Titans, Buffalo Bills, and Boston Patriots. Joe Foss, a legendary World War II hero and former governor of South Dakota, was named the league's commissioner.

It was rough going in the early years. Teams did not try to hire NFL players at first, and rosters were composed largely of rookies and castoffs. The quality of play was often poor, and the fans stayed at home. The Los Angeles team fled to San Diego. Dallas was to switch to Kansas City and become the Chiefs. The Titans ended up in bankruptcy court, emerging as the Jets.

Little by little attendance increased, but what really saved the league was a contract with NBC for television rights which enabled the teams to share in a $36 million jackpot. "After I signed that contract [in 1964]," Joe Foss said, "people stopped asking me if we were going to make it. Everyone knew we were."

The war between the two leagues grew hot in 1966. Al Davis, who was the Raiders' coach and general manager at the time, replaced Foss as commissioner, and embarked on a bold plan of signing established NFL players. Davis's Oakland team announced it had Roman Gabriel, quarterback for the Rams, under contract, and John Brodie of the 49ers was said to be going to the Oilers.

The merger soon followed. On June 8, 1966, the AFL and NFL agreed to form a combined league of 24 teams, expanding to 26 teams by 1968. The two leagues played separate schedules until 1970, but agreed to meet in a championship game—the Super Bowl—in 1967.

In May, 1970, three NFL teams—the Cleveland Browns, Baltimore Colts, and Pittsburgh Steelers—joined the AFL teams to create the American Football Conference. The other NFL clubs became the National Football Conference. Beginning in 1970, the Conference champions met annually in the Super Bowl.

American Professional Football Association

The first professional football league. Formed during September, 1920, in Canton, Ohio, the Association consisted initially of 13 teams: the Akron Pros, Buffalo All-Americans, Canton Bulldogs, Chicago Cardinals, Chicago Tigers, Cleveland Panthers, Columbus Panhandles, Dayton Triangles, Decatur Staleys, Detroit Heralds, Hammond Pros, Rochester Jeffersons, and Rock Island Independents.

The Association was reorganized the following year, and Jim Thorpe was elected league president. He served for a year, being replaced by Joe F. Carr, who represented the Columbus Panhandles. The American Professional Football Association

7

was renamed the National Football League in 1922. Eighteen teams were active in league play that year. The Canton Bulldogs were the NFL's first champion.

APFA

See American Professional Football Association.

AstroTurf

See synthetic turf.

Atlanta Falcons

NFL team, 1966 to present.

audible

The signal shouted by the quarterback at the line of scrimmage which serves to change the play called in the huddle. The practice is also known as checking off or calling an automatic.

The quarterback calls an audible—or "audibilizes"—when confronted with a defensive formation he did not anticipate. There are games when a quarterback may use only two or three audibles. Other times, he may call only a handful of plays in the huddle. "But you can't call too many audibles," Joe Namath once said, "because you wind up having the defense dictating your strategy."

automatic

See audible.

B

back, n.

While the term "back" usually refers to a member of the offensive backfield—the quarterback or either of the two running backs—it also applies to members of the defensive secondary, to either of the safeties or cornerbacks.

backer-up

Now obsolete, the term "backer-up" was once used to describe the defensive player (or players) who played behind the line and in front of the deep backs. Today the position is known as linebacker.

backfield

On offense, the backfield consists of the quarterback and the players who line up behind him. Thus, the term usually refers to the quarterback and the two running backs. But it can also include the tight end (in the case of the tight I formation).

On defense, the deep backs—the two cornerbacks and two safeties—comprise the backfield.

back judge

A member of the six-man officiating team, the back judge lines up from 15 to 17 yards from the line of scrimmage on the defensive team's side of the ball, and on the same side of the field as the line judge. He looks for pass interference and, with the field judge, rules on field-goal attempts. He also makes decisions on out-of-bounds plays on his side of the field.

backward pass

See lateral.

balanced attack

In 1973, the year that O. J. Simpson set all those rushing records, becoming the first player ever to exceed 2,000 yards for a season, O. J.'s team, the Buffalo Bills, hardly challenged for the championship of their division. The next year O. J. was much less spectacular, but the Bills were competitive from the very first game. The reason for the change was a sharp improvement in their passing attack. The Bills, at last, had balance, a balanced attack.

As Paul Brown once put it, the best teams are always those that achieve a 50–50 balance in yards gained rushing and passing. On any given play from scrimmage, they are just as likely to run as to pass. The defense can never relax.

balanced line

Ⓣ Ⓖ Ⓒ Ⓖ Ⓣ

balanced line

An offensive alignment in which an equal number of players aré positioned on each side of the center.

ball-control offense

A conservative style of attack characterized by an emphasis on running plays, with occasional short passes. A team that employs ball control is usually seeking to keep possession for a sustained period of time to protect its lead.

Baltimore Colts

AAFC team, 1947–1949.

NFL team, 1950, 1953 to present; won Coastal Division championship (Western Conference), 1968; won Western Conference championship, 1958, 1959, 1964, 1968; won Eastern Division championship (American Conference), 1970; won American Conference championship, 1970; won NFL championship, 1958, 1959, 1968; won Super Bowl V (1971).

band squad

See taxi squad.

Battles, Cliff

Hall of Fame, 1968.

Battles

Before the Redskins played in Washington, Boston was the team's home and Braves its name. Cliff Battles, a splendid breakaway runner out of West Virginia Wesleyan, was the team's star. "He plays football because he loves it," the team's press book said of Battles, "and the rougher the game, the wider his smile."

In 1933, his second year with the team, Battles led the league in rushing, and did it again in 1937, gaining 838 yards. He thus became the first man to capture the rushing title twice.

The year 1937 was also memorable for his team, which by that time had been shifted to Washington. In the championship game, the Redskins vs. the Chicago Bears, Battles, on the first play from scrimmage, gathered in a Sammy Baugh pass and raced 42 yards with it. Not long after, he scored the game's first touchdown. The Redskins won, 28–21, to capture their first NFL title.

That winter, Battles, who had been earning about $4,000 a year, wrote to Redskin owner George Marshall and asked for a raise. He had, after all, led the league in rushing and carried the Redskin attack in several key games.

All Battles wanted was another $1,000 or so. But

11

Marshall turned him down. Battles reacted by signing with Columbia University as a backfield coach.

Pro football thus lost a colorful performer. As for the Redskins, it took them until fairly recent times to develop a running back with skills the equal to those of Cliff Battles.

Baugh, Sammy

Hall of Fame, 1963.

Baugh

He was a rancher in his later years, slim and wiry, and with the same deep-set blue eyes. He would rise before dawn, slip into a pair of blue jeans, grab a cup of coffee, then it was out to the barn to saddle his horse.

This was west Texas, the town of Rotan, about an hour's drive north of Sweetwater. Sammy Baugh put his money into a ranch there where he raised cattle. Counting what he leased as well as what he owned, it came to 35,000 acres, a pretty good-sized spread considering Sam's biggest paycheck was $21,000.

Some people say Sammy Baugh was the greatest quarterback in the history of pro football. If he wasn't, he came awfully close. Surely no other quarterback had the impact upon the game that he did. When George Marshall signed Baugh for his Washington Redskins in 1937, the forward pass was used only out of desperation. To advance the ball, the tailback ran with it or handed it to someone else who did. Baugh, with his whiplike right arm, helped to change that, establishing the forward pass as a standard method of attack.

When Baugh retired in 1952, the NFL record manual was awash with his name. Remarkably, many of the records he set are still on the books. In 1945 he completed 128 out of 182 passes, giving him a 70.33 completion percentage, the all-time high for a season. He led the league in passing six times, another record.

Baugh holds records as a punter, leading the

league in punting four times. He also played as a defensive back, and he is one of the handful of players who holds the record for intercepting four passes in a game.

But it's for his passing that Baugh will be remembered. Sid Luckman, as quarterback of the Chicago Bears, a contemporary of Baugh's, once called Sam the "nearest thing there is to passing perfection.

"He's so automatic that he hardly ever looks at his receivers, and he cuts the ball loose so quickly that opposing linemen seldom have a chance to smear him or force him to hurry his passing to the point of inaccuracy."

Several times following his retirement as a player, Baugh was lured back into pro football. In 1960 Harry Wismer hired Sammy to coach the New York Titans of the American Football League. Baugh stayed two years. In 1964 Sammy coached the Houston Oilers. Three years later he was an assistant coach with the Detroit Lions for a short time.

Obviously, ranching, not coaching, was his forte. Or playing the game. As he approached his 60th year, he looked, according to visitors to his ranch, as if he could still boom a punt 50 yards or so, or whip the ball to a fast-breaking receiver.

Bednarik, Chuck

Hall of Fame, 1967.

When Chuck Bednarik broke in with the Philadelphia Eagles in 1949, pro football was going through a period of technical change. For one thing, the day of the linebacker was beginning to dawn. The new 4–3 defense called for a player who could lurch forward to plug a hole in the line, swing wide to stop a sweep, and get back quickly to defend against a pass.

The man had to be tall, strong, and agile. The Giants had Sam Huff to play the role. The Lions had Joe Schmidt. In Philadelphia, it was Bednarik.

Bednarik

Bednarik did all the things a linebacker had to do, but he did each with a certain ardor. Once, in the final minutes of an important game against the Giants, the Eagles leading 17–10, Frank Gifford caught a pass and broke into the open. Only Bednarik and the Eagles' safety had a chance to tackle him.

"He saw me coming," Bednarik says, "but he made the mistake of taking his eye off me for a second to check the safety. When he did that, I ran right through him. He went down and the ball went up." Bednarik might also have said that Gifford went out, which he did. He was, in fact, unconscious for 36 hours.

Chuck Noll, then a guard with the Cleveland Browns, once made the mistake of smashing a forearm across Bednarik's mouth, driving his front teeth through his lips. Three years went by. Then one day the Browns were playing the Eagles, and Bednarik looked across the line to see Noll.

"Let's get that guy," he said to a teammate. "We high-lowed him. It took three guys to cart him off the field."

Bednarik's style must have made him an awful lot of enemies. But it also earned him All-Pro honors nine times.

The crowds loved him. In the 13 years he played for the Eagles, the fans never booed him once. Maybe they were afraid to.

Bell, Bert

Hall of Fame, 1963.

"For me there was never anything but football," Bert Bell once said. Indeed, it was true. His father was the Attorney General of the state of Pennsylvania and a brother became its governor, but Bell, a little round man with a gravelly voice, had no desire for either politics or government service.

In 1933 he organized a syndicate that bought the Frankford Yellowjackets, and he moved the team from the suburbs into Philadelphia proper, renaming it the Eagles. He was the club's president, manager, coach, bookkeeper, cashier, and press agent. He later sold his interest to become a part owner of the Steelers.

Other club owners persuaded Bell to become the league's commissioner in 1946, a post he held until his death in 1959. During his tenure Bell helped to achieve a better competitive balance among the various teams by improving the schedule-making process. When a betting scandal threatened, he formulated realistic rules and regulations concerning the gambling menace.

It was Bell who set the merger terms when the National League absorbed the All-America Football Conference in 1949. And it was Bell who saw the wisdom of "blacking out" television sets in home cities when the local team played there.

Pro football prospered during the 1960s and came to enjoy a lofty status on the American sports scene. Bert Bell and the policies he established must be given part of the credit.

belly back, v.

On a sweep or other running play to the outside, the movement of the ball carrier away from the line of scrimmage to either gain momentum or allow the blocking to form.

Berry, Raymond

Hall of Fame, 1973.

"For every pass I ever caught in a game," Don Hutson once said, "I caught a thousand in practice." Raymond Berry could have said the same thing.

Berry was not the fastest receiver in the league, nor was he elusive by nature. But in his 13-year career with the Baltimore Colts, he never stopped hustling. He was, as Tex Maule once observed, "a made receiver."

Berry failed to make his high school team until his senior year, and during his college career at

15

Berry

Southern Methodist he caught only 33 passes. Baltimore drafted him in 1955, but not enthusiastically.

The Colts didn't have a more dedicated player in camp that summer. Berry perfected his patterns by drawing key routes on adhesive tape he taped to his wrist. He posted signs in his locker, such as, "Look the ball into your hands, Raymond."

"I spend hours every day studying game movies of Hirsch and the other great ends who played in the league," Berry once said. "I could copy some of the moves they made exactly, with all of the fakes, just the way I saw them on the screen. But there were others I couldn't do because I wasn't as fast as some of those guys and not as big as others. You have to squeeze the best out of what you have."

Berry, by actual count, developed 88 different maneuvers to get free. "You couldn't leave the practice field," Johnny Unitas once observed, "until Raymond had run through each of his routes at least once."

There were days that the Unitas-to-Berry combination was virtually unbeatable. In the championship playoff game against the Giants in 1958, with the Colts winning in overtime, Berry caught 12 passes for 178 yards, and frequently he was double-covered.

In a crucial play in the overtime period, Unitas sent Berry down one sideline. When halfback Carl Karilivacz moved to cover him, Berry faked, turned, then headed in a new direction. Karilivacz got so tangled up in his own feet that he fell down, and Berry was in the clear. Unitas motioned him to go even deeper, then pitched him a strike. Shortly after, Alan Ameche plunged into the end zone for the game-winning touchdown.

Raymond (never Ray) was the league's leading receiver for three consecutive years beginning in 1958, and when he retired in 1967 he held the record for career receptions with 631 (a record later to be erased by Don Maynard). No one ever got more out of hustling.

Bidwill, Charles W.

Hall of Fame, 1967.

The Cardinals used to be in Chicago, and when they were, Charley Bidwill owned and operated the franchise. He bought the club in 1933 for $50,000.

There must have been many times he figured he'd made a terrible investment. The Cards frequently occupied last place in the standings and were always near the bottom in terms of total gate receipts.

Their chief problem was that they had to play second fiddle to the Bears. It has been said that even Bidwill himself rooted for the Bears against his own team in the years that the Bears were winning championships and the Cards were the league doormats.

In the 15 years that Bidwill ran the team—he died in 1947—the Cardinals had only two winning seasons and lost money every year. To persevere, the dictionary says, is "to persist or remain constant to a purpose or idea in the face of obstacles and discouragement." That was Charley Bidwill.

birdcage

The type of facemask worn by a lineman, made of thin steel tubing coated with rubber.

Birmingham Americans

WFL team, 1974; won WFL championship, 1974.

Birmingham Vulcans

WFL team, 1975.

blackout, n.

In 1950, several years before the television networks began to demonstrate any genuine interest

birdcage

in pro football, the Los Angeles Rams, who had been promised a financial guarantee if attendance was adversely affected, began telecasting home games within their home territory. Attendance nose-dived, and the television sponsor suffered severe losses.

Deeply troubled by the experience, NFL teams formulated a blackout policy, declining to televise home games for hometown fans. Several times in the years that followed, the league's right to do this was upheld in the courts.

The policy was modified somewhat in 1966 when the league began to permit telecasts of other games into teams' home territories on home-game days. Then, in September, 1973, the policy was all but revoked when Congress adopted a measure requiring that any NFL game that was sold out 72 hours prior to kickoff, had to be made available for local telecast.

BLESTO-VIII

One of pro football's scouting combines—the others are CEPO and QUADRA—the members of which gather and share information on college prospects. The teams affiliated with BLESTO-VIII are the Chicago Bears, Detroit Lions, Philadelphia Eagles, Baltimore Colts, Miami Dolphins, Minnesota Vikings, Buffalo Bills, and Pittsburgh Steelers.

blind-side block

A block directed at a player by an unseen opponent.

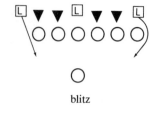

blitz

blitz

A surprise defensive maneuver in which one or more linebackers and/or safeties charge across the line of scrimmage in an effort to sack the quarterback. While blitzing can have a stunning effect, costing the offense a substantial loss of yardage, it leaves the defense vulnerable to quick, short passes. A blitzing team is usually gambling.

block, blocking, v.

To check a defensive player by legal body contact. The offensive player is permitted to use any part of his body above his knees. However, if he uses his arms he must keep them close to his body.

blocked kick

Any punt, field goal, or try-for-point attempt that is deflected or stopped by the defensive team. In the cast of punts and field-goal attempts, the ball becomes "free" following a block and may be recovered and advanced. When a try-for-point attempt is blocked, the ball is declared dead and may not be advanced.

blocking back

In the single-wing formation, the back who lines up directly behind one of the guards, and whose chief assignment is to protect the ball carrier. *See* single wing.

blue formation

A variation of the T formation used in short-yardage situations in which the fullback is positioned behind the quarterback, while the halfback is set to the strong side.

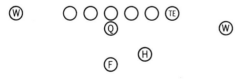

blue formation

bomb, n.

A long, long pass thrown with the intent of scoring a touchdown.

bootleg, n.

A play in which the quarterback conceals the ball by holding it against his hip following a fake hand-off. The bootleg is sometimes used in goal-line situations, with the flow of the play going in one direction and the quarterback in the other and into the end zone.

bootleg

Boston Bears

AFL team, 1940.

Boston Braves

NFL team, 1932; renamed Boston Redskins following 1932 season.

Boston Bulldogs

AFL team, 1926. NFL team, 1929.

Boston Patriots

AFL team, 1960–1969; won Eastern Division championship, 1963. NFL team, 1970; renamed New England Patriots following 1970 season.

Boston Redskins

NFL team, 1933–1936; won Eastern Division championship, 1936; franchise transferred to Washington following 1936 season.

Boston Shamrocks

AFL team, 1936, 1937; won AFL championship, 1936.

Boston Yanks

NFL team, 1944–1948; franchise transferred to New York following 1948 season.

box formation

An offensive formation similar to the single wing and used in the late 1930s by the Green Bay

box formation

boxman

Packers. It differed from the conventional single wing in that the line was balanced and the halfback positioned inside the right end. Used earlier by Notre Dame teams, it was sometimes called the Notre Dame box. The formation was judged to be more effective than the single wing on running plays to the weak side.

boxman

The member of the chain crew who is responsible for operating the down marker.

bread-and-butter play

When Vince Lombardi coached the Green Bay Packers, he sometimes referred to the power sweep as the team's bread-and-butter play, its payoff-the-mortgage play. The term refers to a team's most effective offensive weapon, the play it frequently uses in "must" yardage situations.

Brodie, John

Player of the Year, 1970.

Like the Golden Gate Bridge and Coit Tower, John Brodie was a San Francisco landmark. When he retired in 1973 after 17 seasons with the 49ers, the city just didn't seem the same.

Brodie was a rookie in 1957, watching from the bench as the team lost to Detroit in a conference playoff game. It was Brodie who served as tailback in 1960 and 1961 when coach Red Hickey was tinkering with the shotgun formation. Brodie managed to survive that, then endured the seasons of 1963 and 1964, when the 49ers won a total of six games. The fans booed Brodie at football luncheons and threw beer cans at him at Kezar Stadium.

Brodie won All-Pro honors in 1965, hitting on 61.9 percent of his passes, 30 of which went for touchdowns. But the 49ers won only half their games that year, and again the fans made Brodie shoulder the blame.

Coaches came and went quickly and quietly, like the Bay Area fog—Frankie Albert, Hickey, Jack Christiansen, and Dick Nolan. Other quarterbacks came, too. Billy Kilmer was one; George Mira and Steve Spurrier were two others. But no one ever unseated Brodie.

Then in 1970 everything seemed to fall in place. Gene Washington developed into one of the league's best pass receivers, and Ken Willard proved a dependable running back. The club acquired Bruce Gossett, giving them a capable kicker, something they had always lacked.

Brodie

Brodie went out and won the Western Division title that year. Suddenly he was Mr. Wonderful, winning a truckload of awards.

Brodie wasn't surprised. "The way they pick these things you have to play on a winning team," he said. "They never pay attention to losers."

His teammates agreed that Brodie had always been an outstanding quarterback; it was just that no one noticed. "The fact that we didn't win was never his fault," said veteran tackle Ken Rhode. "He's no different this year. It's just that he had receivers who could catch the ball, and his protection was good."

Brodie and the 49ers, as if to show their winning in 1970 was no fluke, captured the Western Division championship again in 1971 and did it a third time in 1972.

Brodie became one of only five passers in football history to pass for more than 25,000 yards, and one of only four to complete more than 2,000 passes.

Brodie shrugs when you mention the statistics. But the championships are another matter. He always felt he was a winner. The championships helped him to prove it.

23

Brooklyn Dodgers

NFL team, 1930–1943. AAFC team, 1946–1948; club merged with the New York Yankees for 1949 season.

Brooklyn Horsemen

AFL team, 1926.

Brooklyn Lions

NFL team, 1926.

Brooklyn Tigers

AFL team, 1936. NFL team, 1944.

brown formation

A variation of the T formation in which the fullback takes a set position behind the quarterback, while the halfback is positioned to the weak side.

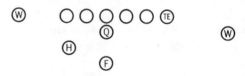

brown formation

Brown, Jim

Most Valuable Player, 1957, 1965; Hall of Fame, 1971.

For the nine years he played for the Cleveland

Browns, Jim Brown was the greatest of all running backs, and he is frequently rated as the best running back in football history.

He compiled an extraordinary list of achievements. Besides being named Most Valuable Player twice, he was the NFL's Rookie of the Year in 1957 and a Pro-Bowl selection every year he played. With more than 12,000 yards, he is No. 1 on the league's all-time rushing list, and the No. 2 man is more than a mile behind him.

Brown was 6-foot-2; he weighed 230. As these statistics imply, he was a punishing runner, but he was unusual in that he had quickness to go with his power. He also had stamina, durability, and the balance of a high-wire performer.

Willie Davis, an All-Pro defensive end for the Green Bay Packers who played against Brown, once described what it was like to tackle him: "We called a blitz, and I had the responsibility inside, and they ran a draw with Brown carrying. It was me and him, one on one. Well, I hit him, hit him good, and we both went down, and it was one of the few times in my life when my whole body was aching. Only my pride made me get up."

Born in Georgia, Brown grew up on Long Island, New York, and graduated from Manhasset High School in 1953 after winning 13 letters in five sports. While attending Syracuse, he won All-America honors as a halfback in football and as a midfielder in lacrosse.

Brown's name is everywhere in the NFL record manual. These are the rushing records he holds:

Most seasons leading league—8
Most consecutive seasons leading league—5
Most attempts, lifetime—2,359
Most yards gained, lifetime—12,312
Most games, 100 yards or more—58
Highest average gain, lifetime—5.2
Most touchdowns, season—19
Most touchdowns, lifetime—106

Brown used to hold the record for the most yards gained in a season. O. J. Simpson of the

Jim Brown

Buffalo Bills, who rushed for 2,003 yards in 1973, broke it. Willie Davis voiced the opinion of fans of Jim Brown when he said, "If Cleveland ever decided Jim was going to get 2,000 yards in a season, he would have gotten it."

Brown retired after the 1965 season to pursue a motion picture career. He quickly became a Hollywood star. Naturally.

Brown, Larry

Most Valuable Player, 1972.

When Vince Lombardi took command of the Washington Redskins in 1969, people expected him to build the same kind of overpowering ground attack that had been so effective for him in Green Bay. And that's exactly what he did—or was beginning to do—until his death in 1970.

Larry Brown, a rookie in 1969, was the man that Lombardi chose to power the Redskins' running game. At halftime of the opening game of the 1969 season, Lombardi told the starting running backs that they were being replaced by Brown and Charlie Harraway, who had just been obtained from the Cleveland Browns. Brown and Harraway quickly became the best running combination in the history of the Redskins.

Lombardi told Brown that he could gain 1,000 yards a season, if he wanted to pay the price, the price being the pain and suffering he'd have to endure. Brown stood 5-foot-11 and weighed 195 pounds. Being crunched to the ground by men who are considerably taller and 50 or 60 pounds heavier can cause some agonizing moments, indeed, some agonizing seasons.

Brown grew up in a section of Pittsburgh known as The Hill. "You wouldn't go there and stand on a corner," he once said. "You had to be rough just to survive. There were no playgrounds. I learned to play football on concrete."

While Brown was always quick, he was successful because of his toughness and determina-

Larry Brown

tion. He punished himself to get that extra yard. "He's not only a scary runner," Redskin quarterback Sonny Jurgensen once said, "taking those horrible spills all the time, but he's also a scary blocker. The way he blocks, I swear he's going to kill someone, or maybe himself."

Brown made his recklessness pay. He gained 1,125 yards, best in the league, in 1970, and 1,216 yards in 1972. He was the mainstay of the Redskin attack that season, which saw the team take the National Conference crown, but lose to the Dolphins in the Super Bowl.

Brown's 860 yards in 1973 gave him a career total of 5,037 yards. Jim Brown and O. J. Simpson were the only other runners in NFL history to gain more than 5,000 yards in their first five seasons.

The price was high, however. Brown suffered so many leg injuries he lost count, and more than once he was hospitalized because of them. Injuries sharply reduced his effectiveness in 1974, and he did not carry the ball with nearly the frequency he had in the past. The price, he realized, kept getting higher all the time.

Brown, Paul

Hall of Fame, 1967; Coach of the year, 1953, 1972.

"I was with Buffalo in the old All-America Conference," Abe Gibron, later coach of the Chicago Bears once recalled, "and we played the Browns three times. Every time I looked across the field I saw this little guy on the sidelines and I wondered how he was able to put together such a team.

"When I went with the Browns, he still seemed a little small, but I was impressed by the way he handled negotiations. And when I got to my first Browns' camp I was really impressed."

The "little guy," of course, was Paul Brown, a giant among the game's coaches. Anyone who has ever had any contact with him comes away just as impressed as Gibron was.

It was Brown who was the first to organize

27

Paul Brown

coaching, developing a full-time staff and carefully planned practice sessions. Playbooks, game plans, and the calling of plays from the sidelines are other Brown innovations.

If his contributions to the game don't impress you, his record may. As coach of the Cleveland Browns in the All-America Football Conference, beginning in 1946, Brown won the league championship four consecutive years, and the team continued as champions in 1950 after switching over to the NFL. In 13 NFL seasons, Brown won seven divisional titles and three league championships.

After a five-year hiatus, Brown came back to pro football in 1968 as head coach and general manager of the Cincinnati Bengals. Although he had a squad made up largely of rookies and castoffs, the Bengals were never a pushover team, and in 1970, their third year of existence, Brown guided them to a division title. They won the division crown again in 1973.

One day when Brown was coaching the Browns, a promising rookie showed up at camp wearing a T-shirt, soiled pants, and shabby sneakers. "I'm sorry," Brown said to him icily, "there's been a mistake. See the business manager. He'll arrange your transportation home."

If Brown's attitude has changed over the years, no one has been able to detect it. He still believes in and enforces strict discipline. He treated the players' strike in 1974 as a personal affront, defying the strikers and not without success, if you measure success in the terms of numbers of defectors. No one ever accused Paul Brown of mellowing.

During the 1974 season the Bengals defeated the Colts in a game that marked Brown's 200th coaching victory. "I don't pay any attention to those things," he said afterward. The next week his Bengals were to play the Steelers, and to Brown that was the only thing important at the time.

Brown, Roosevelt (Rosey)

Hall of Fame, 1975.

Offensive linemen hardly ever make the Hall of Fame. Only four have been inducted in the past 25 years or so—they are Chuck Bednarik (who was known chiefly as a linebacker), Lou Groza (a kicker), Jim Parker, and Roosevelt Brown.

A 6-foot-3, 255 pounder, Brown became a starting offensive tackle for the New York Giants in his rookie season of 1953, then held the job for 13 years. He also reinforced the Giants' defensive line in goal-line situations.

During Brown's career, the Giants won six divisional titles and, in 1956, the NFL championship. Brown himself won Lineman-of-the-Year honors that season. He was an All-NFL performer for eight consecutive years beginning in 1956. After his retirement as a player, Brown was an assistant coach for the team and later became a scout.

brush block

Quick, light contact on the part of an offensive player, to delay a defensive man's charge. Usually the blocker has a second assignment. For example, an offensive lineman will brush block a defensive lineman before hitting a linebacker, or a tight end will brush block a lineman before heading downfield for a pass.

buck, n.

Virtually obsolete; a term used to describe a dive play, a quick thrust into the line.

Buffalo All-Americans

APFA team, 1920, 1921. NFL team, 1922, 1923, 1925.

Buffalo Bills

AAFC team, 1947–1949; won Eastern Division championship, 1948. AFL team, 1960–1969; won Eastern Division championship, 1964–1966; won AFL championship, 1964, 1965. NFL team, 1970 to present.

Buffalo Bisons

NFL team, 1924, 1927, 1929. AAFC team, 1946; team renamed Buffalo Bills following 1946 season.

Buffalo Indians

AFL team, 1940.

Buffalo Rangers

NFL team, 1926.

bullet pass

A hard-thrown pass that travels on a rod-straight line.

bump and run

Kent McCloughan was a cornerback for the Oakland Raiders for six years beginning in 1965. Toward the end of his career, McCloughan had difficulty covering some of the young speedsters coming into the league. He did, that is, until he developed a new defensive technique. He would line up opposite the receiver to which he was assigned, and when the man broke across the line of scrimmage, McCloughan would belt him, then run with the man for a few steps, then, if he thought it was necessary, belt him again, and so on down the field. Perhaps it should have been called the belt and run; "bump and run" really doesn't suggest the violence involved.

There was nothing illegal about the practice since the rules permitted defensive players to make contact with prospective receivers until the ball was thrown. The bump and run became widely used throughout the American Football League and was adopted by many NFL teams following the merger.

You don't hear very much about the bump and run any more. The reason you don't is because of a rule change that became effective in 1974 that stated that once the receiver has advanced three or more yards downfield, he can be bumped only once. The penalty for violating the rule is five yards and an automatic first down. Kent McCloughan would never have approved.

buttonhook

See hook.

C

See center, n.

cab squad

See taxi squad.

call, v.

To select an offensive play.

Canadeo, Tony

Hall of Fame, 1974.

When the Packers' Tony Canadeo was elected to the Hall of Fame, it was as a running back, and largely for what he did in the 1949 season—rush for 1,052 yards for a last-place Green Bay team. He was only the third player in National League history to cross the 1,000-yard mark.

But the smallish Canadeo, known as the "Gray Ghost" because of the color of his hair, could have been categorized as a quarterback. Throughout his 11-year career with the Packers, he frequently filled in at that position, and in 1943, the year that Cecil Isbell retired, Canadeo passed for 875 yards and nine touchdowns.

Canadeo also won praise as a defensive back and was often an interception leader. He ran back kickoffs. He punted and returned punts. And in 1951 when the Packers were short on receivers, Canadeo starred in that role, catching 22 passes and averaging 10.3 yards per catch.

"Canadeo shouldn't be classified as a runner,

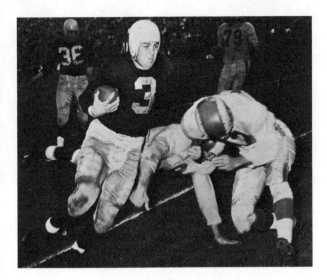

Canadeo

passer, or defender," Don Smith of Pro Football's
Hall of Fame once said. "Just 'football player.'
It's the only title that seems appropriate."

Canadian Football League

Suite 908, 11 King St., Toronto 105, Ontario.

The Canadian Football League is composed of
four Eastern Conference teams—Montreal, Ot-
tawa, Toronto, and Hamilton—and five in the
Western Conference—Winnipeg, Saskatchewan,
Edmonton, Calgary, and British Columbia. The
season opens during the first week in August,
about the same time NFL teams are playing the
first preseason games, and continues until mid-
November, with teams playing a 14-game in-
terlocking schedule. The early start is necessary to
avoid the below-freezing temperatures, indeed,
below-zero temperatures, of late November and
December. Weather is an important factor through
most of the season. Significantly, the program
book for a recent championship game had a folded
sheet-plastic rainhat taped to the inside cover.

Playoffs follow the regular season schedule. The second place team in each conference meets the third place team, with the winner playing the first place team for the conference championship. The two conference champions then meet for the league crown.

At a quick glance, Canadian football seems to be very similar to the American version. The center snaps the ball back to the quarterback who either hands-off to a running back or scampers back to throw to one of three or four receivers. Defensive strategy and tactics appear the same; there's a rush line, a defensive secondary, and linebackers in between. When the opposition runs the ball, the defensive men charge; on passes they drop off.

The game is made up of four 15-minute quarters. There's unlimited substitution, with players streaming on and off the field every time the ball changes hands. They sell hotdogs at games, the same tasteless kind they sell at games in the States. You can buy a knit hat in the colors of your favorite team, and a program costs a dollar.

Canadian Football League

But there are some differences. A team is given only three downs to make a first down, a rule that has many implications. One thing it means is that it's difficult to get a first down by running the ball, so you see plenty of passing. And the field is wider, and since it is, the passing is frequently the rollout type. There are no gimpy quarterbacks in Canada.

You don't get much tactical football. You seldom see a quarterback directing a long drive, picking apart the opposition, getting a few yards on an off-tackle slant, a few more on a flare pass, and then, when it's third and two, sending his fullback up the middle. The trouble is that a few yards is never enough; you need a big chunk every time. After Marv Levy had left George Allen in 1972 as coach of the Redskins' special teams to take over the Montreal Alouettes, someone asked him what was the biggest difference he encountered. "It was the realization," he said, "that you have to start getting your punting teams ready after first down."

Not only is the field wider, it is also longer. It is 110 yards long and 65 yards wide, with 25-yard end zones. Try to put a Canadian field in the old Yankee Stadium and one of the end lines, called "deadlines," would be somewhere out on River Avenue.

1881291

To help fill the bigger field, Canadian football teams have 12 players on each side. On offense, the added player is a backfield man, sometimes called a slotback, other times a wingback. He usually lines up on the left side, inside the wide receiver on that side, the one that used to be called the split end. On defense, the twelfth man is called a rover and stationed in between the two safeties. Exactly where he lines up depends on the offensive alignment and the game situation.

On each of its three downs, the attacking team is given 20 seconds to put the ball in play, as compared to 30 seconds in the NFL. This quickens the game's pace. Audibles are seldom called; there's usually not enough time. "First-sound" or "quick-count" snaps are more common than in the States.

A touchdown counts as six points; a field goal, three points; a safety, two points; and a conversion following a touchdown—referred to as a *convert*—one point. A team can also score one point by means of a rouge.

There are two ways of scoring a rouge. One way is when a punt or missed field goal goes into the end zone and is recovered by a defensive player who is then tackled, a type of play that can lead to some frantic moments. Quarterback Don Gault, a free agent at the New York Jets' training camp in 1973 and a man who had played a season for the Edmonton Eskimos, recalled a game in which the Eskimos were losing by one point and the team's punter booted the ball into the opposition end zone. When the returner saw that he was going to be trapped, he kicked the ball out again, which you are also permitted to do. "Then," according to Gault, "our man picked it up and kicked it back into the end zone to score a point. I thought there was a penalty there somewhere with all that

35

kicking, and I asked the coach about it, but all he said was, 'Ssshhh.'"

A rouge can also be scored when a punt or missed field goal goes out of bounds beyond the deadline. Joe Theismann, who quarterbacked the Toronto Argonauts before switching to the Washington Redskins, in 1974, recalls the Argos winning a game, 21–20, on a rouge. "We were inside their 20-yard line late in the game and we punted one past the end zone and into the stands. There was no way they could run it back."

Another original aspect of the kicking game is the rule covering punt returns. The ball must be returned—no fair-catching—and, further, the receiving team cannot block for the man doing the returning.

The same rule covers field-goal attempts that are short of the goal line. They must be returned without benefit of blocking.

Another difference concerns the movement of the backfield. In the NFL, at the snap, only one backfield man can be in motion, and he is not permitted to move forward, only laterally or away from the line. But in Canada, every player in the backfield is allowed to move in any direction. Sometimes it looks like there's been an explosion back there.

When kicking off under Canadian rules, the ball is spotted on the kicking team's 45-yard line. This means that the ball has to travel 65 yards to go into the end zone. And instead of kicking off after a field goal, the ball goes over to the team scored upon. It's first down on the team's 35-yard line.

The system of penalties is much the same. One exception, however, is a 25-yard penalty which Canadian officials assess for rough play or fighting.

Canton Bulldogs

APFA team, 1920, 1921. NFL team, 1922, 1923, 1925, 1926; won NFL championship, 1922, 1923.

Carr, Joe F.

Hall of Fame, 1963.

On April 30, 1921, the members of the American Professional Football Association, meeting in Akron, Ohio, decided to rename their organization, calling it the National Football League. They then elected Joe F. Carr, of Columbus, Ohio, as the new league's first president, and agreed to pay him a salary of $1,000 a year.

These were troublesome times for professional football. Franchises came and went like summer showers. There was a running conflict with the colleges over pro ball's winked-at practice of having college players play under assumed names. Then in 1925, when the Bears signed Red Grange off the University of Illinois campus, and Ernie Nevers, the great Stanford star, agreed to join the Duluth Eskimos, the skirmishing threatened to develop into a full-fledged war. But Carr, a dedicated little man, who also served as president of the American Basketball League, brought peace. He did it by getting the owners to meet and adopt a resolution that said in part: "It is the unanimous decision of this meeting that every member of the National Football League be positively prohibited from inducing or attempting to induce any college player to engage in professional football until his class at college shall have graduated . . ."

The rule, which has remained in effect to this day, served as one of the building blocks on which the pro game developed. It was also Carr, a charter member of the Hall of Fame, who sold Tim Mara on the idea of owning a pro team in New York, and George Marshall of the Redskins and Art Rooney of the Steelers became owners through Carr's efforts.

Before he died in 1939, Carr saw the player draft and the waiver system instituted. He championed the streamlining of the playing rules and the division of the league into conferences with an annual championship playoff. You'd have to say that $1,000 annual salary was money well spent.

37

CB

See cornerback.

center, n.

Someone once calculated that over the course of a season the center snaps the ball back to the quarterback at the line of scrimmage, to the punter on punts, and to the holder on field-goal and try-for-point attempts a total of about 900 times. What's lamentable about this statistic, at least according to the men who play the position, is that no one ever notices the center unless the snap is bad. To be good is to be anonymous.

Some centers snap with one hand; others with two. To some extent, it depends on the quarterback and how he wants to receive the ball. If the quarterback wants it point up, the center will probably have to use two hands. No matter what, the ball has to arrive so that the laces lie across the fingertips of the quarterback's right hand. The two men practice together until a perfect snap is automatic.

Of course, snapping the ball back is only one part of the center's job. He also has an assignment as a blocker on each play. These duties used to be much less demanding than they are nowadays. On the running plays, he was usually assigned to cut down the middle linebacker, a man about his equal in size and weight. In defending on pass plays, he

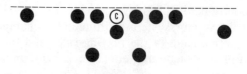

center

helped out a teammate or picked up a blitzer. In more recent years, with odd-front formations replacing the standard 4–3, the center has been looking up to see a big defensive tackle hovering over him. It's made a big difference.

On running plays, the center can, by coming off the ball low, hard, and very quickly, beat the tackle to the punch. On passes, where he has to retreat, it's tougher. The tackle can belt him with an open hand, then grab his jersey and pads and fling him to one side. Most coaches, realizing the center is in a disadvantageous position, assign one of the guards to help him out.

Another problem for the center, and one on which he gets almost no help at all, involves the snap for punts and field goals. The snap itself is not difficult; it's just that it makes him very vulnerable. He has to bend way over to be able to look between his legs at his target. The defensive player can really tee off on him—and does.

In the 1920s, the Bears' George Trafton, an All-Pro year in and year out, played at 6-foot-2 and 220 pounds. Mel Hein, like Trafton, a perennial All-Pro, was the standout center of the 1930s. He stood 6-foot-3 and weighed 230 pounds. Centers of the 1970s are not much bigger, averaging from 230 to 245 pounds.

Centers today are probably not as well known as those of past generations. Offensive guards, who get out and lead the blocking, have taken some of the play away from them. And it seems the fans are always watching the quarterback or the ball carrier.

But not only is the center anonymous, he's also underrated. After all, if he doesn't get the ball to the quarterback, it really doesn't matter what those other 21 guys do.

center, v.

To snap the ball back from the line of scrimmage.

CEPO

One of the three basic scouting combines (along with BLESTO-VIII and QUADRA), the members of which gather and share information on talented college players. Teams affiliated with CEPO include the Cleveland Browns, Green Bay Packers, New York Giants, Washington Redskins, Atlanta Falcons, New England Patriots, New Orleans Saints, and St. Louis Cardinals.

chain crew

The group of three assistants to the officials—a boxman and two rodmen—who handle the first-down yardage equipment. The boxman operates the down marker; the two rodmen handle the poles linking the ten yards of chain that indicate the yardage necessary for a first down. The chain crew is supervised by the referee and the head linesman.

Chamberlin, Guy

Chamberlin

Hall of Fame, 1965.

You can talk about Vince Lombardi and Don Shula, but the winningiest coach in pro football history is Guy Chamberlin. In five years as a coach, he won the league championship four times.

And his record as a player is even better. A tall, slim, swift pass receiver, Chamberlin's playing career covered six seasons, and in five of those his teams won NFL championships.

Chamberlin first came to attention as a halfback and defensive end at the University of Nebraska where he led the Cornhuskers to undefeated seasons in 1914 and 1915. After World War I, Chamberlin was invited by Jim Thorpe to join the Canton Bulldogs, and he was quick to accept. The Bulldogs didn't lose a game that season.

Chamberlin signed with George Halas and his Decatur Staleys in 1920. Like most of the other players, he worked part-time in the Staley starch factory. When Halas shifted the franchise to Chicago, Chamberlin went along. In those two seasons, the team lost only two games.

Chamberlin became player-coach of the Canton Bulldogs in 1922, guiding the team to an undefeated season. They didn't lose any games in 1923, either. Everywhere Chamberlin went, it was the same—in Cleveland as coach of the Bulldogs and in Frankford, Pennsylvania, as coach of the Yellowjackets. Only in 1925 did he allow his record to become tainted, when the Yellowjackets finished sixth in a 22-team league.

But the next year, the Yellowjackets were back in contention for the title. They faced the Bears in a crucial game late in the season. Chamberlin, playing end, broke through to block Paddy Driscoll's try-for-point attempt, and the Yellowjackets went on to win, 7–6.

Chamberlin is a member of both the Professional Football Hall of Fame and the College Football Hall of Fame. During induction ceremonies for the last-named, Earl (Red) Blaik described Chamberlin appropriately, calling him "a man who never learned how to lose."

Charlotte Hornets

WFL team, 1974 (franchise transferred to Charlotte from New York in midseason), 1975.

Chicago Bears

NFL team, 1922 to present; won Western Division championship, 1933, 1934, 1937, 1940–1943, 1946; won Western Conference championship, 1956, 1963; won NFL championship, 1932, 1933, 1940, 1941, 1943, 1946, 1963.

Chicago Bulls

AFL team, 1926.

41

Chicago Cardinals

APFA team, 1920, 1921. NFL team, 1922–1959; merged with Pittsburgh Steelers in 1944 and operated during season as Card-Pitt; won Western Division championship, 1947, 1948; won NFL championship, 1925, 1947; franchise transferred to St. Louis following 1959 season.

Chicago Fire

WFL team, 1974.

Chicago Rockets

AAFC team, 1946–1949.

Chicago Staleys

APFA team, 1921; won APFA championship, 1921; renamed Chicago Bears following 1921 season.

Chicago Tigers

APFA team, 1920.

check off

See audible.

Christiansen, Jack

Hall of Fame, 1970.

The Detroit Lions have always managed to excel

defensively over the past couple of decades, especially in the case of the defensive secondary. Such players as Lem Barney, Bruce Maher, Dick LeBeau, and Night Train Lane helped win the Lions a reputation for defensive superiority.

The tradition goes all the way back to 1951—to the defensive backs who played with Jack Christiansen and became known as "Chris's crew." They helped the Lions to win four division championships and three league titles. Christiansen was the left safety, and Jim David, Yale Lary, and Carl Karilivacz were other members of the unit.

There was no better defensive backfield in pro football during the period from 1951–1958. "Chris's crew" was responsible for 24 interceptions in 1953 alone, with Chris himself making 12 steals. "Detroit had the defense and Chris was the leader," Mac Speedie of the Browns, one of the best pass receivers of the day, once said. "We had one standard rule when we played Detroit—never throw into his area."

Lanky and loose-gaited, Christiansen played college football at Colorado A & M. Dutch Clark, one of the Lions' all-time greats, recommended him to Detroit coach Buddy Parker. Christiansen was a success right from the beginning.

"He's tough and he tackles hard," Dub Jones of the Cleveland Browns once said of Christiansen. "But he's a great defensive player because he's always looking 'through' the receiver to the passer. As soon as the ball leaves the passer's hand, he releases on his man and he's after it."

An All-League choice six times, Christiansen was also known for his talents as a punt returner. During the 1951 season, he returned four punts for touchdowns, a record. When he ended his career in 1958, he had returned a total of eight punts for touchdowns, a record no other returner has approached.

During the 1960s, Christiansen served as head coach of the San Francisco 49ers for several years. In 1972 he signed a long-term contract to become head coach at Stanford.

Christiansen

43

chucking

chucking

A rulebook word used to describe the "bump" phase of the bump and run. "Chucking," says the rulebook, "is a means of warding off a receiver . . . by contact with a quick extension of the arm or arms followed by a return of the arm(s) to a flexed position." Simply, it is a rap, a belt, a hit in the head. A defensive player is not allowed to "chuck" a receiver more than once.

✓Cincinnati Bengals

AFL team, 1937, 1940, 1968, 1969. NFL team, 1970 to present; won Central Division championship (American Conference), 1970, 1973, 1980

Cincinnati Colts

APFA team, 1921.

Cincinnati Reds

NFL team, 1933, 1934; franchise transferred to St. Louis in midseason, 1934.

Clark, Earl (Dutch)

Hall of Fame, 1963.

The list of quarterbacks in the Pro Football Hall of Fame includes such names as Sammy Baugh, Otto Graham, Sid Luckman, Bobby Layne, Y. A. Tittle, Norm Van Brocklin, and Bob Waterfield. Dutch Clark's name is on the list, too. Significantly, he's a charter member.

Clark's first years as a professional were spent with the Portsmouth (Ohio) Spartans, an NFL team from 1930–1933. Born in Fowler, Colorado,

Clark attended Colorado College, signing with the Spartans in 1931. When the franchise was switched to Detroit in 1934 and renamed the Lions, Clark went along.

In the years that followed, the Lions were often the dominant team in the National League, winning the NFL title in 1935. Clark won All-Pro honors four straight years beginning in 1934.

Besides passing the ball and drop kicking (he led the league in field goals in 1932), Clark was well known for his skill as a ball carrier. One of his coaches once compared him to "a rabbit in a brush heap," adding, "Just when you expect him to be smothered, he's free of tacklers."

Clark

Clark retired as a player in 1938, then stayed on as head coach. He later coached the Cleveland Rams.

But it's as a player that he's remembered. His talent and appeal were such that he helped to make the Detroit franchise one of the strongest in the league.

Cleveland Browns

AAFC team, 1946–1949; won Western Division title, 1946–1949; won AAFC championship, 1946–1949.

NFL team, 1950 to present; won American Conference championship, 1950–1952; won Century Division championship (Eastern Conference), 1967, 1968, 1969; won Central Division championship (American Conference), 1971; won Eastern Conference championship, 1953–1955, 1957, 1964, 1965, 1968, 1969; won NFL championship, 1950, 1954, 1955, 1964.

Cleveland Bulldogs

NFL team, 1924, 1925, 1927; won NFL championship, 1924.

45

Cleveland Indians

APFA team, 1921. NFL team, 1923, 1931.

Cleveland Panthers

APFA team, 1920. AFL team, 1926.

Cleveland Rams

AFL team, 1936. NFL team, 1937–1942, 1944, 1945; won NFL championship, 1945; franchise transferred to Los Angeles following 1945 season.

clipping

Blocking a defensive player from the rear—usually across the back of the legs—and in an area beyond the line of scrimmage. Clipping results in a 15-yard penalty which is paced off from the point of the infraction.

clothesline, v.

To strike an opponent, usually a receiver breaking downfield, across the neck or face with an extended forearm. Clotheslining is now illegal.

coffin corner

Any corner of the playing field within ten or so yards of the goal line. Punters, when they are close enough to the opposition goal to do so, aim for the coffin corner. Punting the ball out of bounds just short of the coffin corner means that the opposition will take over the ball at a point dangerously close to its goal line.

coin toss

Thirty minutes before the game begins, the referee calls the opposing captains together at the center of the field for the coin toss. The visiting captain announces which side of the coin will fall face up.

The winner of the toss makes one of two choices. He either decides whether his team will kick or receive, or he designates the particular goal his team will defend. The loser gets the remaining choice.

At the end of the first half, both captains meet with the referee to announce their choices for the second half. This time the loser of the pregame toss chooses first.

The two captains also meet with the referee in the center of the field three minutes before game

coin toss

time. It's at this time that the referee indicates which team will kickoff and which goal the receiving team will defend. "No toss is simulated at this time," the NFL rulebook stresses.

Columbus Bullies

AFL team, 1940; won AFL championship, 1926.

Columbus Panhandles

APFA team, 1920, 1921. NFL team, 1922.

Columbus Tigers

NFL team, 1923–1926.

combination

Any pass pattern in which two or more receivers work together to outwit the defensive coverage, as in the case of a crossing pattern.

compensation rule

See Rozelle rule.

completion

A pass legally caught.

Conerly, Charlie

Most Valuable Player, 1959.

While he now ranks as one of the most hallowed

quarterbacks in the long history of the New York Giants, Charlie Conerly suffered through many bleak seasons before he ever saw his team win anything. "Suffered" is the appropriate word.

In Conerly's first years with the Giants, key positions were often filled with rookies or aging veterans. Every time Conerly dropped back to pass, it seemed as if two or three opposition players went back with him. There were never any competent receivers to throw to, and the running game was almost zilch.

The fans came to identify Conerly with the team's ineptitude. They booed him and booed him. Signs hung from the stands that read BACK TO THE FARM, CONERLY and GET A NEW QUARTERBACK. Conerly and his wife seldom left their apartment. "We were afraid we'd be recognized," he said.

Tall and lean, Conerly bore a physical resemblance to Sammy Baugh. And his passes, like the Slinger's, were crisp and accurate. He had been a college hero at Ole Miss, and then a military hero with the U.S. Marines in the South Pacific. No one had ever booed him. No one had ever considered booing him.

Conerly quarterbacked the Giants to winning seasons in 1950 and 1951, but the next year a downhill slide began, reaching its low point in 1953 when the team finished with a 3–9 record, worst in its history up to that time. It got so that Conerly was hearing boos in his sleep.

When the season was over, Conerly returned to the tranquillity of his Mississippi farm and announced that he was retiring. He was 32 at the time, and he felt as though he had taken enough fan abuse and physical punishment to last him the rest of his lifetime. But the Giants made a coaching change, replacing Steve Owen with Jim Lee Howell, and Howell prevailed upon Conerly to return.

Charlie guided the team to the conference title in 1956, and then to a stunning 47–7 win over the Bears in the championship game. He and the Giants were back in the title game again two years later, this time to face the Colts. Ten of Conerly's

14 passes went for completions that afternoon, producing one Giant touchdown and setting up another, but few remember his brilliance. Johnny Unitas and the Colts triumphed in overtime.

The next year, 1959, was Conerly's best. After missing two midseason games with an injured leg, he came back to lead the Giants to another Eastern Conference title. He also won the league passing title that year.

The fans honored him with Charlie Conerly Day. The signs that hung in Yankee Stadium now read CHARLIE FOR PRESIDENT and CHARLIE, WE LOVE YOU.

Charlie was still throwing passes for the Giants in 1961 at the age of 40. But that was his last season. Of his final years with the Giants, he once remarked, "When I had a good day, they would call me the Old Pro. But when I had a bad one, I was the Old Man."

Connor, George

Hall of Fame, 1975.

A much-publicized All American at Notre Dame, George Connor was the No. 1 draft pick of the Chicago Bears in 1948. George Halas used Connor as a two-way tackle at first, but the young man's quickness and aggressiveness were such that he was later switched to linebacker.

It didn't make any difference where he played, Connor always excelled. He won All-Pro honors as an offensive tackle in 1951 and 1952, also as a defensive tackle in 1952, and as a linebacker in 1953 and 1955, the year that he retired.

conversion

The score made in a try-for-point attempt following a touchdown. Usually a conversion is achieved by means of a placekick, but it can be done by running or passing. *See* try-for-point.

Conzelman, Jimmy

Hall of Fame, 1964.

What was pro football like in the scruffy, ragtag days of the 1920s? Jimmy Conzelman knew as well as anyone.

"Those were the days when the cure-all for any injury was iodine and four fingers of bourbon," he once said. "The chief requirement for coaching was an off-tackle play.

"You had eighteen men on the roster. One time in Milwaukee we had three players injured, so the owner put on a uniform and sat on the bench, just to give us a look of depth.

"The first season I played, the sport was considered such a lowly occupation that I returned home without telling anybody where I had been or what I had been doing."

Jimmy Conzelman started in 1920, playing halfback for George Halas's Decatur Staleys. He went from the Staleys to the Rock Island Independents, where, at 23, he became the youngest head coach in pro history.

He coached two NFL champion teams—the Providence Steamrollers in 1928 and the Chicago Cardinals in 1947. He had the Cards back in the championship the following year, but they were beaten by the Eagles.

Conzelman's interests and talents extended beyond the world of professional football. At one time or another, he was an author, actor, boxer, baseball executive, newspaper publisher, radio broadcaster, public relations executive, and a raconteur and after-dinner speaker par excellence. As Conzelman himself once put it not long before his death in 1970, "I've done almost anything and everything I wanted to."

cornerback

Consider the poor cornerback. He has to cover the fastest, trickiest men on the field. Yet he never

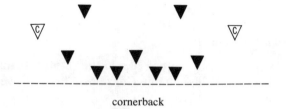

cornerback

makes the first move himself; he's always reacting. Seventy-five percent of what he does he has to do while running backwards. When he makes a mistake, everyone in the stadium knows it.

"The most important part of playing cornerback is not physical but mental," Lem Barney of the Detroit Lions, perhaps the finest cornerback of recent times, once said. "You've got to know your opponents. You've got to be prepared. What does this team, this quarterback, this receiver like to do in such and such a situation? You study the films and you play the game and you find out."

While the cornerback is primarily concerned with stopping passes, he also has certain responsibilities on running plays, working closely with the safety in this regard. Before the tackle can be made, however, they must force the play to the inside and strip away the blockers.

But it's the passes that cause cornerbacks the sleepless nights. Some try to control the receivers by intimidation, hitting a man with a shoulder or a forearm as he comes off the line. Others try to outwit the receiver by carefully studying him in films and scouting reports. Still others rely on distracting conversation.

How successful are they? Well, if you've glanced at any passing percentages recently, you know that cornerbacks are a long way away from solving their problems.

corner backer

A term used to describe either one of the outside linebackers.

corner linebacker

Either one of the outside linebackers; the right or left linebacker.

corner route

A pass route in which the receiver's final cut is toward the corner of the field; also called a flag route.

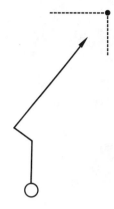

corner route

Coryell, Don

Coach of the Year, 1974.

Don Coryell turned the St. Louis Cardinals from perennial losers into division champions. He did it in 1974, his second year with the team, using an offense that didn't mind putting the ball into the air. "I want a quarterback who can explode the ball, particularly against the zone defense," Coryell said. "I like to score points. There are two things I have to have—a quarterback who can really throw and receivers who can catch."

Jim Hart was Coryell's strong-armed quarterback. In the spring of 1973, Coryell told Hart, who had shuttled in and out of the lineup under previous coaches, "You're my No. 1." Hart responded by developing into one of the league's most dangerous passers.

A college coach at San Diego State beginning in 1961, Coryell built teams around a strong passing attack. Among his quarterbacks were Don Horn and Dennis Shaw, both of whom became NFL quarterbacks.

Coryell entered the ranks of college coaches in 1957 when he was named head coach at Whittier College, succeeding George Allen there. After three winning seasons, Coryell became an assistant coach at the University of Southern California, then moved on to San Diego State. His Aztec teams had winning streaks of 21 and 25 games.

Coryell

When Coryell guided the Cards to the NFC's Eastern Division championship in 1974, it marked the first title for the team since 1948, when the franchise was located in Chicago. It was moved to St. Louis in 1960.

counter play

A type of running play in which the flow of the play is sent in one direction and the ball carrier goes in the other.

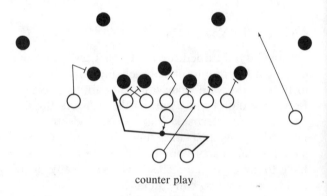

counter play

cover, v.

To defend against a potential pass receiver.

crackback block

A block usually delivered by a wide receiver who starts downfield as if running a pattern, then turns back to take out a linebacker or defensive end. The block must be executed above the waist.

crawling

An attempt to advance the ball after the official's whistle has sounded. Crawling can result in a five-yard penalty.

crossbar

The horizontal bar connecting the goalpost upright.

cross block

A maneuver by two offensive linemen whose paths crisscross as they carry out their blocking assignments.

crossing pattern

A pass pattern by two receivers who line up on opposite sides of the formation and whose routes crisscross as they break over the middle. The pattern can be run by two wide receivers, a wide receiver and the tight end, or even involve one of the running backs.

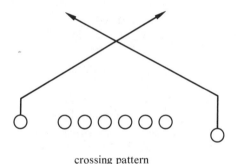

crossing pattern

Csonka, Larry

Most Valuable Player, Super Bowl VIII (1974).

Talk about Larry Csonka's style and you talk about power running. Darting, dashing, and hip swiveling—that's for people like O. J. Simpson. Straight-ahead power. That's what 240-pound Larry Csonka is all about. "He's like tackling a

55

Csonka

bulldozer with 9.5 speed,'' an opposition player once said.

A farmboy from Ohio, Csonka set scoring records and won All-America honors at Syracuse University. The Dolphins selected him in the first round of the 1968 draft.

His first years with the team were marred by head injuries, and more than a few people suggested that he quit the game. In time, Csonka came to rely on his forearms more than his head. He himself has another explanation: "My head-aches went away," he says, "when the blocking got better."

Csonka powered the Dolphin teams that won three consecutive American Conference titles beginning in 1971, and two Super Bowl games. In each of those three seasons, Csonka rushed for more than 1,000 yards.

Csonka was the unanimous choice for the MVP award in Super Bowl VIII, in which the Dolphins handled the Minnesota Vikings with relative ease. The first eight times he carried the ball, all in the first quarter, he gained 64 yards, scoring one touchdown and setting up another. The game was Dullsville after that.

Csonka finished the afternoon with 145 yards gained rushing, a Super Bowl record. Viking quarterback Fran Tarkenton said of him, "He just may be the best man ever at what he's paid to do."

Not long after the Super Bowl, Csonka, along with teammates Paul Warfield and Jim Kiick, sold his considerable talents to the World Football League or, more specifically, to the franchise owned by Toronto's John Bassett and which was to be located in Memphis. The NFL was rudely jolted by Csonka's decision. But to the league's linemen and defensive backs, it was the best news in years.

cup

See pocket.

curl

See hook.

cut, v.

Any quick change of direction by a running back or receiver.

cut-off block

Often this term does not refer to a block in the literal sense, but simply to movement on the part of an offensive lineman which permits him to seal off a defensive player's path to the ball carrier.

D

Dallas Cowboys

NFL team, 1952; franchise transferred to Baltimore following 1952 season. AFL team, 1960–1962; won Western Division championship, 1962; won AFL 1968, 1969; won Eastern Division championship (National Conference), 1970, 1971, 1973; won National Conference championship, 1970, 1971; won Super Bowl VI (1972).

Dallas Texans

NFL team, 1952; franchise transferred to Baltimore following 1952 season. AFL team, 1960–1962; won Western Division championship, 1962; won AFL championship, 1962; franchise transferred to Kansas City following 1962 season.

Dawson, Len

Most Valuable Player, Super Bowl IV (1970).

As quarterback Len Dawson of the Kansas City Chiefs began his 18th professional season in 1974, he could look back on a career studded with notable games.

He was twice a Super Bowl quarterback, a losing quarterback in Super Bowl I, a winner in Super Bowl IV. He was the quarterback in the "longest game in history," when his team, the Dallas Texans, beat the Houston Oilers in the 1962 American League championship. And he was the losing quarterback in an even longer "longest game in history," the 1971 American Conference playoff in which the Chiefs lost to the Miami Dolphins.

Dawson

It would take several pages to list all of Dawson's statistical achievements. Four times he was the American League's leading passer, and he holds most of the AFL's all-time passing records. He once threw six touchdown passes in a game.

"He may be the most accurate passer the game has ever known," Hank Stram, Dawson's coach for many years, once said of him. "Although he doesn't throw as deep as most quarterbacks or, for that matter, as far as most, he picks his spots and is deadly when he does throw."

It was Stram who recruited the lean, boyish-faced Dawson for Purdue when Stram was the Boilermakers' backfield coach. And it was Stram who claimed Dawson for the American League's Dallas Texans in 1962. By that time, Dawson had spent three years with the Pittsburgh Steelers and

59

two years with Cleveland. But he had seldom played; he was a benchwarmer.

Quarterbacking the Dallas Texans, who became the Kansas City Chiefs in 1963, was never terribly difficult. The team had an outstanding defensive unit and also featured a solid running game. Dawson threw enough to keep the opposition honest.

During those years, Dawson was seldom hailed by the pro football establishment, even though he was twice named the AFL's Player of the Year. His critics never let it be forgotten that he was an NFL reject, playing in what was thought to be a weaker league.

Dawson got a chance to still the criticism in Super Bowl I, but his performance that afternoon was less than heroic, and the Green Bay Packers were easy winners.

Three years later the Chiefs were back in the Super Bowl, this time to face the Vikings. The Chiefs led, 16–0, at halftime, but early in the third quarter the Vikes came surging back, narrowing the gap with a touchdown.

Dawson reacted by marching the Chiefs downfield, capping the drive with a 40-yard touchdown pass to Otis Taylor. The game's outcome was never in doubt after that, and Dawson was never again looked upon as a second rater.

Dayton Triangles

APFA team, 1920, 1921. NFL team, 1922–1929.

DE

See defensive end.

dead ball

Any ball which, under the rules, is no longer in play.

Decatur (Illinois) Staleys

APFA team, 1920; franchise transferred to Chicago following 1920 season.

defensive backfield

The four-man unit that consists of the two corner-backs and two safeties.

defensive end

Junious (Buck) Buchanan, 6-foot-7, 285 pounds, who distinguished himself as a defensive end for the Kansas City Chiefs for a bit more than a decade beginning in the early 1960s, once summed up his mission: ''To ring the quarterback's bell.'' Like all defensive ends, Buchanan was supposed to stop off-tackle thrusts and wipe out the blockers on sweeps, but ringing the quarterback's bell, that's what Buchanan always figured he was getting paid for.

To accomplish this, it takes a human of unusual size. Defensive ends are big, very big, 6-foot-6 or so and 260 pounds and up. Yet they're also very agile. Indeed, the trend in recent years has been toward ends who feature speed and quickness.

The right mental attitude is also important. You have to have the ambition to ring bells.

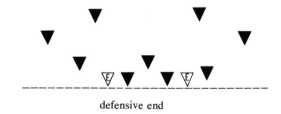

defensive end

defensive holding

Illegal use of the hands by a defensive player. The penalty is five yards and an automatic first down.

When the infraction occurs, it's usually on a pass play, with a defensive player holding a receiver's jersey to prevent him from running his pattern. If such holding occurs after the ball is released, it's called pass interference.

defensive line

The "front four"—the two tackles and two ends.

defensive tackle

The tackle position is the heart of the defense. It's where everything happens.

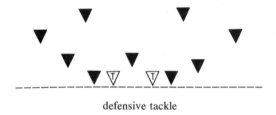

defensive tackle

It used to be that coaches would plug the position with the biggest body on the roster. The legendary Big Daddy Lipscomb was 6-foot-6, 284 pounds. The Giants had Rosey Grier, 6-foot-5, 285 pounds. If King Kong ever wandered into camp, he would have been tried at tackle.

Size is still important, but speed and versatility are now added requirements. Henry Jordan, a Green Bay defensive tackle during the team's glory years whose playing weight never reached 250, convinced coaches that size wasn't everything.

Like the defensive ends, the tackle's No. 1 job is to stop the ball carrier, or at least to scramble the blockers so that the linebackers can shoot in and bring the man down. His other assignment is to rush the passer. To a tackle, happiness is a sacked quarterback.

delay, n.

See draw play.

delay of game

Any action—or inaction—by either team which prevents the ball from being put in play promptly. The penalty is five yards. Delay-of-game infractions are usually called in cases where the offensive team fails to snap the ball within the allotted 30 seconds.

delay pass

Any pass pattern in which the primary receiver blocks or fakes a block before running his pass route. Usually the delay pass involves one of the running backs or the tight end, since the defensive players assigned to cover these men may go elsewhere if they can be made to believe they are not potential receivers.

Denver Broncos

AFL team, 1960–1969. NFL team, 1970 to present.

Detroit Heralds

APFA team, 1920, 1921.

Detroit Lions

NFL team, 1934 to present; won Western Division championship, 1935; won Western Conference championship, 1952–1954, 1957; won NFL championship, 1935, 1952, 1953, 1957.

Detroit Panthers

NFL team, 1925, 1926.

Detroit Wheels

WFL team, 1974; failed to complete season.

Detroit Wolverines

NFL team, 1928.

direct pass

A pass from the center to a backfield man or other player positioned several yards behind the line of scrimmage, as in the case of the center's snap to the punter, or to the quarterback in the shotgun formation.

direct pass

disqualified player

A player who is banished from the game for committing any one of a number of offenses, including kneeing or kicking an opponent, striking him with the fists, flagrant roughing of the passer or kicker, or for what the rulebook calls any "palpably unfair act."

dive play

A quick-hitting running play in which the back takes the quarterback's handoff and hits straight into the line. Its success depends on the back's quickness and also his ability to cut to the right or left, should the predetermined hole be blocked.

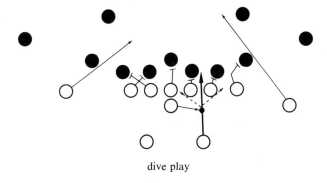

dive play

Donovan, Art

Hall of Fame, 1968.

Johnny Unitas is the all-time favorite among fans of the Baltimore Colts. But Art Donovan ranks a close second.

Donovan, a big, round tackle, with a rollicking sense of humor, is identified with Baltimore's championship years of 1958 and 1959. Donovan remembers those years, of course, but he also has some vivid memories of earlier days with the Colts—of 1950, for example, his rookie season.

The 1950 Colts dropped all seven of their preseason games, ten of their 12 regular season games, and then dropped right out of the league. The next season things were even worse. Playing with the

65

Donovan

New York Yanks, Donovan saw the team win only one game, and then the franchise was traded and transferred to Dallas.

Donovan stayed with the team. After playing four games at the Cotton Bowl before thousands upon thousands of empty seats, the Dallas franchise was turned back to the league. For the second half of the season, Dallas was a road team, traveling gypsylike from city to city. Their only win that year came on Thanksgiving Day in Akron, Ohio, when they beat the Bears before 3,000 paying customers.

Thirteen of the Dallas players caught on with the Colts when they resumed operation in 1953. Among them were defensive end Gino Marchetti, All-Pro cornerback Tom Keane, and Donovan. Coach Weeb Ewbank arrived the next year and, shortly after, Jim Parker, Big Daddy Lipscomb, Lenny Moore, Raymond Berry, and Johnny Unitas signed on. The championship years soon followed.

Donovan played an important role in the Colts' success, winning All-Pro recognition four times. But considering those first three seasons, Donovan should have been honored not so much as a player, but as a survivor.

double coverage

The guarding of one pass receiver by two defensive players. Usually one of the defenders will pick up the receiver as he leaves the line of scrimmage, and the other will move to cover him as he breaks deep.

double-double

A type of zone pass defense in which there are two zones deep and five short. Its name is derived from the fact that both wide receivers are double-covered, first by the cornerbacks as they leave the line of scrimmage and then, when they get deep, by the safeties.

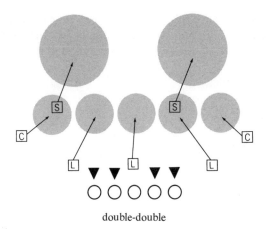

double-double

The double-double is used mostly in third-and-long-yardage situations, that is, when a gain of seven or eight yards is needed. It's difficult to complete a pass of that distance because the linebackers and cornerbacks create a picket-fence effect in the short zones. There's just no room there.

double foul

A rule infraction by both teams on the same down.

double-team, v.

To assign two offensive players to block a defensive lineman.

double-wing formation

A variation of the T formation in which a halfback is positioned just to the outside of the weak-side

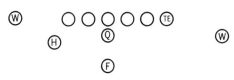

double-wing formation

67

tackle, and the fullback sets up behind the quarter-back. The double wing is used as a passing forma-tion, since it serves to get the halfback downfield quickly.

down, n.

An offensive play.

down-and-in

A pass pattern in which the receiver breaks straight downfield, then cuts over the middle.

down-and-out

A pass pattern in which the receiver races straight downfield before cutting toward the sideline.

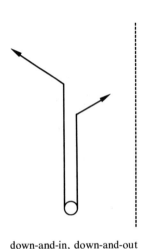

down-and-in, down-and-out

downfield

To the offensive team, any portion of the field beyond the line of scrimmage.

down marker

A metal rod approximately seven feet in length at the top of which is mounted a set of four numbered cards—1 to 4—which are used to designate the up-coming down. On each play, the down marker is also used at the sideline to spot the location of the ball; also called a down box or down indicator.

draft, n.

In May, 1935, the late Bert Bell, who owned the Philadelphia Eagles at the time, proposed that the

NFL adopt a player-selection system in which ready-to-graduate college players would be chosen by teams inversely according to the league standings; the last-place team would get first choice, next to last second choice, and so on. In February, 1936, the National League held the first of its annual selection meetings, an event commonly known as the draft.

Legend has it that Bell hit upon the idea of the draft in an effort to obtain top-drawer college talent for his Eagles, perennially one of the league's weak-sister teams. If the innovation did Bell's team any good, it was never reflected in the standings. In the five years that followed the institution of the draft, the Eagles won a total of ten games, and they never managed to have a winning season until 1943, a year they did enjoy a significant increase in playing talent, not by virtue of the player-selection proceedings, but through a merger with the Pittsburgh Steelers.

What happened to the Eagles, their year-in, year-out lack of competitiveness, should have been a tipoff that the draft really doesn't always serve to equalize the league's playing talent, something its proponents have been claiming since the days of Bert Bell.

Suppose the Miami Dolphins win the Super Bowl and the New Orleans Saints end up last in their division with the worst record in pro football. The following January the Saints would pick first in the draft. The Dolphins, in the first round, would pick last, or 26th.

In the second round, the Saints would begin again by choosing player No. 27. The Dolphins would select No. 52. The Saints, beginning the third round, take No. 53. The Dolphins then choose No. 78. The Saints' next pick is No. 79.

And so it goes through the ensuing rounds. The Dolphins choose No. 104; the Saints, No. 105. The Dolphins, No. 130; the Saints, No. 131. Obviously, the Saints are not making any headway.

Over the 17 rounds of the draft, the Dolphins and Saints choose 16 players who have virtually identical ratings. (Indeed, the Dolphins, in each instance, get a one-place edge over the Saints.)

The advantage to the Saints is that they get a No. 1 pick in the draft as compared to the final choice, No. 442, which goes to the Dolphins. This one player is likely to have superstar potential, but the important thing to remember is that it is only *one* player.

All of this shouldn't imply that the draft isn't important in building a team to championship strength. But doing so requires the services of scouts who are knowledgeable and perceptive in the evaluation of talent, and even then it is a long process, requiring several years. It never happens overnight.

draw play

A running play that looks initially like a pass, with the offensive linemen dropping off to pass block and the quarterback pedaling back, his arm cocked as if to throw. But as the defensive linemen charge in, the quarterback slips the ball to a running back who sifts his way through the onrushing defenders. Frequently the draw play is used against a hard-charging defensive line. If it's successful, they won't be charging quite so hard.

Clyde (Bulldog) Turner, the Bears' All-League

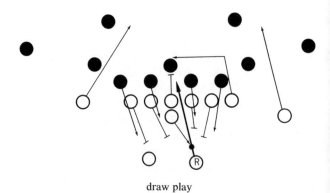

draw play

center during most of the 1940s, once claimed credit for originating the draw play. The Bears were playing the Packers, and Buckets Goldenberg, a Packer guard, kept diagnosing Chicago's pass plays, dropping off the line and covering a receiver as soon as the ball was snapped.

"Let's fake a pass and give the ball to the fullback," Turner told Bear quarterback Sid Luckman. "Then let him come right here where I am because there's no one here but me." When the Bears tried it, the fullback galloped as far as the safety before the Packers realized what had happened. The next year the play was included in the Bears' playbook, becoming a consistent ground gainer.

Driscoll, Paddy

Hall of Fame, 1965.

Before the days of specialization, the ambition of many young football players was to be a "triple threat" man, to be able to run, pass, and punt. Paddy Driscoll did better. He could run, pass, punt, *and* drop kick. A "quadruple menace," he was once called.

Driscoll

Driscoll was a college star at Northwestern, the team captain in 1916. During World War I, he enlisted in the Navy and was stationed at the Great Lakes Naval Air Station. He starred for the Bluejacket team that won the 1919 Rose Bowl, booting a field goal and throwing a touchdown pass to a speedy end named George Halas. After, Halas wanted Driscoll for his Decatur Staleys, but Paddy had already signed with the Chicago Cardinals.

When Halas shifted his team from Decatur to Chicago, a spirited rivalry developed with the Cards, and whenever the two teams opposed one another it seemed to bring out the best in Driscoll. In 1922, the Cards and Bears met twice, and the Cards won both games, 6–0 and 9–0, with all the points coming on Driscoll's drop kicks.

When Halas signed the great Red Grange in 1925, he introduced him to the Chicago fans in a game against the Cards on Thanksgiving Day that year. A capacity crowd jammed Wrigley Field hoping to see Grange put on a dazzling show.

But Driscoll was the center of attraction. Every time he punted the ball, he angled it away from Grange, and the Redhead never got loose once. The game ended in a scoreless tie.

As the teams were leaving the field, several thousand fans booed loudly. "It was a shame to hear those fans boo Grange," Driscoll said to his wife afterwards. "It wasn't his fault."

"Don't feel sorry for Grange," she said. "They were booing *you*."

Halas couldn't take it any longer. He went to the Cards and purchased Paddy's contract.

Driscoll remained with the Bears as a player until 1929, then stayed on as an assistant coach, and later became head coach. He guided the Bears to a Western Conference championship in 1956. Still later, he served as director of research and planning for the Bears.

drop

drop, n.

In punting, the release of the ball to the kicking foot. Poor kicks, say many coaches, are more the result of poor drops than any other single factor. The drop has to be as short as possible, with the hand releasing the ball as close as possible to the kicking foot.

drop kick

Dropping the ball to the ground and kicking it just as it rebounds used to be the accepted method of booting field goals and extra points. The ball was held in both hands, point down. The kicker tilted the ball back slightly as he dropped it, aiming his toe at a spot an inch or two below the middle. The ball traveled end-over-end.

Drop kickers were just as accurate as field-goal kickers are today, and they could get good distance. In an exhibition game in 1923, the Toledo Maroons beat the Kansas City Cowboys, 3–0. The points were scored on a 40-yard drop kick by Jim Thorpe.

The drop kick began to wane in popularity during the 1930s as the ball began losing its melon shape. With the slimmer, sharp-pointed ball, drop kickers were not always able to get a true bounce. Then in the 1940s, specialists like Lou Groza and Ben Agajanian began to demonstrate the remarkable consistency that was possible by place kicking.

The rules still permit the use of the drop kick for field-goal or try-for-point attempts. But high school and college coaches don't teach it any more, and pro coaches look upon it in much the same way they regard the single-wing formation and cardboard shoulder pads.

In his book, *The Secrets of Kicking the Football,* Dr. Edward J. Storey hailed the drop kick as being a superior weapon to the place kick. It's easier to learn, said Dr. Storey, and it can be executed quicker. And, in the case of a bad pass from center, it's much easier to get the kick away. In addition, since no holder is necessary, it gives the kicking team another blocker.

Dr. Storey admits that "today's football is easier to slice or hook than the old wide pre-1934 ball." But, he adds, "The problem is no greater in the drop kick than it is in the place kick." Dr. Storey notwithstanding, don't look for any drop kicks in the very near future.

drop kick

DT

See defensive tackle.

Dudley

Dudley, Bill

Hall of Fame, 1966.

Up until they began to achieve some degree of eminence in the early 1970s, the Pittsburgh Steelers were always among the lowliest of teams. Being inept was their stock in trade for more than 40 years.

There was, in fact, only one bright spot in the team's otherwise drab history. That occurred in the mid-1940s when a smallish halfback named Bill Dudley was smashing the opposition. Only 5-foot-10, 175 pounds, not particularly fast, but very elusive, Dudley led the NFL in rushing in 1946 and, as one of pro football's last 60-minute-a-game performers, also led in interceptions. He was the NFL's Player of the Year that season. It must have been a very easy choice.

Dudley also returned kickoffs and punts and did the team's place kicking. He expected his teammates to play with the same dedication and enthusiasm that he displayed. When he thought that someone was shirking his duty, he lectured him. This didn't win him any friends, but it helped to stop the Steelers from losing so much.

A college star at the University of Virginia where he set a national collegiate scoring record, Dudley was the Steelers' No. 1 draft choice in 1942. He led the league in rushing that season, won Rookie-of-the-Year honors, and became a favorite of the fans. His efforts helped the Steelers to finish second in their division that season, the first winning season in the history of the team.

Three years of military service followed. In his first appearance in a Steeler uniform following his discharge, Dudley scored two touchdowns in leading the Steelers to an upset win over the Chicago Cardinals. The next morning a headline in a Pittsburgh daily newspaper proclaimed: THAT MAN IS BACK.

Franco Harris, Terry Bradshaw, and Andy Russell are some others who are Pittsburgh heroes today. But real Steeler fans rate Bill Dudley with the best of them.

Duluth (Minnesota) Eskimos

NFL team, 1924, 1926, 1927.

Duluth (Minnesota) Kellys

NFL team, 1925.

E

Edwards, Turk

Hall of Fame, 1969.

One of pro football's first big men with good speed, the Redskins' Turk Edwards has been called one of the greatest linemen of them all.

He played for Washington State University from 1929–1931, then signed with the Boston Braves, who became the Redskins the next year. The franchise was switched to Washington in 1937. Edwards' playing career spanned nine seasons, after which he became the team's coach and, later, a Redskin vice-president. A tackle, Edwards won All-Pro recognition four times.

While Edwards was easy-going off the field, he was all business during the game once the game began. "When he got mad," a teammate once recalled, "he could handle one whole side of the line by himself." Since Edwards was 6-foot-2, 260 pounds, the best way to play him, as Lewis Atchison once suggested, was "gently and politely."

Edwards

eligible receiver

Any one of the five offensive players permitted to catch a forward pass—the two wide receivers, the two running backs, and the tight end. The quarterback and 11 members of the defensive team are likewise eligible receivers.

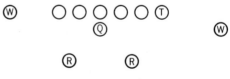

eligible receivers

encroachment

Movement by a player, usually a lineman, across the neutral zone before the ball's snap in which he makes contact with an opposing player. The penalty for encroachment is five yards.

end

Either of the two pass receivers who line up on opposite sides of the formation. *See* wide receiver. Also, the tight end or defensive end (which *see*).

end around

A running play in which a wide receiver or tight end, after hesitating at the line of scrimmage, wheels around to circle behind the quarterback and takes a handoff from him.

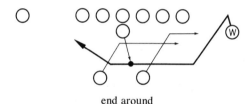

end around

end line

The boundary line at each end of the field; the end of the end zone.

end zone

The area between the goal line and the end line. It is 160 feet wide and 30 feet deep.

77

Evansville (Indiana) Crimson

NFL team, 1922.

Ewbank, Weeb

Coach of the Year, 1958.

Weeb Ewbank, who retired in 1973 at the age of 66, will always be remembered as the only coach to win championships in both the American and National Leagues.

Usually described as "a little round man," Ewbank directed the Baltimore Colts to NFL titles in 1958 and 1959. After he was relieved of his duties in Baltimore following the 1962 season, he signed with David (Sonny) Werblin, owner of the New York Jets.

Ewbank

Known for his organizational talents, Weeb organized the Jets all the way to the Super Bowl. There the team scored one of pro football's greatest upsets, whipping the heavily favored Baltimore Colts, 16–7. Ironically, the Colts were owned by Carroll Rosenbloom, the man who had fired Weeb several years before.

Weeb was never accused of being a disciplinarian. "I never had to force guys to practice," he once said. "I never wanted to. I never had to yell at them. I always believed in treating them like men."

extra point

The one-play, one-point scoring opportunity given a team that scores a touchdown. *See* try-for-point.

F

face bar

A horizontal length of plastic or metal tubing fastened to the helmet to protect the wearer's face. Since it is less likely to obstruct a player's vision than is a face mask, the face bar is worn by quarterbacks, running backs, and receivers.

face bar

face mask

The piece of protective equipment fastened to the helmet and consisting of horizontal and vertical lengths of metal tubing that is meant to protect the wearer's face.

face-masking

Grasping an opponent's face mask, usually that of a ball carrier, in an effort to halt his forward progress. Face-masking results in a 15-yard penalty.

fair catch

When a punt receiver believes he has no chance of advancing the ball, he has the option of signaling for a fair catch. This means he can make the catch without interference, but he is not permitted to advance the ball.

To signal a fair catch, the receiver raises one arm above his head while the ball is in flight. In attempting the catch, should he muff the ball, it's treated as any fumble.

fair catch

fake

Any movement by an offensive player meant to deceive the opposition, as in the case of a fake kick, fake pass, and so on.

Fears, Tom

Hall of Fame, 1970.

It was said that the 1951 Los Angeles Rams, the NFL champions that year, could score almost at will. They had what they called the Bull Elephant Backfield in Deacon Dan Towler, Tank Younger, and Dick Hoerner. They had two of the finest quarterbacks of all time in Bob Waterfield and Norm Van Brocklin.

81

Fears

And they had the flashiest ends of the day in Elroy (Crazylegs) Hirsch and Tom Fears. Both set records by the helmetful. Both are Hall of Famers.

Fears, a good-sized man at 6-foot-2, 220 pounds, lacked somewhat in speed and elusiveness, but he made up for it in his ability to outsmart the opposition. In 1948 he bacame the first rookie ever to win the NFL's pass-receiving title, and he won it again in 1949 and 1950.

In a game against the Green Bay Packers in 1950, Fears caught a record 18 passes. Many of the other records he established have been broken, but that one still stands.

Fears retired as a player in 1959, embarking on a career as coach. The results have been mixed. He served as an assistant coach for the Rams, Packers, Falcons, and Eagles. He has been head coach of the Saints and, in 1974, the WFL's California Sun. Coaching has had its rewards, but catching passes was much simpler.

field goal

Three points, earned on a play from scrimmage when a placekick (or drop kick) travels over the

field goal

crossbar and between the goalpost uprights. Field goals attempted and missed when the line of scrimmage is beyond the 20-yard line result in the defensive team taking possession of the ball at the line of scrimmage. When a field goal is attempted and missed from inside the 20-yard line, the defensive team takes possession at the line of scrimmage.

field judge

The member of the officiating team who covers kicks as part of his set of responsibilities. Stationed deep behind the defensive team—as much as 25 yards from the line of scrimmage—the field judge makes rulings on fair catches, clipping on kick returns, and, together with the back judge, rules on whether field-goal attempts are successful.

On pass plays, the field judge keeps an eye on the receivers and the actions taken against them by defensive players. He rules on infractions in-

83

volving holding and illegal use of the hands, and he often makes the decision as to which team has recovered a loose ball.

The field judge is also responsible for timing the interval between plays (it must not be more than 30 seconds) and timing the intermission period between halves.

field of play

Pro football's playing field is 360 feet long and 160 feet wide. The end zones are each 30 feet deep.

Each of the hashmarks, that is, the inbound lines, is 70 feet, 9 inches from the nearest sideline. The sidelines and the end lines are out of bounds.

The goal line is actually in the end zone. A player with the ball in his possession scores a touchdown when the ball is on or over the goal line.

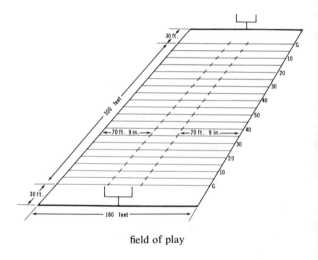

field of play

field position

The yard line or general area of the field where the ball is put in play. Suppose a punt is downed on a team's two-yard line; the team would be said to have "poor" field position. But taking over the ball within the opposition's territory is usually rated as "good" field position.

53 defense

During the early 1970s, the 53 pass defense was frequently used in prevent situations. It was developed by Bill Arnsparger when he was assistant head coach of the Miami Dolphins.

One thing that confused people about the 53 was its name. It had nothing to do with the way the players were aligned. Instead, it was a term derived from the uniform number of Bill Matheson, the Dolphin linebacker who made it work.

The alignment was 3–4, actually, with one of the front linemen being replaced by a linebacker, giving the team four linebackers. The extra linebacker could get down in a three-point stance for a pass rush or stay erect to drop back and cover the pass. "When executed properly," said Arnsparger, "the offense doesn't know who's coming and who's dropping off."

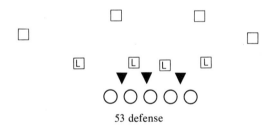

53 defense

fill

A blocking maneuver in which an offensive player, usually a backfield man, moves in to plug a hole created by a pulling guard or other lineman assigned to lead a sweep or to trap block.

flag

See penalty marker.

flag route

See corner route.

flanker

The wide receiver positioned on the same side of the formation as the tight end. Usually he is set six to seven yards outside of the tight end and a yard or two behind the line of scrimmage.

The Los Angeles Rams, when coached by Clark Shaughnessy, introduced the flanker. In a game against the Bears in 1949, when the Rams broke from the huddle, they lined up with three receivers. Tom Fears was set to the left side, split about ten yards away from the tackle on that side. Elroy (Crazylegs) Hirsch was set to the other side as the flanker. In between Hirsch and the right tackle, the Rams slotted Bob Shaw, the third receiver. The Rams enjoyed such spectacular success with the formation that it or one of its variations soon came to be adopted by every team.

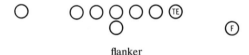

flanker

flare pass

A short pass thrown to a point close to the line of scrimmage to a running back cutting toward the sideline. Sometimes the back fakes into the line

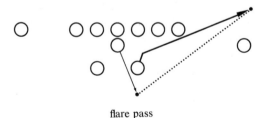

flare pass

before making his cut, or he may first set up as if to pass block, in which case the play is called a delay flare. A flare pass is sometimes referred to as a swing pass.

flat

The area of the field extending laterally to the sideline from the ball; a short-pass area.

flex

A distinctive alignment of the defensive front four introduced by Tom Landry, coach of the Dallas Cowboys, and later used by the San Francisco 49ers. Instead of all four linemen taking their set positions at the normal distance from the ball (no less than a foot), one of the tackles and an end on the other side played 12 to 18 inches off the ball. Landry believed that the flexed linemen were better able to pursue laterally in the case of a sweep or other play to the outside.

flip-flop, n.

A defensive maneuver in which a team's two safeties exchange areas of coverage just before the ball is snapped. Flip-flopping is sometimes necessary in order for the strong safety to be lined up on the same side of the field as the tight end. Some teams don't bother to flip-flop, assigning their safeties to play a particular side of the field no matter how the offensive team aligns itself.

flood, v.

To send two or more pass receivers into the same zone of defensive coverage. "Flooding" an area

87

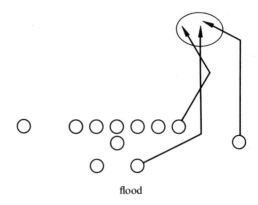

flood

has the obvious intent of overwhelming the coverage in that area.

Florida Blazers

WFL team, 1974.

flow, n.

The direction in which a running play moves.

fly pattern

A pass route in which a wide receiver races straight downfield as fast as he can go; also called a go pattern.

fold block

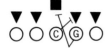

fold block

A blocking maneuver in which an offensive player steps back from the line of scrimmage to allow a teammate to get an unobstructed blocking angle on a defensive player. For example, a guard will step back to allow the center to fire out at the defensive tackle. The guard will then block the middle line-backer.

football

The football—its shape—has had a sharp influence on the character of the pro game. In pro football's early days, the ball was more pumpkinlike, and it was almost impossible to throw it accurately. Little by little, the rulemakers began slimming it down, and as they did, the passing game increased in importance.

The ball specifications now in effect were established in 1941. They state that the ball must take the form of an "inflated rubber bladder enclosed in a pebble-grained leather case." Its shape, says the rulebook, must be that of a prolate spheroid, which means its polar axis must be longer than its equatorial diameter; it must be cigar-shaped. It must also bear the NFL logo and Pete Rozelle's signature.

Other specifications are as follows:
long axis: 11 to 11¼ inches
long circumference: 28 to 28½ inches
short circumference: 21¼ to 21½ inches

For every game, the home team furnishes two dozen footballs, which the officials check for pressure (no less than 12½, no more than 13½ pounds) and weight (no less than 14 and no more than 15 ounces).

Football Writers Association of America

Box 1022, Edmond, Oklahoma 73034.

Founded in 1941, with approximately 1,000 members, the Football Writers Association of America is composed of newspaper and magazine sportswriters who cover college and professional football. The organization holds its annual meeting in Chicago at the time of the All Star Football Game, usually the first week in August.

formation

The alignment of either the offensive or defensive team; also called a set.

Fortmann, Danny

Hall of Fame, 1965.

Pro football adopted the player draft in 1936, and the first year it was in effect the Chicago Bears used it to good advantage. George Halas's first choice was Joe Stydahar, who was to become an All-Pro tackle for the Bears. His second selection showed equal foresight. He picked Danny Fortmann, a little-known college player out of Colgate. Fortmann, a guard, played next to Stydahar in the Bear line and, like him, was an All-Pro performer several times.

Fortmann lacked the size of the other Bear linemen, weighing less than 200 pounds. But he had agility, a necessary quality when Halas installed the T formation in 1940.

In the eight years that Fortmann played for the Bears, they won their division title six times and the NFL crown four times.

It was Fortmann's interest in a medical career that led him to play football, for he used his salary to finance his medical education. Today he is Dr. Daniel F. Fortmann, a Burbank, California, orthopedic surgeon.

forward pass

A ball thrown toward the opposition goal line. The passer must be behind the line of scrimmage when he throws, says the rulebook, and the pass may be touched or caught by only one eligible receiver.

foul, n.

Any violation of a playing rule.

4–3 defense

The standard pro football defensive alignment of recent years. It employs a front "four"—two big, tenacious ends, and two tackles of similar size and character—and "three" mobile, aggressive line-backers. Two cornerbacks and two safeties complete the unit.

During the 1970s, teams began to use more and more variations of the basic 4–3. *See* odd-man line, gap defense, stack defense, goal-line defense.

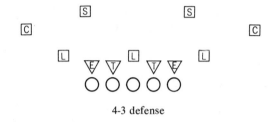

4-3 defense

Frankford (Pennsylvania) Yellowjackets

NFL team, 1924–1931; won NFL championship, 1926.

free agent

Any player who is not drafted by an NFL club and who joins a team by invitation. In addition, the term applies to a player who is waived by all teams (*see* waivers).

A player can also become a free agent by playing out his option (*see* option clause). The National Football League Players Association contended that in such cases a free agent wasn't really "free," since the Rozelle rule (which *see*) deterred teams from signing free agents.

free kick

A play in which the defensive team is restrained from interfering with the kicker. For example, the

91

kicks used at the beginning of each half and following touchdowns and field goals are types of free kicks.

A free kick can also follow a safety. In this case, the team scored upon puts the ball in play by means of a punt or placekick (or drop kick), and the receiving team is not permitted to rush the kicker. A free kick is also allowed—but rarely used—on the first play following a fair catch. In such cases, the receiving team returns the kick as if it were a conventional punt or field-goal try.

free safety

A decade or so ago, when most teams used man-to-man pass coverage, the cornerbacks were assigned to guard the side receivers, while the left safety covered the tight end. But the right safety had no specific receiver to cover, and so was "free" to help out wherever he was needed. *See* safety.

freezing the linebackers

A play action or any other faking maneuver by the quarterback which is intended to keep the linebackers from dropping off into their coverage zones.

frequency chart

The Rams are to play the 49ers. The Rams want to know what the 49ers are likely to do when they have the ball third-and-seven between midfield and the opponent's 40-yard line. If the 49ers pass in such a situation, what type of pass are they likely to use? Who are the most likely receivers? What success have the 49ers had with the play? The frequency chart, always an important part of a team's game plan, answers these questions.

By definition, the frequency chart is a detailed breakdown of how a team's offensive and defensive units have reacted and performed on each play of a particular game. The information that is charted is derived from scouting reports and game films.

By analyzing a frequency chart, a team is sometimes able to discern certain tendencies for the opposition. For example, a defensive unit may show an inclination to blitz on second-down-and-long-yardage situations, or a particular quarterback may have a tendency to pass on second-down-and-short-yardage situations.

During the game, each team keeps a frequency chart on the other. The coaching staff may consult the chart in formulating game strategy, both on offense and defense.

front four

The defensive linemen, the two tackles and two ends.

fullback

In the T formation, the running back who lines up three or so yards directly behind the quarterback, or is set to the strong side. *See* running back.

full-house backfield

An offensive formation with three set backs. The normal pro alignment calls for only two set backs.

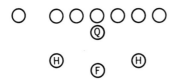

full-house backfield

93

fumble, n.

A ball that is in play after having been dropped or otherwise mishandled. Either team may recover and advance a fumble.

fumble

future list

See taxi squad.

Gabriel, Roman

Most Valuable Player, 1969.

Someone once asked quarterback Roman Gabriel to rate the other National League quarterbacks. "Over here," he said, "you've got Brodie, Namath, and Jurgensen, the picture passers. Then there are guys who don't necessarily look good throwing the ball, but they get the job done.

"Then you've got the complete quarterback, the guy who doesn't throw interceptions, can pass, and call good plays."

Gabriel himself belonged in the last-named category. Indeed, of all the passers active in 1974, no one had a lower percentage of interceptions than Gabriel (3.29 percent). It wasn't that he was conservative. He had the ability to flick the ball 50 yards or so in the blink of an eye, and occasionally did. In addition to his skills, Gabriel had the advantage of being big—6-foot-4, 220 pounds—and very durable.

As quarterback of the Los Angeles Rams for years, and during the 1960s, Gabriel was more closely identified with the team than any other player. The No. 1 draft choice of the Rams in 1962 following an All-American career at North Carolina State, Roman weathered several coaching changes before becoming the team's starting quarterback. That was in 1965.

In the years that followed, the Rams took on a bridesmaid-but-never-a-bride image. The team would lose only two or three games a season, but the ones they lost were always critical ones.

Finally, in 1969, the Rams seemed ready to claim the jackpot. They wrapped up the championship of the Coastal Division quickly, winning their first 11 games.

Gabriel

In the Western Conference title match against the Vikings, the Rams rolled up a 17–7 lead at halftime, with Gabriel completing 11 of 14 passes, two of them for touchdowns. But the Vikings came roaring back to win, 23–20.

"When it first hit me that we had blown the championship, I couldn't breathe," said Gabriel. "I felt like I had been slugged in the stomach with an anvil."

A year went by, and the defeat still bothered him. "It's still with me," he said. "I bump into it every time I turn around."

The season of 1969 remained a high point in Gabriel's fortunes. The Rams' owner, Dan Reeves, died in 1971, and wholesale changes followed. As one aspect of the change, Gabriel was traded to the Philadelphia Eagles.

The trade did not make Eagle fans happy. To get Gabriel, the club gave up the league's No. 1 receiver, Harold Jackson, plus running back Terry Baker, plus two first-round and one third-round draft choices. "There's nothing left," the fans lamented.

But Gabriel performed with brilliance, transforming the Eagle offense from the third worst in the NFL to the second best. He was the only passer in the league to throw for more than 3,000 yards in 1973. The Eagles still had some shortcomings, to be sure, but Gabriel gave them something they hadn't had for years—hope.

game ball

The ball awarded to a player or coach in recognition of outstanding effort in a team's victory.

game films

In the week before a game, players view films of games that feature their upcoming opponent, and coaches carefully analyze them. Game films play a vital role in developing strategy.

Game films, unlike live telecasts or video-taped or filmed re-creations of games seen on the screen, are shot with wide-angle lenses, so that every player is seen during every minute of the game. In the case of home TV coverage, the cameras follow the ball, and thus the quarterback and running backs play starring roles.

Also, a game film is not one individual film, but several different films, one devoted to defense, another to offense, a third to the kicking teams, etc., etc. Some teams order close-up views of the action as well as wide-angle coverage.

An NFL rule makes mandatory that opposing teams exchange films. Each must have the films of its two most recent games in the hands of the other team at least by the Tuesday morning preceding their meeting.

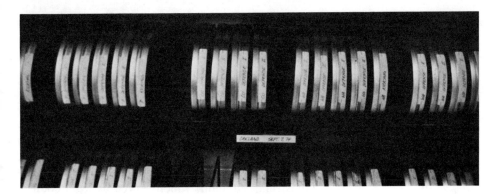

game films

game plan

The strategy formulated by one team to beat an opponent. There is a separate game plan for the offensive and defensive teams. Prepared by the coaching staff from scouting reports and game films, each game plan is several mimeographed pages in length and contains frequency charts, short critiques of the enemy team's principal players, plus a ready list, a selection of 20 or so plays that the coaches feel will be effective.

games

See stunting.

gap

The space between adjacent linemen at the line of scrimmage.

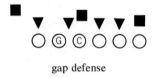

gap defense

gap defense

A variation of the basic 4–3 defense in which a defensive tackle lines up in the gap between the center and the weak-side guard.

Garvey, Edward (Ed)

Once called "the Thomas Jefferson of pro football" by *New York Times* columnist Dave Anderson, bright, articulate Ed Garvey became the executive director of the National Football League Players Association in 1971. After graduation from the University of Wisconsin Law School in 1969, Garvey joined the Minneapolis law firm of Lindquist and Vennum, which served as legal counsel to the NFLPA. Before his appointment as executive director, he was the Association's general counsel.

Gaudaur, J. G. (Jake)

According to a recent study, the offensive center is often the brightest member of the line. He's ambitious, tenacious, precise, and stubborn rather than explosive in demeanor.

Many of these characteristics apply to J. G. (Jake) Gaudaur (rhymes with guitar), a one-time center for the Hamilton Tigers in the Canadian Football League. Today he's the league's commissioner.

Gaudaur signed his first pro contract in 1940 at the age of 18. He became captain of the Tigers, a director of the team, its president, president of the CFL's Eastern Football Conference, and then president of the league itself. He was named the league commissioner in 1968.

Gaudaur will tell you that Canadian football is the greatest thing since the founding of the Hudson's Bay Company. "The pace of the game is quicker, much quicker, than in the NFL," he says. "There's much more of an emphasis on speed and agility." Because he is built like a center, you are inclined to agree with him.

George, Bill

Hall of Fame, 1974.

Joe Schmidt of the Detroit Lions and Sam Huff of the New York Giants are usually thought of as being pro football's first linebackers. But not in Chicago. There the credit goes to the Bears' Bill George.

A muscular 235 pounds, with close-cropped black hair and a swarthy appearance, George played 15 years in the National League, all except one of them with the Bears. He was the man who

99

George

called defensive signals for the team and he was an All-Pro choice six times.

George came to the Bears in 1952 after an All-America career at Wake Forest. His becoming a pro linebacker, specifically a middle linebacker, happened partly by accident. He was a lineman in his first season with the Bears, first a tackle, later a guard. In a game during his second year with the team, he saw that the Bears were vulnerable to quick passes to the running backs because there was no protecting the middle. The defensive ends were being pulled to the outside by the receivers.

"I told George Connor, our defensive captain, that I was pretty sure I could stop that sort of thing by pulling back off the line before the play started," George once recalled. "Connor said, 'Go ahead and try it,' and that's how it started. Two passes hit me in the midsection that day and I even held one for an interception."

Exceptionally fast and strong, George pioneered many of the techniques used by linebackers today. Abe Gibron, a teammate, once said of him, "Guys like Joe Schmidt and Sam Huff, although they were fine players, got all the credit because they played with teams that were always in contention. But as far as I'm concerned, George was tops."

George did get to play on one championship team, the 1963 Bears. They were a team that featured a rock-ribbed defense, allowing opponents an average of only ten points per game over the season. They destroyed Y. A. Tittle and the New York Giants in the title match, 14–10.

George obtained his release from the Bears in 1965 and played one season for the Rams. He served briefly as an assistant coach for the Bears in 1972.

goal line

The line that separates the field of play from the end zone. An imaginary vertical plane is said to rise from the goal line, and a player scores a touchdown by penetrating that plane.

goal-line defense

When a team's end zone is threatened, the outside
linebackers move up to the line of scrimmage. The
cornerbacks and safeties move up close, too,
playing the prospective pass receivers on a man-to-
man basis.

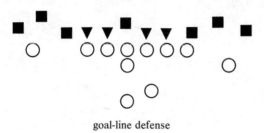

goal-line defense

goalpost

The two poles at each end of the field which are
18½ feet apart. They are connected by a crossbar
which is ten feet above the ground and positioned
directly above and parallel to the end line.

The vertical posts must extend at least 20 feet
above the crossbar. The distance used to be ten
feet. The added ten feet, intended to make it easier
for officials to tell good kicks from bad, is known
as the Baltimore extension, a most appropriate
term.

In the Western Conference playoff game of 1965,
the Colts vs. the Packers, the Colts led, 10–7, with
1:58 to play. In came Green Bay's Don Chandler
to try a field goal. He kicked from the 25-yard line,
sending the ball high and to the right. Packer fans
gasped. "No good! No good!" a radio broadcaster
proclaimed. But the official posted beneath the
crossbar raised both arms. The score was tied and
the Packers went on to win in overtime.

In the weeks that followed, Chandler's kick was
the subject of much controversy. Was it really

goalpost

good? Newspaper and magazine photographs and television replays never answered the question conclusively. Some pictures seemed to depict the ball missing; with others, the ball looked as if it went right over the goalpost. It depended on the photographer's angle. Before the next season opened, however, ten feet were added to each of the uprights—the Baltimore extension.

Of course, the actual goal is not limited to the height of the uprights. According to the rules, the goal is a plane that "extends indefinitely" above the crossbar (and within the outer edges of the posts).

The slingshot goalposts, known officially as the single standard type, were first used in the Pro-Bowl game in January, 1967, and the following season they began to appear in end zones every-

GRAHAM, OTTO

where. They're mandatory now. Goalpost color
has been standardized, too. The rulebook says
they must be painted "bright gold."

go pattern

See fly.

Graham, Otto

Hall of Fame, 1965.

In the ten years that Otto Graham quarterbacked
the Cleveland Browns, beginning in 1946, the team
achieved a remarkable record. Never once from

Graham

103

1946–1949, the years the Browns were members of the All-America Football conference, did they fail to win the league title. And when the Browns switched to the NFL, they kept right on winning—three more league titles in the next six years. In those ten years, the Browns lost only 13 games.

Graham didn't do it all by himself, of course. He had a pile-driving fullback in Marion Motley, the best running back of the day. He had fast and clever ends in Mac Speedie and Dante Lavelli. He had The Toe, Lou Groza, the league's highest scorer. And there was Paul Brown, the man who put all the parts together in a manner that was to win him billing as a coaching genius.

But mostly it was Graham. He could throw long or short, and he did for the sideline pass what Babe Ruth did for the home run. "I was accurate. I was very accurate," Graham says. "A coach would tell me where to throw the ball and how to throw it, and I'd do it. It was a gift, a God-given talent."

Graham did more than pass, however. He played safety on defense for several of his seasons, and even ran back punts and kickoffs. As a tailback at Northwestern, Graham had been well schooled in how to run with the ball, a fact documented by the NFL record manual. Of the eight NFC championship records that Graham holds, four have to do with rushing and scoring.

Otto became football coach and athletic director at the U.S. Coast Guard Academy in 1959. Pro-football teams kept making him coaching offers, and in 1966 the Redskins made him one he couldn't refuse. But it was not a happy experience. Graham's Redskins were feeble, and after three seasons he was glad to return to the serenity of New London, Connecticut, and the Coast Guard Academy.

"I'm happy where I am," Graham said recently. "What happened with the Redskins made me grow up. I suddenly realized that life wasn't a bowl of cherries."

Grange, Harold (Red)

Hall of Fame, 1963.

A streak of fire, a breath of flame;
Eluding all who reach and clutch;
A gray ghost thrown into the game
That rival hands may rarely touch . . .

That's how Grantland Rice once described Red Grange, who sprinted to fame and a tidy fortune during the 1920s, the Golden Age of Sport, as it was called. They had many nicknames for Grange. They called him the "Galloping Ghost," the "Flying Terror," the "Illinois Cyclone," and the "Wheaton Wizard" (Wheaton, Illinois, being his hometown).

Grange

But Grange, a charter member of the Pro Football Hall of Fame, did almost all of his galloping, flying, and cyclonic sprinting as a college player at the University of Illinois. There he gained 3,637 yards, scored 31 touchdowns and, more importantly, captured the imagination of the entire nation.

His on-the-field achievements as a member of the Chicago Bears were not nearly so gaudy. Indeed, one of his contemporaries has called Grange "a flop as a pro player," and there's probably a case that can be made for that argument. But Grange has enormous importance, not so much for what he did *in* the game as what he did *for* it.

Professional football before Red Grange was a scruffy, ragtag business, hardly noticed by the American sports fan and condemned by college coaches. "When I joined the Bears in 1925, I would have been much more popular had I joined the Capone mob," Grange once said.

Grange made his debut as a professional at Wrigley Field, Chicago, on the morning of Thanksgiving Day, 1925, and such was his popularity that he attracted the first sellout crowd in the history of the Bears. The game marked the beginning of a frantic exhibition tour that took Grange and a supporting cast of Chicago players into the population

105

centers of the Northeast and then back into the Midwest. They played ten games in 17 days. A swing through Florida followed, and then, early the next year, it was on to the West Coast, to Los Angeles, San Francisco, Portland, and Seattle.

Almost everywhere huge crowds turned out to see the ghost gallop. At New York's Polo Grounds, after the 65,000 available tickets had been sold, fans stormed the gates. Once the game began, the crowd cheered Grange's every move, and when he intercepted a pass in the final period and raced 30 yards for a touchdown, they roared their approval. It didn't matter that the play cost the Giants the game. In the week that followed, the road show played Washington, D.C., Providence, and Boston.

Grange, whose contract specified that he had to play at least 30 minutes of every game, soon became worn and exhausted, and his body ached in a hundred places. The game scheduled for Detroit had to be canceled because of his injuries.

Every time he did play, he earned big headlines. And big money. A Chicago newspaper published a daily boxscore of Grange's earnings and said he was averaging $300 an hour, 24 hours a day. He signed endorsement contracts for hats, dolls, soft drinks, candy bars, and a meat loaf.

Grange rested two weeks before the tour headed into Florida, with stopovers at Coral Gables (where tickets went for $20), Jacksonville, Tampa, and Miami. Following a one-night stand in New Orleans, the caravan moved on to the Pacific Coast.

The game in Los Angeles drew 70,000 fans, the largest crowd ever to see a pro game, and Grange earned $18,000 for his afternoon's work. In San Francisco, he was hailed in a parade up Market Street and honored at a City Hall reception.

Grange pocketed over $100,000 for his efforts, but in terms of what he accomplished for pro football he was underpaid. "Grange gave it [pro football] respectability," Arthur Daley once wrote. "As the idol of America, he was a powerful force of public opinion, and he definitely altered the image of the pro game in the minds of the fans.''

Unable to come to terms with the Bears for the 1926 season, Grange joined the New York franchise of a rival league, the American Football League, established by his manager, C. C. Pyle. The league did poorly, and the following year, as part of his agreement to abandon the league, Pyle was given the NFL franchise in New York City. Grange, of course, was the team's star.

In the third game of the season, played at Wrigley Field, Grange was sprinting downfield for a pass when George Trafton, The Bears' big center, piled into him, severely damaging Grange's knee. It was months before he attempted walking.

Later Grange tried a comeback, and was successful at it, rejoining the Bears in 1929 for six seasons. Although he won All-League recognition a couple of times, he was less than spectacular. He once described himself in those years as ''a straight runner . . . and the woods are filled with straight runners.''

No college football player since Grange has attained the superstar status he held. Few, if any, pro players have. By virtue of his eminence, he launched pro football on the road to $400,000 quarterbacks, $100,000,000 stadiums, and recognition as the national pastime.

Grant, Bud

Coach of the Year, 1969.

"I don't feel a coach can afford the luxury of emotion in a game," Bud Grant said often. Anyone who ever saw Grant's Vikings perform on television knew that. Grant was a familiar figure, standing tall and erect, wearing a peaked Vikings cap and a telephone headset. He stared out at the action, his face a mask.

Football was strictly business to Bud Grant. He was not a cheerleader, not a back-thumper. "He

Grant

coaches basic, well-disciplined football, with no garbage,'' the Packers' Dan Devine once said of him.

The No. 1 draft choice of the Philadelphia Eagles in 1950, Grant played both offensive and defensive end before shifting to Canada in 1953 following a contract dispute. There he led the league in receptions three times and when he turned to coaching—the Winnipeg Blue Bombers were his team—he won four Grey Cup championships. He became head coach of the Vikings prior to the 1967 season.

His early Viking teams put an emphasis on defensive muscle, while the offense lived and died by the run. When quarterback Fran Tarkenton arrived in 1972, the Viking attack became more creative. Still, the passing game consisted mostly of quick tosses to the backs.

Grant has gotten more out of conservatism than William F. Buckley. Through the 1974 season, his teams had won five division and two conference championships and one NFL title.

As one might expect, Grant took the success very much in stride. In 1970, when the Vikings played in Super Bowl IV, Grant told reporters: "We didn't outcoach anybody. Maybe we outplayed and outhustled some teams. But it wasn't the coaching, it was the execution. We don't win with mirrors or gimmicks. There are no short cuts. You win with hard work and good players.''

Green Bay Packers

APFA team, 1921. NFL team, 1922 to present; won Central Division championship (Western Conference), 1967; won Central Division championship (National Conference), 1970; won Western Division championship, 1936, 1938, 1939, 1944; won Western Conference championship, 1960–1962, 1965–1967; won NFL championship, 1929–1931, 1936, 1939, 1944, 1961, 1962, 1965–1967; won Super Bowl I (1967), Super Bowl II (1968).

Grey Cup

Grey Cup

Besides money and the title, the champions of the Canadian Football League's Eastern and Western Conferences play for the Grey Cup, which has been the symbol of football supremacy in Canada since 1909, the year Earl Grey, the Governor-General at the time, donated the silver-plated trophy for "the rugby-football championship of Canada." In the early years it was intended only for amateur competition, but when the pro version of the sport mushroomed in popularity, colleges dropped out. The Cup was formally turned over to the CFL by the Canadian Amateur Football Association in 1966.

gridiron

A term, now seldom used, to describe the football field. In the early 1900s, the field was laid out in true gridiron fashion, that is, with both horizontal and vertical chalk lines. Parallel to one another and only five yards apart, the additional lines gave the field an appearance of a checkerboard.

109

The rules in those days stated that a team had to advance five yards in three downs or give up the ball. Passing was not permitted. To advance legally, the ball carrier had to cross the line of scrimmage at a point at least five yards from where the snapper-back (the center) had put the ball in play. The lines that ran parallel to the sidelines helped the referee enforce this rule.

grounding

See intentional grounding.

Groza, Lou

Hall of Fame, 1974.

Groza

When big, broad-shouldered Lou Groza joined the Cleveland Browns of the All-America Football Conference in 1946, the kicking game had little tactical importance. A field goal was something a team "settled for." It was attempted only on rare occasions and never from very long distances. Groza, who earned the nickname "The Toe," helped change all that. When he retired after a couple decades of placekicking, people were complaining that the preeminence of the kicking game was beginning to ruin the sport.

Groza's 13 field goals in 1946 established a new high for the pro game, and gave an indication of what was possible. The 23 field goals he booted in 1953 stood as the record until 1962. In all, he led the league in field goals five times.

Because of his nickname and the fact that he kicked so many field goals (234) and so many extra points (641), many people have forgotten that Groza also played tackle. Indeed, he was All Pro at the position six times.

When Groza signed on with the Browns, there was no roster space for a kicking specialist. "I always considered myself a tackle," says Groza. "I'd work on my kicking after practice. Sometimes it was tough to get a holder and snapper to work with me. Our punter, Horace Gillom, also played end. Now they have kickers who never played football in their lives."

Groza calls the 1950 championship against the Los Angeles Rams the most exciting game of his career. "We messed up an extra-point try," he says. "The snap was bad and the holder, Tommy James, never got it down. He threw a pass to Tony Adamle that went through his hands. We were losing, 28–27, the last time we got the ball. With just 28 seconds to go, I kicked a field goal from the 16 and we won it, 30–28. They gave me a ride around town on a firetruck."

guard, n.

Either of the two offensive linemen on either side of the center. *See* offensive guard.

Guyon, Joe

Hall of Fame, 1966.

Jim Thorpe was the most noted Indian player in football's early days. But there were many others—Pete Calac, Woodchuck Welmus, Mount Pleasant, Red Fang, and Little Twig and Big Twig.

And there was one other, Joe Guyon, almost as well known as Thorpe in those days. Guyon, a halfback, succeeded Thorpe as an All-American at Carlisle, and then teamed with him as Thorpe meandered his way through pro football, with stop-overs in Canton, Cleveland, Rock Island, New York, and several other places. In the eight years Guyon played professional football, he averaged about a team a year.

Guyon had a reputation as a devastating blocker and to tackle him, it was said, was like trying to tackle a propellor blade. He was also known for the zest he displayed when playing defense. "He loved to hurt a player, and then while the guy was

stretched out he'd do a war dance around him,''
said Century Milstead, a tackle with the New York
Giants in the 1920s. Barry Gottehrer in his book,
The Giants of New York, observed that Guyon
"graduated from Carlisle with a degree in vi-
ciousness.''

Guyon was also a professional baseball player
with the Louisville Colonels of the American Association. He settled in Louisville after his playing
days were over, and used to coach junior football
there, an indication that he must have mellowed.

Halas, George

Hall of Fame, 1963; Coach of the Year, 1963, 1965.

"George Halas didn't invent football," Arthur Daley once wrote. "It just seems that way."

For half a century and more, anyone the least bit familiar with the pro game knew about George Halas, identifying him with the Chicago Bears. But Halas's involvement with the sport predates the Bears and even the National Football League itself.

Halas was born in Chicago, grew up there, and attended the University of Illinois, where he studied civil engineering and played end on the football team and right field on the baseball team. After a tour of duty with the Navy during World War I, Halas played some minor league baseball, then got a job in the bridge department of the Chicago, Burlington, & Quincy Railroad.

This doesn't sound like the profile of someone who one day would be called "The Father of Pro Football," but in 1920 his life changed. He had been playing semipro football for the Hammond (Indiana) Pros, when he came to the attention of A. E. Staley, a Decatur, Illinois, starch manufacturer. Staley asked Halas to round up some players and coach a football team under the company's banner.

One problem was the schedule. Halas wrote to Ralph Hay, the manager of the Canton, Ohio, Bulldogs and suggested that they organize a league. Thus, on September 17, 1920, Halas, Hay, and representatives of nine other teams met in Hay's Canton automobile showroom and formed the American Professional Football Association, which later became the National Football League.

Halas

The Staley Company dropped football the next year, whereupon Halas moved the team to Chicago.

In 1921, Halas, then 26, the Bears' player-coach, won the NFL's first championship.

In 1925, Halas, a mature 30, signed Red Grange off the campus of the University of Illinois, and for two months Grange and the Bears barnstormed the country, making millions aware of pro football for the first time.

In 1932, 1933, and 1934, Halas's Bears, with Bronko Nagurski in a starring role, were the scourge of pro football.

In 1940, Halas, then 45, unleashed quarterback Sid Luckman and the T formation to defeat the Redskins, 73–0, in the NFL title game.

In 1946, the Bears won the NFL championship again. Halas, 51, was still running things.

From 1946 through the mid-1970s, the Bears won only one championship. Halas was assailed in the press as being "too old" to run the team. He was called "El Cheapo." Columnist William Barry Furlong characterized him as having a personality with "all the warmth of broken bones."

But Halas was always able to shrug off such criticism. "There's an old saying," he liked to say, "to this effect—anger doth a bonehead make."

From time to time through the years, however, Halas did relinquish his coaching duties. Then in 1968, at 73, he retired as head coach for good.

But he still remained active, firing coach Jim Dooley in 1972, replacing him with Abe Gibron. He signed up Jim Finks in 1974 as general manager and chief of operations. "I'm going to take it a little easier now," he said. He was 79, an enthusiastic and optimistic 79, to be sure.

Myron Cope, in his book, *Broken Cigars,* asked Halas what principles he followed through all those years. "Louis Nizer, the great attorney," said Halas, "wrote a book in which he said, 'Nothing is work unless you'd rather be doing something else.' Well, that's the principle I've been following for years. I prefer doing football to anything else in the world."

halfback

The running back who is positioned three or so yards behind the quarterback and usually set to the left side of the backfield alignment.

halftime

The 15-minute intermission between halves.

Hall of Fame

See Professional Football Hall of Fame.

Hammond (Indiana) Pros

APFA team, 1920. NFL team, 1922–1926.

handoff, n.

The exchange of the ball from one offensive player—usually the quarterback—to another.

handoff

✓hang time

The amount of time a punted ball remains in the air. For example, Hank Stram, former coach of the Kansas City Chiefs, wanted his punters to "hang" the ball for 4.5 seconds, thus giving the coverage team sufficient time to get downfield.

Harris, Franco

Most Valuable Player, Super Bowl IX (1975).

When Franco Harris won the MVP trophy in Super Bowl IX for helping to destroy the Minnesota Vikings, setting records with 34 carries and 158 yards, it capped a brilliant season for the Steelers' prize running back.

Against the Buffalo Bills in the first of the playoff games, Harris exploded for three touchdowns in the first half. And when the Steelers faced the Oakland Raiders for the conference crown, Harris ripped big holes in the Raider line and scored two more touchdowns.

During the regular season, Harris topped 1,000 yards rushing for the second time in his career, quite an accomplishment since his career was only three years in length. He had come to the Steelers in 1972, a first draft choice from Penn State.

A 230-pounder, measuring 6-foot-2, Harris moved exceptionally well for a big back, and was equally valuable inside or out. He won Rookie-of-the-Year honors in 1972 but was hampered by injuries in the season that followed.

Franco was healthy again in 1974 and remained so through most of the season. The fact that the Steelers managed to get to the Super Bowl and win it is proof of that.

Harris

Hartford (Connecticut) Blues

NFL team, 1926.

hashmarks

The two series of short lines that run the length of the field, each set of which lines up with a goalpost upright. Officially known as inbound lines, each series of hashmarks is 70 feet, 9 inches from the near sideline. If a play ends between the hashmarks and the sideline, the ball is next put in play at the closest hashmark.

head linesman

One of the members of the officiating crew. On plays from scrimmage, the head linesman straddles the line of scrimmage on the same side of the field as the chain crew. He watches for offsides, other infractions of rules involving line play, and illegal formations. He helps the other officials on passes and runs to his side of the field, and he rules on out-of-bounds plays. He also supervises the chain crew.

head linesman

Healey, Ed

Hall of Fame, 1964.

When Chicago Bears owner George Halas purchased Ed Healey's contract from the Rock Island Independents for $100 in 1922. Healey became—or so many historians say—the first football player to be sold. That's not the only reason the sale is unusual; it may have been the only one to be motivated out of outright fear.

Healey, who once gave serious consideration to a career as a heavyweight boxer, played left tackle for the Rock Island team. One November afternoon, the Independents faced the Bears at Wrigley Field. Halas was at right end for the Bears, an assignment that put him directly across the line from Healey.

The game, played on a muddy field, entered the final stages with neither team having scored. A contributing factor may have been that Halas kept holding Healey, grabbing his jersey sleeve and throwing him off balance. Healey complained to the officials, but to no avail, the Bears being the home team, an important factor in that day.

Healey knew how to solve the problem. He drew back his brawny fist and let it fly at Halas's head. But somehow he lost his footing and his fist whizzed by Halas's left cheek and plunged into the muck.

Halas stared in disbelief. Healey's arm was buried up to the wrist. The incident took place on Sunday. On Tuesday Healey was told to report to the Bears.

There Healey remained for seven years, winning All-Pro honors as a tackle each year. The position seemed to suit him perfectly. "I thrived in the explosiveness that playing in the line presented you," Healey once told Myron Cope. "Fear was remote in my makeup. I mean, I loved bodily contact. I just thrived on it. I ate it up." George Halas would surely have agreed.

Hein, Mel

Hall of Fame, 1963.

Think of the great passing quarterbacks, and you think of Johnny Unitas and Sammy Baugh. Think of the outstanding running backs, and the name Jim Brown is the first to come to mind. Mel Hein, who played for the New York Giants for 15 seasons beginning in 1931, has that kind of identification with the center's position.

An All-American at Washington State, Hein was one of the first notable college players to join the pro ranks. He won All-Pro honors as a center six times, was the NFL's Player of the Year in 1938, and is a charter member of the Hall of Fame.

While Hein, who stood 6-foot-3 and weighed 235, won all of those honors as a center, it's not as a center that he wants to be remembered, but as a backer-up, the position he played on defense. The backer-up of the 1930s and 1940s is the middle linebacker of today. "I made my name backing up the line," Hein once told me. "And I made it by bumping into some pretty tough people. Besides, who ever remembers an offensive center?"

Although Hein was an aggressive player, he was also a gentleman. Gouging, kneeing, piling on, and other and similar transgressions were not in his repertoire.

Toward the end of his career, the Giants held a "Mel Hein Day" at the Polo Grounds. Mayor Fiorello La Guardia made a speech, and Hein received a new car loaded with gifts. But when the Giants took the field, they lost to the Dodgers, 14–6. "We're sorry we didn't win for Mel," said Giant halfback Hank Soar afterwards. "But, hell, every day the Giants have played in the last ten years has been Mel Hein Day."

Hein

helmet

The player's protective headgear, made of shell plastic and fitted with sponge pads or other cushioning material.

Henry, Wilbur (Pete)

Hall of Fame, 1963.

Pete Henry, a two-way tackle in pro football's leather-helmet days, didn't look like a football player. He was a round man—6-feet tall, 260 pounds. They called him "Fats."

But to go with his bulk, he had surprising agility. At Washington and Jefferson College, he was a

Henry

tackle on Walter Camp's All-America team in 1919, and the next year he joined the Canton Bulldogs. The same day that he signed his contract, the American Professional Football Association was organized in Canton, but the biggest headlines in the Canton paper that day were Henry's.

He played nine years as a professional, winning All-Pro recognition three times. When, in 1950, *Collier's* magazine chose a mid-century All-America team, Pete Henry was there at tackle.

In the latter stages of his pro career, Henry punted and placekicked. And when he swung one of those ponderous legs into the ball, it went some-place. He once boomed a punt 94 yards, an NFL record for many years. And he still holds the record for the longest drop kick in professional football—50 yards.

Like many players of an earlier time, Henry really cared about the game. His diary is part of a collection of Henry memorabilia on exhibition at the Hall of Fame. An entry for one winter day reads: "Now that football's over, I don't know what to do."

Herber, Arnie

Hall of Fame, 1966.

When Arnie Herber, who was to become one of pro football's first great passers, began playing football for the Green Bay Packers, it was 1930, and the pay was $75 a game. That didn't matter to Arnie. He was just happy to be a member of the team.

He had been born in Green Bay, grew up there, and had gone to Green Bay's West High. He sold programs at Packer games and later was a club-house boy.

Since Herber had played high school football and also had a couple of years of college experience, coach Curly Lambeau decided to give him a tryout. Lambeau figured that even if he didn't per-form well, he might, being a hometown boy, sell some tickets. You can guess what happened. Herber had an outstanding day, and even threw the game-winning pass. Lambeau forgot all about his being a drawing card.

Handicapped by extremely pudgy fingers, Herber gripped the ball with his thumb over the laces in order to prevent wobbling and impart a spiral quality to the throw. It may have been unusual, but it worked. Herber was the league's leading passer in 1932, 1934, and 1936. Three times he led Green Bay to the NFL championship.

Herber was handicapped by a leg injury in 1937. A new passer named Cecil Isbell started alternating with him and finally supplanted him. Herber retired in 1940, but not permanently. During the World War II player shortage, the New York Giants convinced him to make a comeback.

He helped steer the team to the Eastern Division championship in 1944, but they were beaten in the playoff by, of all teams, the Packers. The next season was much less of a success, and when it was over Herber went back to Green Bay, this time for good.

Herber

Hewitt, Bill

Hall of Fame, 1971.

No one ever had to consult his program to pick out Bill Hewitt on the football field. He was the player without a helmet.

But Hewitt didn't end up in the Hall of Fame by reason of his bareheadedness. For nine seasons in a career that began in 1932, Hewitt was a fleet two-way end for the Bears, later the Eagles, and for one season, the merged Philadelphia-Pittsburgh club.

Hewitt had such quickness in getting off the line that newspapers of the day called him "The Off-side Kid." Officials who worked games in which he played insisted that he seldom, if ever, was actually offside; it just looked that way. Hewitt later admitted he was often able to get a telltale in-

121

Hewitt

dication of the impending snap by watching the center's fingers.

One of Hewitt's most glittering moments came in the 1933 NFL title game, the Bears vs. the Giants. In the game's closing minutes, the Bears trailing, Hewitt improvised a play in the huddle. Bronko Nagurski faked a plunge into the line, then threw a pass to Hewitt who lateraled to Bill Karr. Karr scored the game-winning touchdown.

Such razzle-dazzle was another of Hewitt's trademarks. A favorite maneuver of the Bears' was for Hewitt to get the ball on an end-around and wind up throwing a long pass.

Hewitt retired in 1939, then tried a comeback with Philadelphia-Pittsburgh in 1943. He did not have one of his better seasons. Perhaps it was the long layoff. Or maybe it was the problems he had in trying to cope with the passes thrown by a young left-handed quarterback named Allie Sherman.

Or it may have been a new rule that hampered Hewitt. For the first time in his career, he was made to wear a helmet.

Hinkle, Clarke

Hall of Fame, 1964.

There's debate as to who was pro football's greatest fullback in the era before the rules were changed to encourage forward passing. Some say Bronko Nagurski, others Ernie Nevers. But still others cite Clarke Hinkle.

Whereas Nagurski had size and strength, and Nevers was simply relentless, Hinkle's success was built on his fierce determination. "He'd get so fired up before a game, he'd be glassy-eyed," a teammate once recalled. "If we lost, he'd weep."

At Bucknell in his senior year, Hinkle was the nation's leading scorer, and he helped to give the college its finest football years. He was named the Most Valuable Player in the East-West game in 1932, and the day after the game Curly Lambeau signed him to a contract with the Packers calling for him to be paid $125 a game.

"What Lambeau didn't know at the time," Hinkle once said, "was that I wanted to play so badly that I would have signed for nothing." With the Packers, Hinkle played nearly every play of every game for ten years, and in that period Green Bay was either a champion or a close challenger eight times.

Don Smith of Pro Football's Hall of Fame once described Hinkle as "a hard-knocking runner . . . but he could turn the corner as well as hit the middle. He was an excellent faker and many times he would draw the defense to him while [quarterback] Arnie Herber and later Cecil Isbell unleashed a long pass. . . ." Hinkle's rushing records lasted for years.

Hinkle was just as tenacious on defense, a savage tackler who seemed to thrive on contact. A Green Bay lineman of the 1930s once recalled that

Hinkle

123

if the Packer line was doing its job, stopping the ball carriers cold, Hinkle would become impatient. "Hey, you guys," he'd yell. "Let someone through and give me a chance. I want to hit somebody!"

Someone once said that you didn't need to know Hinkle's number to pick him out on the field. You just waited until you heard a sharp *thwack!* That's where Hinkle would be.

Hirsch, Elroy (Crazylegs)

Hall of Fame, 1968.

Crazylegs. It was the perfect nickname.

As a pass receiver for the Los Angeles Rams during their championship seasons of the late 1940s

Hirsch

and early 1950s, Roy Hirsch, with his dazzling speed and shiftiness, won recognition as one of the most elusive ends of all time. "You've heard about guys who can zig and zag," Ram quarterback Norm Van Brocklin once said. "Well, Hirsch has got a 'zog' and a couple of varieties of 'zugs.'"

Hirsch's specialty was catching long passes. He grabbed them the same way that Willie Mays used to catch long fly balls to center field, running at full tilt with his back to the oncoming ball, then reaching out to take it over his shoulder. In 1951, a year he won the NFL's pass-receiving title, Hirsch was involved in touchdown throws that covered 72, 76, 79, 81, and 91 yards.

He gained a record 1,495 yards that season, and, with 102 points, led the league in scoring. He caught touchdown passes in 11 consecutive games. Most of his records have been equalled or surpassed, but that one still stands.

After Hirsch retired as a player in 1957, he stayed with the Rams as general manager and later as an assistant to club president Dan Reeves. Still later, he accepted a post as athletic director at the University of Wisconsin.

hitch and go

A pass pattern in which the receiver breaks straight downfield, fakes to the right or left, then races downfield again.

hitch and go

hitting the seam

A method of attacking the zone pass defense in which the quarterback seeks to connect with a receiver cutting into the gap, or "dead" area, between coverage zones.

holder

Just as quarterbacks need sure-handed receivers and running backs require blockers, so the holder

125

holder

is vital to the success of the kicker. On field-goal attempts, he puts one knee to the ground at a point about seven yards from the line of scrimmage and holds his hands about chest high as a target for the center. When he catches the snap, he quickly spins the ball so that the laces are away from the kicker's toe, then he places the ball on the turf, tilting it slightly toward the kicker, and he holds it steady with his index finger. He has about one second to do all of this.

Because the job requires a player who is skilled in handling the ball, it's often a quarterback who serves as the team's holder. During all those years that Sonny Jurgensen was awing everyone with his daring passing, he was also the Redskins' holder. Bart Starr held for the Packers. George Blanda had Ken Stabler; Garo Yepremian had Earl Morrall.

"In practically every kicking situation, the center and the holder are as important as the kicker," Jim Bakken, kicker for the St. Louis Cardinals, once said. "There's delicate timing involved, which is not possible to achieve unless the same people work together in practice all the time."

Honolulu Hawaiians

WFL team, 1974, 1975.

hook, n.

A pass pattern in which the receiver breaks straight downfield, then doubles back a step or two to face the passer; also called a curl.

hook

Hornung, Paul

Most Valuable Player, 1961.

"You have to know what Hornung means to this team," said Vince Lombardi in his book, *Run to Daylight.* "In the middle of the field, he may be only slightly better than an average ballplayer, but inside the 20-yard line, he is one of the greatest I have ever seen. He smells the goal line."

To Lombardi, Hornung was exactly what a halfback should be. He had good speed, was difficult to bring down in the open field, and was cool and skilled in executing the option pass. He could catch passes. He could block. In addition, Hornung also kicked field goals and extra points.

Hornung

Thanks to his versatility, Hornung led the league in scoring for three consecutive years beginning in 1959. In 1960, with 176 points (15 touchdowns, 15 field goals, and 41 extra points), he established a season record for scoring that no one has ever threatened.

Tall, blond, and extremely personable, Hornung arrived in Green Bay in 1957, two years before Lombardi got there. From Louisville, and one of the most famous high school athletes in the city's history, Hornung went to Notre Dame where he played quarterback and played it well enough to win the Heisman Trophy.

The seasons at Green Bay before Lombardi were difficult. Hornung was used at one position after another—quarterback, halfback, and fullback.

He still managed to lead the 1958 Packers in scoring.

Once Lombardi arrived, Hornung began winning a reputation as one of the game's best "money" players. In crucial games when the Packers got within scoring range, it was Hornung who was frequently called upon to get the ball into the end zone. If he didn't do it one way, he'd do it another.

When Green Bay whipped the New York Giants in the 1961 NFL championship game, 37–0, it was Hornung who started the scoring avalanche with a touchdown in the second period. He then went on to account for a total of 19 points, a playoff-game record.

The next year Hornung injured a knee and was sidelined for several games. The year that followed was worse. Hornung, along with Alex Karras, a tackle for the Lions, was suspended for betting on games and for what the NFL described as "transmitting information for betting purposes." The suspension lasted a year.

When Hornung returned to the Packers in 1964, there were games in which he showed flashes of his former skills, but not enough of them. Lombardi allowed him to be taken by the New Orleans Saints in the expansion draft in 1967. But because of a previous injury, he never played for the Saints.

During his better years with the Packers, Hornung was sometimes called the "Golden Boy" by the press, and following his retirement as a player, he managed to retain his golden image. His smiling face continued to be seen in magazine advertisements, he was in demand as an after-dinner speaker, and he pursued a successful career as a sports commentator.

Houston Oilers

AFL team, 1960–1969; won Eastern Division championship, 1960–1962, 1967; won AFL championship, 1960, 1961.

NFL team, 1970 to present.

Houston Texans

WFL team, 1974; franchise transferred to Shreveport during 1974 season.

Howley, Chuck

Most Valuable Player, Super Bowl V (1971).

They called Super Bowl V, Dallas vs. Baltimore, the Blunder Bowl. It was a zany affair, an afternoon of fumbles—six of them—interceptions, tipped passes, and broken plays. A field goal by Jim O'Brien with five seconds remaining won it for Baltimore. It was a victory the Colt players accepted happily but with some chagrin.

When it came to awarding the outstanding player trophy, the sportswriters present voted for a member of the losing team. They voted for Chuck Howley, the right linebacker for the Cowboys.

Howley

Howley made several key tackles, assisted on others, and intercepted two passes. The second was a ball thrown by Earl Morrall just as the fourth period began. Howley made the interception in the end zone, killing a Colt scoring threat.

A six-time All Pro, Howley had been a mainstay of the Dallas defense since 1961, the year the Cowboys had obtained him from the Chicago Bears. He had played in Chicago for three years, winning a reputation for his quickness and his ability to anticipate plays. Because of a knee injury he sustained in 1959, the Bears were doubtful about his future and traded him to Dallas.

Just one year after the debacle they suffered at the hands of the Colts, the Cowboys were back in the Super Bowl, this time to play the Miami Dolphins. Howley excelled again, making tackles at critical times and recovering a fumble that led to the first Dallas score. The Cowboys won, 24–3. Although he didn't win the MVP award, that's the Super Bowl that Howley prefers to remember.

129

Hubbard

Hubbard, Cal

Hall of Fame, 1963.

A huge mountain of a man, Cal Hubbard played either tackle on a number of pro teams during the 1920s and 1930s. Some of his opponents said that he was big enough and strong enough to play both positions at the same time.

Hubbard began his career with the New York Giants in 1927, moved to the Green Bay Packers in 1929, back to the Giants in 1936, and finished up with the Pittsburgh Steelers, also in 1936. Wherever he went, the championship usually went with him. He played on a total of four NFL titleholders.

Hubbard stood 6-foot-5 and weighed 265. He was menacing not only because of his size and strength but also by virtue of his attitude. He gloried the game, in smothering the ball carrier or delivering a crunching block.

During his years with the Packers, he served as the team's policeman. Every team had one in those days. When an opponent was found to be playing dirty, it was the policeman's duty to teach the wrongdoer a lesson.

Hubbard relished the assignment. Lou Evans, a teammate of Hubbard's, once told of being slugged across the mouth by a lineman across from him. " 'This guy is killing me,' I said to Hubbard. And I told him I was going to tell the referee. Hubbard was shocked. 'Lord, no, don't do that,' he said. 'Don't get the referee excited. Wait until we get on defense. Then we'll take care of him.' "

Through much of his career, Hubbard spent his summers as a baseball umpire. He worked his way up through the minor leagues and into the majors and, in 1952, became the supervisor of umpires for the American League. Hubbard's success had to be expected. Behind the plate or when working the bases, he was always a formidable figure, and when he made a decision, no one argued.

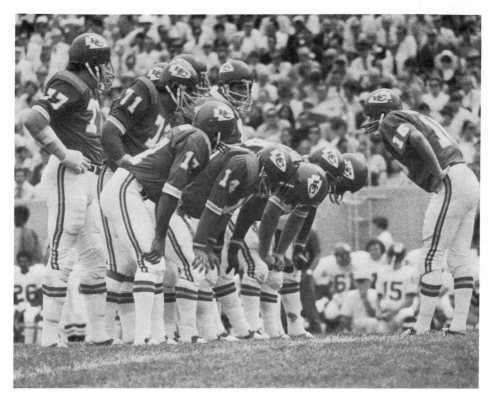

huddle

huddle

A team's huddle is not a mere random gathering, but is formed according to careful instructions set down in the playbook. The rallying point is the center, who takes his position seven yards behind the point where the ball has been spotted down. The guards flank the center, and the tackles move in next to the guards. The receivers and running backs line up on the other side. The quarterback is at one end. "Look at the quarterback's eyes," the playbook may say. "No talking. Give the quarterback information only if he asks for it."

A few teams—the San Diego Chargers are one—prefer the open huddle, with the players arrayed in two lines facing the quarterback. It's said to discourage unnecessary talk.

131

Hunt, Lamar

Hall of Fame, 1972.

When 26-year-old Lamar Hunt was rebuffed in his attempts to acquire a franchise in the National Football League in 1958 and 1959, he went out and formed a league of his own—the American Football League. "The idea just hit me," he once said, "while I was flying home from my last attempt to buy the Cardinals."

Hunt had more than simply an idea going for him. He had zillions of dollars, his father being H. L. Hunt of the Hunt Oil Company, one of the world's richest men. By the fall of 1959, he also had half a dozen other people lined up who were interested in owning American League franchises, and had sufficient money to support their interest.

What happened—the ultimate success of the league, the merger with the National, the Super Bowl—is well known. But it was never easy. "We had an obviously inferior product and a hare-brained idea," Hunt once told Jack Olsen. "We *should* have been scared."

Hunt's own team, the Dallas Texans, fought the Dallas Cowboys for three years, then tried Kansas City. There Hunt developed a winning team, which he had reluctantly renamed the Chiefs, indeed, a Super Bowl winner, and a $43-million-dollar stadium, one of the finest football showplaces in the country.

The Chiefs and professional football are not Hunt's only interests. Not by any means. He is co-owner of a professional soccer team, the Dallas Tornadoes, a minority owner of the Chicago Bulls of the National Basketball Association, and the majority owner of World Championship Tennis, the professional tennis tour. There are several other things, but these are the most important.

Sports Illustrated says that Hunt's investments in sports are worth $50 million. "Czar" is the term that is now sometimes used to describe him.

He has one other distinction. He's the one who thought of the term "Super Bowl."

Hutson, Don

Hall of Fame, 1963.

Up until fairly recent times, whenever a new and flashy pass receiver came upon the pro scene, he was invariably hailed as "a second Hutson." Hutson was the yardstick against which all other receivers were measured. When he retired in 1945, it required a full page in the NFL record manual to list the scoring and receiving marks he had established.

The Packers were Hutson's team. He was scouted and signed by Curly Lambeau, one of the founders of the Green Bay club. Lambeau first saw Hutson perform as a college player at the University of Alabama in 1934. "He would glide downfield," Lambeau said, "leaning forward as if to steady himself close to the ground. Then, as suddenly as you gulp or blink an eye, he'd feint one way and go to the other, reach up like a dancer, gracefully squeeze the ball, and leave the scene of the accident—the accident being the defensive backs who tangled their feet up and fell trying to cover him."

The very first time he got into a game as a Packer, Hutson caught a pass, outmaneuvered the defense, and raced across the goal. The play covered 83 yards.

That's the way it was for the next 11 years. Hutson was the league's pass-reception leader eight times and the scoring leader five times. A charter member of the Hall of Fame, Hutson is now an automobile dealer in Racine, Wisconsin.

Anyone who has any doubts as to Hutson's value only has to look at how the Packers fared in the years he was with the team. They won four Western Division titles and three NFL championships. Not until 1945, his final year with the team, did they fail to finish first or second, and that year they were third.

Hutson

I formation

A variation of the T formation in which the half-back and the fullback line up directly behind the quarterback. The Buffalo Bills liked to run O. J. Simpson out of the I because he'd be set deeper than normal, and thus have an extra second or so to size up the blocking and pick a hole.

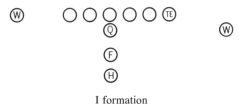

I formation

illegal procedure

Movement on the part of a member of the offensive line after the team is set and before the ball is snapped. The movement is usually back or to one side, as compared to straight-ahead movement, in which case the player would be offside. The penalty for illegal procedure is five yards.

inbound lines

See hashmarks.

ineligible receiver

An offensive player, normally an interior lineman (a tackle, guard, or center), not permitted to catch a forward pass. In addition, ineligible receivers are not permitted downfield until after the ball is thrown. The penalty for violating the rule is 15 yards.

injured reserve

A term used to describe the status of an injured player who is not a member of the club's active roster. He does not count against the club's 47-man player limit (the 40-man active roster and the seven-man taxi squad). He is permitted to attend team meetings but cannot take part in practice sessions. In order to be reactivated, he must clear waivers.

injured waivers

See waivers.

injury

Football, a team physician once observed, is "not so much a contact sport as a collision sport." Because it is, injuries are frequent. By December, there is not a player who is not hurting.

The National Football League sends out a report on significant injuries every week, and individual teams also issue such reports. Some of the terms commonly used in reporting injuries are defined in the paragraphs that follow.

Contusion: The most common injury in football, a bruise. Usually it's not serious, although when it occurs in the front of the thigh it can be extremely painful and debilitating. Then it's sometimes referred to as a charley horse.

Sprain: When the ligaments associated with a particular joint are wrenched beyond their normal range, the resulting damage is a sprain. In seriousness, it can range from the damage of a few fibers to the complete rupture of a ligament.

Strain: Whereas a sprain refers to ligaments,

135

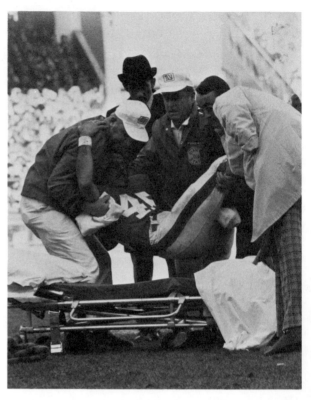

injury

strain has to do with muscles. Strains can be caused by overstretching a muscle or by overuse.

Dislocation: Once, during a game involving the University of Alabama under coach Paul (Bear) Bryant, a player dislocated his finger, and it jutted out from his hand at an unusual angle. He started screaming and stamping his feet. Bryant walked over to the man, looked at the injury, and snorted, "Nobody ever died of a goddamn little dislocated finger," then walked away. Bryant's statement is probably true. A dislocation is a displacement of a limb from its normal position in a socket or a joint. Players frequently remedy dislocated fingers on the field between plays.

Concussion: Any violent, jarring blow to the head, any shock, can be termed a concussion. A concussion can range from mild—a brief period of mental confusion—to severe, which implies a period of prolonged unconsciousness or amnesia.

Separation: Usually relating to a shoulder injury, a separation occurs when the outer end of the collarbone becomes detached from the top of the shoulder blade.

Torn cartilage: Knee injuries sometimes involve cartilage, the tough, white, fibrous connective tissue that is attached to the articular surface of the tibia, the large bone of the lower leg. The term "torn cartilage" can refer to almost anything from an actual tear to a complete break. Such damage prevents the knee from functioning properly; it locks. Surgery to remove the damaged tissue is the normal solution.

Most fans aren't terribly interested in the medical nature of a player's injury. What they want to know is whether the man is going to be able to play. The team the player is going to be facing wants to know that, too. So coaches are asked to rate injured players as to their expected availability. These are the terms they use, along with the official meaning for each:

    probable—likely to play
    possible—might play
    questionable—status uncertain
    doubtful—probably won't play
    definitely out—won't play

in motion

See man-in-motion.

inside

In the case of the offensive line, the area between the two tackles. A running play up the middle or to either side of either of the guard positions, is said to be heading "inside."

137

interception

intentional grounding

An infraction of the rules in which a passer purposely throws an incomplete pass in order to avoid being tackled behind the line of scrimmage or to prevent an interception. The rulebook judges intentional grounding to be a serious matter, and 15 yards and loss of a down is the penalty.

interception

A pass caught by a defensive player.

interference, n.

The offensive players who block in front of the ball carrier; also, the blocking done by said players.

interior linemen

The members of the offensive team aligned between the receivers—the two guards, two tackles, and the center.

Jacksonville Sharks

WFL team, 1974, 1975.

Joe F. Carr Trophy

An award given from 1938 through 1946 to the NFL's Most Valuable Player. Winners were: Mel Hein, New York Giants (1938), Parker Hall, Cleveland Browns (1939), Ace Parker, Brooklyn Dodgers (1940), Don Hutson, Green Bay Packers (1941, 1942), Sid Luckman, Chicago Bears (1943), Frankie Sinkwich, Detroit Lions (1944), Bob Waterfield, Los Angeles Rams (1945), and Bill Dudley, Pittsburgh Steelers (1946).

juke, v.

To feint or fake.

K

See kicker.

Kansas City Chiefs

AFL team, 1963–1969; won Western Division championship, 1966; won AFL championship 1966, 1969; won Super Bowl IV (1970). NFL team, 1970 to present; won Western Division championship (American Conference), 1971.

Kansas City Cowboys

NFL team, 1924–1926.

keeper

A running play in which the quarterback maintains possession of the ball and charges into the line.

Kenosha (Wisconsin) Maroons

NFL team, 1924.

key

Any small movement on the part of a player which serves to tip off an opponent as to the upcoming play. For example, the direction in which a player happens to be looking may key the side of the field to which the play is going. The positioning of a player's feet may indicate the direction in which he's going to be heading after the snap.

keying

To watch an opponent for a telltale sign or signs that will serve to indicate the upcoming play. The quarterback may key on the movement of the safeties to get an idea of what type of zone defense the opposition is using. Linebackers often key on the running backs, defensive backs on the wide receivers.

kicker

Kickoffs and field-goal and try-for-point attempts are handled by the team's placekicking specialist

kicker

141

or, simply, the kicker. Rarely is a kicker also a punter, and vice versa.

Not only must the kicker be skilled in getting his foot into the ball so as to achieve height, distance, and accuracy, but he also must be cool-headed under pressure. Get tense, and you're bound to miss.

Up until the mid-1960s, every kicker employed the same style, standing several feet behind the ball, striding forward two-and-one-half steps, then kicking, punching the ball with the hard, square toe of his kicking shoe, aiming at a point a few inches below the middle. Then along came Pete Gogolak, a Hungarian soccer player from Cornell University. Some friends got him to try kicking a football. He approached the ball more from the side, taking seven or eight steps, and he lofted it high and far by using his instep, not his toe. After starring with the Cornell football team, Gogolak signed with the Buffalo Bills of the American League in 1964. The following year he set an AFL season record for field goals.

Pro football general managers needed no further convincing, and began to search the soccer-playing nations of the world for prospective field-goal kickers. Their success is evidenced by a quick scanning of the NFL rosters. Among the place-kickers listed, there's the Jets' Bobby Howfield, from England, the Bengals' Horst Muhlmann, from Germany, and the Dolphins' Garo Yepremian, an Armenian who came to the United States by way of Cyprus. Indeed, well over half of all kickers are now soccer stylists. Toe-kickers are not exactly a vanishing breed, but their future is less than glistening.

kicking tee

The three-inch plastic stand which holds the football in an upright position for kickoffs. Use of the tee is not permitted on field-goal or try-for-point attempts.

kicking tee

kicking unit

A special team of players used on kickoff plays. *See* special team.

kickoff, n.

The placekick used to begin play at the start of each half and following a touchdown or field goal.

The ball is spotted down on the kicking team's 35-yard line. To be a legal kick, the ball must travel ten yards or be touched by the receiving team. Once this happens it's a free ball, and anyone can cover it.

When the ball goes over a sideline without being touched by the receiving team, it must be re-

143

kicked. There's a five-yard penalty for an out-of-bounds kick, meaning that the ball is placed down on the 30-yard line.

Kiesling, Walt

Hall of Fame, 1966.

As a player, a guard out of St. Thomas of Minnesota College, as an assistant coach, and ultimately as a head coach, Walt Kiesling gave almost half a century to pro football.

A big man, almost 270 pounds, he joined the Duluth Eskimos in 1926, stayed for a couple of years, then moved on to Pottsville, and later Chicago, playing for both the Cards and the Bears. When, in 1929, Ernie Nevers scored a record six touchdowns in a game against the Bears, it was Kiesling who did the blocking for him.

He was an All-League selection in each of the four years he played for the Cardinals, and the one season that he was a member of the Bears the team went undefeated. Green Bay was next for Big Kies, then Pittsburgh.

Kiesling was the Steelers' head coach in 1941 when the team finished with a 7-4-1 record. While that may seem at first glance like a modest achievement, Steeler fans were enthralled. It was the first winning season in team history.

When quarterback Bobby Layne was traded to the Steelers in 1958, Kiesling was still there as an assistant coach. Layne asked Kiesling how long he had played professional football.

Kiesling grinned. "Until they wouldn't let me suit up any more," he said.

Ill health forced Kiesling to give up coaching. He died in 1962.

Kinard, Frank (Bruiser)

Hall of Fame, 1971.

When the All-America Football Conference set up shop in 1946, about 100 NFL players switched over to the rival league. Of that number, only one man who had earned All-Pro honors in the NFL also managed to win the same recognition in the AAFC, and that was Bruiser Kinard.

A native of Pelahatchie, Mississippi, Kinard was a two-time All-American tackle at the University of Mississippi. He was drafted by coach Potsy Clark of the Brooklyn Dodgers in 1938. While it is often forgotten, the Dodgers were a powerful team in the pre-World War II era, and just missed winning division titles in 1940 and 1941.

Bruiser was a Dodger mainstay for seven seasons, winning renown as a smothering tackler and deadly blocker, particularly on the shovel-pass play that the Dodger team was noted for. Five times Kinard won All-League honors.

The Dodgers, their player strength sapped by the war, folded after the 1944 season. In 1946 Kinard was back in pro football with the New York Yankees of the newly organized All-America Conference. The Yankees won their division championship in 1946 and 1947, but could never manage to beat the Cleveland Browns in the title playoff. Of course, no one else could either. Kinard retired as a player in 1947.

In 1971, while serving as athletic director at the University of Mississippi, Kinard was elected to membership in the Pro Football Hall of Fame. He was asked whether he wanted "Frank" or "Bruiser" to be engraved on his Hall-of-Fame ring. "Better make it Bruiser," he said. "If it said Frank, no one would know it was mine."

Kinard

Knox, Chuck

Coach of the Year, 1973.

"He's got the things that all winners have. He's out of the same mold—hard-working, dedicated, years of pro experience. He's his own man—like Vince Lombardi, Don Shula, and George Allen." That's how Carroll Rosenbloom described Chuck Knox not long after he had hired the pleasant,

145

Knox

boyish-looking Knox to coach his Los Angeles Rams.

Knox didn't waste any time demonstrating that Rosenbloom had made a canny choice. The Rams of 1973 resembled the champion Dolphin teams, playing confident, no-mistake, ball-control football, but with one other attribute, the ever-present threat of a bomb in the John Hadl-to-Harold Jackson combination. Their record that year was very Miami-like, too—12-2 and a division title. The following year Knox directed the Rams to another division championship, but they lost to the Vikings in the NFL title match, the game resembling a street fight.

Born in Sewickley, Pennsylvania, where his father worked in the steel mills, Knox played tackle at small Juniata College in Huntingdon, Pennsylvania. After graduation, he went into coaching, never playing professional football. His apprenticeship included head-coaching experience with high school teams, two years as a college assistant coach, four seasons with the New York Jets, and six with the Detroit Lions. He was always an offensive specialist.

"When interviewing prospective coaches," Carroll Rosenbloom once said, "I always try to get them mad by asking them: 'What makes you think you can be a head coach?' The good ones react the same way. Before answering, Shula stuck his jaw out a mile. I thought Knox was going to spit in my eyes."

Lambeau, Curly

Hall of Fame, 1963.

When Curly Lambeau, with the financial assistance of the Indian Packing Company, founded the Green Bay Packers in 1919, it marked the beginning of a 32-year career in pro football, one that produced a half dozen NFL championships for Green Bay and more than a score of pro stars. At the time of his death in 1965, Lambeau ranked as the dean of NFL coaches.

A charter member of the Hall of Fame, Lambeau could have won such recognition as a founder of the Green Bay team or as its coach—or as a player. He quarterbacked the Packers from 1919 to 1928, and in that period did much to demonstrate that the forward pass was a legitimate offensive weapon. He once threw 45 passes in a game, and this in a time when quarterbacks were hardly ever air-minded.

Lambeau was a restless, impatient, and explosive individual, and his career was marked by controversy. One day during his tenth season as a player, he raged and ranted at the team between halves for errors he felt had been made. When the resentful players went out onto the field for the second half, they arranged "to open the gates on Curly," stepping aside to let the opposition storm in. The first play from scrimmage was Lambeau's last as an active player.

During the years he coached, the Packers were almost always a contending team. He was the first coach to win three consecutive NFL championships, 1929–1931. And during the late 1930s, Lambeau's Packer teams, featuring the Arnie Herber-to-Don Hutson passing combination, dominated NFL play.

147

But there were frequent factional disputes within the Packer organization, with the wrangling always centered about Lambeau and his method of operation. In February, 1950, he resigned. He coached the Chicago Cardinals for two years, and ended his pro career after coaching the Washington Redskins in 1954.

It's with Green Bay he'll always be identified, however. "During Curly's long leadership, the Packers put Green Bay on the map as the home of rough, rugged football, boasting some of the best football players in football history," says the *Encyclopedia of Football*. "He brought a small town into the big leagues."

Landry, Tom

Coach of the Year, 1966.

Cool, meticulous Tom Landry was the man who developed pro football's 4–3 defense and then fathered the multiple offense to punch holes in it. But he's probably better known for what he did with the Dallas Cowboys. He coached the team from its formation in 1960, saw it lose for five seasons, then win consistently for the next decade. The wins included every sort of division and conference championship, plus, in 1972, a Super Bowl victory.

Landry is usually thought of as a defensive specialist. He played cornerback for the New York Giants for six years beginning in 1950, and in his final playing years assisted as a coach. He became the Giants' defensive coach in 1956, and as such changed the team's umbrella defense into the 4–3 that became standard throughout pro football.

After considering the position of head coach of the Houston Oilers in 1960, Landry accepted the Dallas job. The Cowboys, an expansion team, did not win a single game that year. Landry sought to compensate for the lack of talent by installing a multiple offense, using ten or 11 different formations in a game, with five or six variations of each.

Landry

While Landry's admirers called him a "coaching genius," his detractors accused him of producing "a precise, mechanical brand of football that is so efficient it is boring."

Landry always kept his own emotions under a tight rein. There was no screaming from the sidelines, no locker-room harangues at halftime. "A team that has character doesn't need stimulation," he said.

Lane, Dick (Night Train)

Hall of Fame, 1974.

Of the scores of players in Pro Football's Hall of Fame, none took a more unlikely route in getting there than Night Train Lane, a cornerback for the Rams, Cards, and Lions for 14 seasons beginning in 1952.

149

Lane

Raised by a foster mother in Austin, Texas, Lane played a year of football at Scottsbluff (Nebraska) Junior College, then four years with an army team at Fort Ord in California. Always he was an offensive end.

Following his discharge in 1952, Lane got a job in a California aircraft factory. The work was hot and dirty, and eventually he became discouraged and quit.

While looking for another job, he happened to pass the offices of the Los Angeles Rams, and he stopped in and asked for a tryout. "We'll give you a look," said coach Joe Stydahar, and signed Lane to a free-agent contract.

The Rams tried Lane as a pass receiver at first. He worked diligently to learn the plays and patterns. Tom Fears, the Rams' star receiver, tried to help him. Lane would visit Fears' room every day. Fears had a record player in his room, and it seemed that every time that Lane was there, Bobby Morrow's recording of "Night Train" was playing in the background. It happened so frequently that Fears' teammates began to identify Lane with the recording, calling him "Night Train." The nickname stayed with him throughout his career.

Lane didn't impress any of the Ram coaches until they tried him as a defensive back. Tall and rangy, he had the speed and reactions of a basketball player, plus the size and strength to tackle with authority.

Lane had a brilliant rookie season. His 14 interceptions are still the NFL record for a season. He also led the league in 1954 with ten interceptions.

Despite his achievements, the Rams traded him to the Cardinals. He had too much daring for coach Hampton Poole, who wanted his players to follow the plays as set down in the playbook, and leave being creative to artists and poets.

Once he became a member of the Cardinal team, Lane studied films to see how he might improve. He noticed that some quarterbacks took advantage of him when he played a receiver tightly. So he modified his style, becoming a bit more cautious.

But he never ceased being a dangerous player. When he retired in 1965, he had intercepted 68 passes, more than any other player except Emlen Tunnell.

Vince Lombardi once paid Lane the ultimate tribute, giving Packer quarterback Bart Starr these instructions: "Don't throw the ball anywhere near him. He's the best there is."

lateral, n.

A pass that travels to one side or backward. A lateral is permitted any time during a game and from any point on the field.

When a lateral is intercepted, the player who intercepts can advance. However, if the lateral touches the ground and is then recovered by an opposing player, he is not permitted to advance. The ball is spotted down at the point of recovery.

lateral

Lavelli, Dante

Hall of Fame, 1975.

When the Cleveland Browns of the All-America Football Conference were admitted to the National Football League in 1950, it scarcely affected their penchant for winning. They were the NFL's champions that year, just as they had always been in the AAFC.

The switchover didn't cause wide receiver Dante Lavelli any problems, either. He won All-NFL honors twice, just as he had done in the AAFC.

A native of Hudson, Ohio, Lavelli played two seasons of football at Ohio State. Injuries and wartime service with the army caused him to forsake college for a tryout with the Browns. The lack of experience didn't seem to hurt him, however, for he won Rookie-of-the-Year honors in 1946.

Lavelli's forte was gathering in Otto Graham's long passes without breaking stride. He always seemed to be at his best in championship competition. In the six NFC championship games in which he participated, he caught 24 passes for 340 yards, both records. His 11-season career ended in 1956.

Layne, Bobby

Hall of Fame, 1967.

Slick passing and high living—that was Bobby Layne. In a 15-year career with four different teams, the tall, blond, often chunky quarterback set league records for completions and yardage, steered the Detroit Lions to two NFL championships and, at the same time, helped enrich a generation of bartenders and head waiters.

Bobby was very Texan. Born in Santa Anna, Texas, he played high school football in Dallas and was a college star at the University of Texas.

The Chicago Bears were his first pro team, but he spent only a year there, George Halas trading him to the New York Bulldogs. ''You probably don't remember the Bulldogs," Layne said in his book, *Always on Sunday*. "You shouldn't!"

A helpless team, the Bulldogs won only one game that season—an upset, Layne called it—and then drowned in a sea of red ink, but not before they had traded Bobby to the Detroit Lions.

The Lions finished second in the National Conference in 1951. "But we knew we were on our way to the top," said Layne, who led the league in completions, yards gained passing, and touchdown passes.

And Layne was right. The Lions ended the season in a tie with the Los Angeles Rams, then beat them in the playoff. Against Cleveland in the NFL title game, Layne established his eminence. He drove the Lions downfield early in the second quarter, then scored the touchdown himself from the two-yard line. Later, Doak Walker broke loose on a 67-yard touchdown run, and the Lions won, 17–7.

Bobby had the team back in the title game in 1954 and again in 1957. Both times they faced the Browns, Cleveland winning in 1954, the Lions getting revenge in their next meeting.

During those years, Layne built a reputation as a daring passer and flamboyant leader. He also came to be well known for his partying. He felt, however, the press exaggerated his taste for bright lights and loud music. "If you walk in the front door of a place," he once said, "check your coat, and go over to the bar like anyone else, it takes only ten minutes for the word to get all over town that Bobby Layne's down at so and so's, hymn-singing drunk."

Bobby's last years as a player were spent with the Steelers, and then he tried coaching for a while. Eventually, he gave up football altogether to concentrate on his varied business interests in Lubbock, Texas.

Bobby finds players to be different today. "We always had a helluva lot more fun than players today," he told Charlie Vincent of the Detroit *Free Press*. "We were a lot closer as a group. We used

Layne

to all do things together . . . the whole team. It's not like that now."

LB

See linebacker.

line

See line of scrimmage.

linebacker

Someone once asked several NFL scouts whom they would send behind the lines in wartime to assassinate an enemy leader. The scouts all chose a linebacker.

It was not merely the fact that the linebacker, with his size, strength, and mobility, had the physical qualifications. He also was judged to have the necessary mental and emotional capabilities. You have to have a kind of killer instinct to be successful as a linebacker. You have to know precisely when you should hold your ground, drift back, or charge in. And once it's time to make a move, you have to make it with authority, with brutality, even. When Dick Butkus played middle linebacker for the Chicago Bears, there were games in which he absolutely intimidated the opposition.

For years pro football had players who played the linebacker's position, but hardly anyone noticed. These were simply members of the offensive unit who backed up the line on defense, and who were called backers-up. Then came unlimited substitution and the era of specialization, and with that linebackers achieved status on their own.

In the standard 4–3 defensive alignment, there's a middle linebacker flanked by two outside linebackers. Some teams, an increasing number, use four linebackers on certain occasions, the extra linebacker going into the game in place of either a

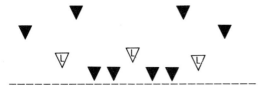

linebacker

lineman or deep back. For example, a team anticipating a short pass may take out a tackle or an end
in favor of another linebacker.

On running plays, the middle linebacker is supposed to either make the tackle or force the ball
carrier into a teammate. Much the same is true on
the sweep, with the outside linebacker usually cutting down the interference so a cornerback or
safety can charge in and make the tackle. As this
implies, the linebacker has to be extremely mobile
and very skilled in throwing off blocks. Dave Rob-
inson, a classic outside linebacker for the Packers
and later the Redskins, had this ability to such a
degree that only a handful of people ever remember seeing him on the ground.

When the quarterback sets up to throw, the
linebackers are responsible for the short zones,
which usually means they're covering the running
backs and the tight end. The strategy they use in
defending against the pass includes blitzing. Sometimes only one of the trio will charge in; other
times two men do; and still other times, all three
go.

There are a few basic differences between
playing outside linebacker on the left side and on
the right. The man who lines up on the left side
usually has to contend with the tight end, which is
no easy matter since tight ends average about 235
pounds and are among the strongest players in the
game.

And playing in the middle is different from
playing either one of the outside positions. By its
very nature, the position involves action and hitting just about every time the ball is snapped. Hall
of Famer Chuck Bednarik, who played both the
middle and outside for the Philadelphia Eagles,

155

line judge

was once asked the difference between the two. "That's easy," he answered. "The corner linebacker plays golf on Tuesday, but not the middle linebacker. He can't lift his arms until the end of the week."

line judge

One of the game officials, the line judge, on plays from scrimmage, straddles the line of scrimmage on the side of the field opposite the chain crew. It's the line judge who is responsible for timing the game, which includes keeping track of time-outs. He supervises the coin toss and he's also the official who fires the pistol to indicate the end of each period.

Like the head linesman, the line judge watches for offsides, other infractions involving line play, illegal formations, and he assists the other officials in runs and passes to his side. He also marks out-of-bounds plays on his side of the field.

lineman

One of the seven offensive players positioned at the line of scrimmage—the center, two guards, two tackles, and two receivers.

line of scrimmage

The imaginary line from sideline to sideline through the ball which separates the offense and defense at the beginning of each play.

live color

The coded signal used by the team's quarterback at the line of scrimmage to announce the calling of an audible. If the live color is red, the quarterback may shout out, "Red, 32 . . . Hut! Hut!" The word "red" alerts the team to disregard the play called in the huddle, and to follow the new instructions. Often the live color is changed during the game.

Quarterbacks call out a color on every play. But in the majority of cases, the color is merely a "dummy" call; that is, it has no special meaning.

Lombardi, Vince

Hall of Fame, 1971; Coach of the Year, 1959.

The scene is a meeting of the Football Writers Association of America in a ballroom of a Chicago hotel just before the College All-Star Game in 1968. Vince Lombardi is at the speaker's stand. He is wearing a powder-blue jacket, black slacks, and a navy tie. The overhead lights glint from his horn-rim glasses.

In answering a question, Lombardi says, ". . . and I could never see any reason why we should lose."

Some writers grin, and there are a few chuckles. But Lombardi is not smiling.

"I mean that gentlemen," he says firmly. "I could never see any reason why we should lose."

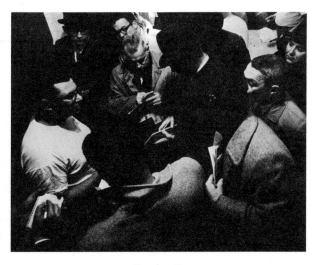

Lombardi

That's the way Lombardi felt. More important, it's the way he was able to get his players to feel. He touched them, moved them, and showed them that they could achieve success beyond what they believed their capabilities to be.

When Lombardi took over the Green Bay Packers in 1959, when he was 46, the team was in a sad state, hovering on the brink of bankruptcy. The previous season they had won only one game of 12. But in Lombardi's first year, virtually the same players won seven of 12 games.

The next year the Packers captured the Western Conference championship, but lost to the Eagles in the NFL title game. Then the parade began, with Green Bay winning NFL championships in 1961, 1962, 1965, 1966, and 1967. They also won the first two Super Bowl contests.

Lombardi always maintained that there was no secret to the success of the Packers. Indeed, it was true. The best of his Packer teams operated with only 12 or 13 plays. Good blocking and good tackling were their main features.

"Coaches who can outline plays on a blackboard are a dime a dozen," Lombardi once said. "The ones who win get inside their players and motivate."

That's what Lombardi was able to do. In achieving this motivation, he often played the role of a militant leader and stern disciplinarian.

"When he says, 'Sit down,' I don't even bother to look for a chair," one player said.

"He's fair. He treats us all the same—like dogs," was tackle Henry Jordan's frequently quoted remark.

Bill Curry, the team's center, once observed that Lombardi "coaches through fear." Bill Curry was traded.

True, Lombardi demanded much, but he gave as much as he demanded. Other coaches have imposed strict discipline and clamored for perfection, but with modest results.

The difference with Lombardi was that he not only believed in discipline for his players, but for himself as well. Indeed, he had a consuming commitment to self-discipline, and it touched every aspect of his life.

He was also a realist. He knew there were players who would never respond to his methods. "I know damn well I can't coach all 640 players in the league," he once said. "I'm only one man. I can only *be* that one man, and I've got to have men who *bend* to me."

The son of an immigrant Italian butcher, Lombardi was born in 1913 in the Sheepshead Bay section of Brooklyn, and grew up there. In college, at Fordham, from which he graduated with honors in 1937, he played guard on the famous line known as the Seven Blocks of Granite.

After graduation, he went to law school for a year, supporting himself by playing minor-league football with the Brooklyn Eagles. In 1939 he joined the faculty at St. Cecilia High School in Englewood, New Jersey, where he taught physics, chemistry, algebra, and Latin, and became head coach of the football team. He stayed there seven years, then returned to Fordham as an assistant coach for two years.

He joined Col. Earl Blaik's staff at the U.S. Military Academy in 1949, and got his first job in pro football in 1954, when head coach Jim Lee Howell of the New York Giants asked him to take over the offense. The offer to join the Packers came five years later.

He retired from coaching in 1967. But in the season that followed he was an unhappy, often forlorn figure. When the Washington Redskins offered him a position as coach and general manager, he accepted.

He worked his magic again in the 1969 season, directing the Redskins to their first winning record in 14 years.

His philosophy was simple, but he was an enigma to many people. Jerry Kramer, in his book, *Instant Replay,* described Lombardi as "a cruel, kind, tough, gentle, miserable, wonderful man whom I often hate and often love and always respect."

In the summer of 1970, Lombardi was struck with what one doctor described as "an extraordi-

159

narily virulent form of cancer." He died in September of that year. People everywhere felt a sense of personal loss.

look-in, n.

A type of short pass wherein the quarterback straightens up immediately after getting the snap, then fires quickly to a receiver slanting over the middle.

loose ball

A ball in play but not in the possession of any player. A loose ball may be recovered by any player.

Los Angeles Buccaneers

NFL team, 1926.

Los Angeles Bulldogs

AFL team, 1937; won AFL championship, 1937.

Los Angeles Chargers

AFL team, 1960; won Western Division championship, 1960; franchise transferred to San Diego following 1960 season.

Los Angeles Dons

AAFC team, 1946–1949.

Los Angeles Rams

NFL team, 1946 to present; won Western Division championship, 1949; won National Conference championship, 1950, 1951; won Western Conference championship, 1955; won Coastal Division championship (Western Conference), 1967, 1969; won Western Division championship (National Conference), 1973, 1974; won NFL title, 1951.

Los Angeles Wildcats

AFL team, 1926.

Louisville Bucks

NFL team, 1922, 1923.

Louisville Colonels

NFL team, 1926.

Luckman, Sid

Hall of Fame, 1965.

George Halas tinkered with the T formation for many years before he found a quarterback who could make the T go, a quarterback who could pivot, fake, handoff, and, most important, pass accurately over long distances. He found him in 1938 in the person of a chunky, dark-haired tailback for Columbia University. His name was Sid Luckman.

But Luckman, born and raised in New York, had little enthusiasm about playing for the Bears. "He thought Chicago was Cowboy-and-Indian country," said George Halas, the Bears' owner. Eventually, however, Halas convinced Luckman to make the move West.

At first Luckman was awkward and unsure of himself, with the pivots and handoffs causing him the most difficulty. The Bears even abandoned the T for a couple of games during 1939. But by the middle of the season, Luckman began to show

Luckman

flashes of the brilliance that were to characterize his career for the next decade.

Never before in pro history and seldom since has a team dominated the game the way the Bears did under Sid Luckman, winning five Western Division championships and four NFL titles. The score of one of their playoff victories, as Arthur Daley once observed, looks like a misprint in the record book. It reads: Chicago, 73; Washington, 0.

As for Luckman himself, he won All-Pro honors five times, and was named Player of the Year in the NFL in 1943. That year Sid's friends in New York honored him with Sid Luckman Day at the Polo Grounds. After the gifts had been presented and the speech-making was over, Luckman expressed his gratitude with a glittering performance.

Seven times that afternoon Luckman connected with Bear receivers for touchdowns, a record that has been equalled several times but never surpassed. The Bears won 56–7. Some day!

Lyman, William Roy (Link)

Hall of Fame, 1964.

In professional football of the early 1920s, each defensive lineman had a fixed area of responsibility which he protected, seldom moving to the right or left, just standing there and waiting. Link Lyman, a Walter Camp All American at the University of Nebraska, who signed with the Canton Bulldogs in 1922, helped change that. Quick and agile, Lyman shifted with the play, watching, probing, sliding, then making his charge.

In Lyman's first three seasons in pro football, he played in only one losing game, and each year his team won the NFL title. George Halas landed Lyman in 1925, and he spent most of the rest of his career with the Bears. He retired in 1934.

In pro football of the 1920s, it was often said that a tackle was merely a fullback with his brains knocked out. Lyman changed that thinking, too.

Lyman

M

Mac

With some teams, the term used to identify the middle linebacker.

man-in-motion

When a running back or receiver turns and runs parallel to the line of scrimmage before the ball is snapped, the man is said to be in motion. The motion man may block or receive a pass, or he may be used to decoy. Only one man is permitted to go in motion, and he cannot run forward until the ball is snapped.

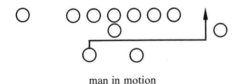

man in motion

man-to-man defense

A type of pass coverage in which members of the defensive secondary are responsible for specific receivers. In the usual man-to-man coverage, each of the cornerbacks covers the wide receiver on his side of the field, while the right safety covers the tight end. The other safety, usually called the free safety, helps out the cornerback on the weak side, or covers a backfield man. The linebackers are responsible for the running backs as they circle out of the backfield.

Assignments can change from play to play, however. For example, a safety on one side of the field may help to double-team the wide receiver on that

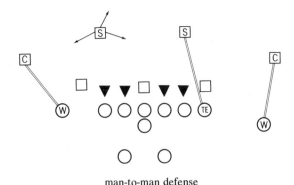

man-to-man defense

side, while the outside linebacker covers the tight end.

Mara, Tim

Hall of Fame, 1963.

According to the book, *Irish Names and Surnames,* by Rev. Patrick Woulfe, the name Mara is Gaelic for merry or mirthful. And, indeed, Tim Mara was a genial sort of person. "The Smiling Irishman," Arthur Daley called him.

He was, that is, until 1925, the year he bought a franchise permitting him to operate an NFL team in New York City called the Giants. It cost him $2,500, but that was only his admission fee. He lost more than ten times that amount in the club's first year of operation.

When Red Grange came to town with the Chicago Bears in December of 1925, he filled the Polo Grounds to capacity, wiping out Mara's losses, and causing him to grin once more. But not for long. The very next season Grange and his manager started a competing team in New York, and the red ink flowed.

Despite the problems, Mara set high standards. He insisted upon players and coaches of the highest caliber, and he hired them on a full-time basis. When the team traveled, everything was first class.

Mara weathered the stock market crash, the Great Depression and, in the 1940s, the encroachment of the All-America Football Conference which put competing teams in New York and Brooklyn.

During the 1950s, things were different. The Giants ranked as one of the most prosperous franchises in a prospering league, and there were smiles galore.

Tim Mara died in 1959. His son, Wellington, is the club's president today.

Marchetti, Gino

Most Valuable Player, 1958; Hall of Fame, 1972.

What do you want in a defensive end? A man who is big, strong, quick, and canny. Having a bit of meanness wouldn't hurt.

From a tactical standpoint, he has to be able to get off the mark fast in rushing the passer, be mobile enough to get outside to turn sweeps in, and have the ability to outmuscle and outsmart the blocking on plays to the inside.

This describes Gino Marchetti, who survived 13 NFL seasons as a defensive end, all but one of them with the Baltimore Colts. He was an All-Pro choice seven times, and when the board of selectors of the Hall of Fame chose the NFL's all-time team in 1969, Marchetti was on it.

Marchetti will always be identified with the Colts-Giants 1958 championship playoff. It's been called the greatest of all football games.

Less than three minutes remained, the Giants led, 17–14, and were struggling to run out the clock. It was third down, three yards to go for a first down. Quarterback Charlie Conerly handed the ball to Frank Gifford who slanted to his left behind the blocking of Roosevelt Brown. Suddenly Marchetti was there, grabbing Gifford and slamming him to the ground a foot short of the first down.

In the pileup that followed, Marchetti was seriously injured. He shrieked in pain as the officials unraveled the players. He had broken a leg bone in two places.

They carried him off the field on a stretcher. Despite the agonizing pain, he refused to be taken to the dressing room. He watched the game from the sidelines, seated on the stretcher, his broken leg propped up with his helmet. He got to see all but the last few plays, as the Colts tied the game, then went on to their thrilling overtime victory.

"I was stretched out on the trainer's table when I heard the guys come into the dressing room," Marchetti once recalled, "and I could tell by the way they were whooping it up that they had won. Then the leg stopped hurting." Later, his teammates voted Marchetti the game ball.

Carroll Rosenbloom, owner of the Colts during Marchetti's years with the team, once credited him with "creating modern defensive-end play." He was, said Rosenbloom, an example of "the ultimate" at the position.

Marshall, George Preston

Hall of Fame, 1963.

As a promoter and idea man, George Preston Marshall, founder, owner, and president of the Washington Redskins, had few equals. It's no wonder the team is a civic institution.

Marshall, charter member of the Hall of Fame, was involved in several other business enterprises before he tried pro football. After his father's death in 1911, he took over the family laundry business, setting up branches throughout Washington. "Long Live Linen" was his slogan. And for a while he was publisher of the old Washington *Times*.

But football was better suited to his talents than anything else. In 1932 he obtained an NFL franchise in Boston and christened the team the

Braves. After five years of financial struggle, he moved the franchise to Washington, renaming the team the Redskins.

There his show-business talents took full flower. He supplied the Redskins with half-time shows that included a 110-piece marching band complete with $25,000 worth of Indian tribal costumes. The team's fight song, "Hail to the Redskins," was hummed and whistled by Supreme Court justices and taxi drivers alike. He also supplied the team with talent, with Slingin' Sammy Baugh and a fine supporting cast. The Redskins won the NFL title in 1937, 1942, and 1943.

Marshall is also remembered for getting his fellow owners to adopt the division of the league into two conferences and to have a title playoff game. He figured in the liberalization of the rule concerning forward passing and the adoption of the waiver rule for players. He was also instrumental in bringing an end to the practice of letting each team formulate its own schedule, permitting the league to do it instead.

Marshall was frequently involved in controversy. The Redskins were the only team in the league to draw the color line. Not until 1962 did the Redskins have a Negro player.

Before Marshall's health began to fail—he died in 1968—he was a familiar figure at Redskin games. If he was not prancing on the sidelines, he would be running the team from his box seat, even down to calling the plays.

At times, though, he seemed to have a greater love for the Redskins' band than the team itself. Once, a blizzard struck Washington several hours before the Redskins were to play the New York Giants. Marshall and his aides began a frantic effort to get the field cleared. An hour before kickoff, Jack Mara, president of the Giants, was standing alone in the stands staring dejectedly out toward the field, which was still buried in snow. Suddenly Marshall was at his side, his face aglow.

"They're coming! They're coming!" Marshall exclaimed. "They'll be here in plenty of time."

167

"The snowplows?" said Mara.

"No," said Marshall. "The overshoes for the band."

Matson, Ollie

Hall of Fame, 1972.

Matson

The only problem Ollie Matson ever gave a coach, Bob Oates once noted, was where to play him. In a 14-year career with four different teams, Matson played halfback, fullback, wide receiver, tight end, and defensive back. No matter where he was assigned, he was usually the best at his position.

Matson played his college football at the University of San Francisco, where he won All-America honors, and was drafted by the Chicago Cardinals in 1952. From the beginning he impressed coaches with his versatility, combining the speed and power of an offensive back with the quickness and finesse of a safety or cornerback.

Pete Rozelle, general manager of the Rams in 1959, wanted Matson—badly. In one of the most discussed trades in football history, Rozelle gave the Cards six players from the Ram roster for Matson, plus two unnamed players, and a draft choice—nine players in all.

Matson was traded to the Lions in 1963, and to the Eagles a year later. He retired in 1966. Unfortunately, he played on only two winning teams in his lengthy career. He, and that marvelous racehorse stride of his, deserved better.

May

With some teams, the term used to identify the middle linebacker.

McAfee, George

Hall of Fame, 1966.

When the great Gale Sayers arrived on the scene in 1965, dazzling fans of the Chicago Bears with his speed and shiftiness, someone asked George Halas to compare the newcomer with George McAfee, a former Bear star. "The greatest compliment you can pay a ball carrier," Halas answered, "is just to compare him with McAfee."

McAfee, a halfback, was the Gale Sayers of his day. A track star at Duke and an All American there, he had a way of luring a tackler with a leg, then shifting direction abruptly and without warning, as Sayers often did. Red Grange called McAfee "the most dangerous man with a football in the game."

McAfee joined the Bears in 1940, the beginning of a period of greatness for the team. They were known as the "Monsters of the Midway." McAfee, however, who never weighed more than 170 pounds, looked out of place among his teammates.

But his size—or lack of it—never seemed to hinder him. Besides his fancy runs on plays from scrimmage, he returned punts and kickoffs, and loved doing it. As a punt-return specialist, he established a career average of 12.78 yards per return, an NFL record that still stands.

To add to his natural speed and elusiveness, McAfee used a "secret weapon." During practice sessions, he wore conventional football shoes but for games he switched to low-cut Oxfords, the type of shoe all players wear today but which were seldom seen in the 1940s.

McAfee and his lightweight footwear helped spark the Bears to NFL championships in 1940 and 1941. After military service, he returned to the Bears in 1945 just in time to take part in a late-season game against the Steelers. Halas promised to use him sparingly, and did—only 12 minutes. But in that time, McAfee scored three touchdowns.

After he retired as a player in 1950, McAfee served as an NFL official—a head linesman—for several years. In 1966, the year he was elected to membership in the Hall of Fame, he gave up officiating to devote his full time to the family oil business in Durham, North Carolina.

169

McElhenny, Hugh

Hall of Fame, 1970.

McElhenny

"The King" was what they called Hugh McElhenny. Tough and casual, he was the preeminent running back of the 1950s, the finest broken-field runner up until the time of Gale Sayers.

Like Sayers, McElhenny had every move in the book, plus a few that weren't there. He could pivot and sidestep, spin and fake. He could change pace and turn on a sudden burst of speed when he needed it.

And McElhenny had power, too, power to break a tackle or bull his way forward for an extra yard or two. "Your moves depend on your field position, the down, the yardage, and your knowledge of the defense and the man you're trying to beat," he said. "But there are times when all the moves in the world won't help you, and the only way to get a couple of yards is by putting your head down and driving straight ahead."

McElhenny was one of the most celebrated college players of his day, and not just because of what he did on the playing field. There were accusations that the University of Washington violated Conference regulations in recruiting him, a charge McElhenny himself never denied. "I've got three cars," he once said, "$30,000 in the bank, the promise of a lifetime job from four companies, and everytime I score a touchdown, some wealthy guy puts ten bucks under my pillow. Hell, I can't afford to graduate."

After he was drafted by the 49ers in 1952, he asked for the kind of money no one ever thought of asking for. Eventually, he signed for $7,000. When San Francisco coach Frankie Albert was introducing McElhenny to his new teammates, he said, "Gentlemen, meet the only college star who took a cut in salary to play pro football."

As a rookie, McElhenny was seldom less than sensational. In a game against the Bears, he gathered in a punt on the 49er six-yard line, shot straight up the middle leaving a pair of wouldbe tacklers in his wake, shifted gears as a tackler appeared on his right, then turned on the speed as the man closed in. He swerved to his left to avoid another man, then cut back to his right again, then zigzagged the rest of the way through the remaining Bear players.

"That," said George Halas, "was the damndest run I've ever seen in pro football." And George Halas had seen an awful lot of runs.

McElhenny was an almost unanimous choice for Rookie of the Year. The competition included Ollie Matson, Babe Parilli, and Frank Gifford.

His best seasons were from 1952–1958. Like every running back, he had his share of injuries, but they never seemed to bother him. Coaches were much more of a problem. He and San Francisco coach Red Hickey were in frequent disagreement.

Hickey put McElhenny's name on the 49ers' "available list" in 1961, allowing him to be taken by the Minnesota Vikings, an expansion team. He played for the Vikings for a couple of years, and then one season with the Giants and one with the Lions before retiring.

While with the Giants, he helped the team win the Eastern Conference title. "Hugh's knees were shot, and I could use him only sparingly," said coach Allie Sherman. "Still, he made valuable contributions. We always knew he would give us his very best."

McNally, John (Johnny Blood)

Hall of Fame, 1963.

Very fast and supremely confident, Johnny Blood, often called the "Vagabond Halfback," played with an assortment of early National League teams, but his best years were spent with the Green Bay Packers in 1929 and most of the 1930s, a period in which the Pack won four NFL titles. Blood contributed 37 touchdowns to the Packer cause, but it's for what he did off the field

McNALLY, JOHN (JOHNNY BLOOD)

McNally

that he's usually remembered. He has been described as the most colorful player of all time.

The son of a wealthy New Richmond, Wisconsin, family, Blood finished high school at 14, attended St. John's College near Collegeville, Minnesota, for a while, and then went on to Notre Dame. Highly regarded as a halfback, he left school abruptly after "borrowing" a motorcycle and heading for Richmond, Virginia, with a young lady in the sidecar.

Football was another of his interests. When he and a friend went to try out for a semipro team, they were told to adopt assumed names if they wanted to retain their college eligibility. They happened to pass a movie marquee that advertised Rudolph Valentino's *Blood and Sand.*

"That's it!" Blood shouted. "You be 'Sand', I'll be 'Blood.'" Johnny Blood he thus became.

Blood played for the Milwaukee Badgers, Detroit Eskimos, and Pottsville Maroons. When he arrived in Green Bay in 1929, his reputation as a hell-raiser preceded him. Green Bay coach Curly Lambeau sought to tone him down. When Blood asked for a salary of $100 a game, Lambeau countered with an offer of $110, provided Blood would promise that he wouldn't drink after the Tuesday of any week in which a game was scheduled.

Blood thought for a minute, then offered a compromise. If Lambeau would make the day Wednesday instead, Blood said he'd play for $100. Lambeau agreed.

Lambeau lectured Blood, fined him, and appointed members of the team to watch over him. But he could not control him.

Lambeau once ordered the squad to report at the railroad station at 3:30 for a trip East. At the appointed time, everyone was there except Blood. The departure time of 3:45 arrived, but there was still no sign of Blood. Lambeau ordered the train to pull out. Ten miles out of the station the brakes screeched and the train jolted to a stop. A car had stopped on the tracks and a man alongside it was waving madly. It was Blood.

Each year during the off-season, Blood floated about the country, taking jobs of every type. He worked as a deckhand on a Pacific freighter, a hotel desk clerk, a bartender, a newspaper reporter, a miner, a croupier in a gambling house, and as a WPA laborer.

In the years following his retirement as a pro player, he returned to college and obtained his master's degree. He listed reading, studying, writing, and meditation as his favorite occupations.

Blood lived in the house in which he was born in New Richmond, Wisconsin. But he seldom could be found there. He never relinquished his vagabond ways.

measuring chain

The ten-yard chain, connected at each end to seven-foot rods, used to indicate the distance that the ball must be advanced for a first down. On a first down, one rod is placed at the sideline at a point opposite the ball. The chain is pulled taut and the other rod is placed in the ground at the sideline ten yards in advance of the ball. Anytime the ball is advanced beyond the second rod, the chain is moved.

When officials are uncertain whether a team has achieved a first down, the chain is brought out onto the field for a careful measurement. Officials use the forward point of the ball in determining whether the first-down point has been reached.

Meg

With some teams, the term used to identify the middle linebacker.

Memphis Southmen

WFL team, 1974, 1975.

Miami Dolphins

AFL team, 1966–1969. NFL team, 1970 to present; won Eastern Division championship (American Conference), 1971–1974; won American Conference championship, 1971–1973; won Super Bowl VII (1973), Super Bowl VIII (1974).

Miami Seahawks

AAFC team, 1946.

Michalske, Mike

Hall of Fame, 1964.

"The Guard of the Century" was what Mike Michalske was called. The gaudy title was first used during Michalske's college days at Penn State when he was clearing the way for Lighthorse Harry Wilson.

And that's what he was called when he moved to the New York Yankees of the American Football League in 1926. There he did the blocking for Red Grange.

After the Yankees folded in 1928, Michalske sold his services to the Green Bay Packers, and he played an important role as Green Bay captured three consecutive NFL championships beginning in 1929. "The Guard of the Century" was an All Pro three times in Green Bay, retiring as a player in 1937.

Another nickname Michalske had was "Iron Mike," one he earned in recognition of his indestructibility. Like all players of his time, Michalske played 60 minutes of every game, but he did it with greater diligence than almost anyone else. "I just never got hurt," he once said, "not until my last season of pro ball when I injured my back. The players used to kid me. They said I must have been getting paid by the minute."

174

middle linebacker

In the normal 4–3 defense, the middle linebacker faces the offensive center, and is usually stationed not more than three or four yards from him. He is flanked by the outside linebackers. *See* linebacker.

Mike

With many teams, the code name for the middle linebacker.

Millner, Wayne

Hall of Fame, 1968.

One of pro football's last two-way ends, Wayne Millner caught the passes of Sammy Baugh during a seven-year career with the Washington Redskins. Having Baugh as your quarterback was something of a mixed blessing. The throws were as perfect as any could be, but no matter how many passes you caught, the headlines always went to Slingin' Sam.

Millner's most memorable game was the 1937 NFL championship. He grabbed down 11 passes that day, an NFL record at the time. And he also established himself as an outstanding "money player." In the third quarter he and Baugh combined a touchdown play that covered 53 yards, and which tied the game, 14–14.

In the final period, after the Bears had moved into the lead again, Baugh hit Millner on a 78-yard touchdown play. The Redskins won, 28–21.

Millner was in the lineup that December day in 1940 when the Redskins were massacred by the Chicago Bears, 73–0. A few weeks after the game, a newspaper man asked Millner whether he thought the game's outcome would have been any different if Charlie Malone hadn't dropped a Baugh pass in the end zone early in the first quarter. Millner grinned, then uttered an often-quoted remark: "Hell," he said, "the score would have been 73–6."

Milwaukee Badgers

NFL team, 1922–1926.

Milwaukee Chiefs

AFL team, 1940.

Minneapolis Marines

NFL team, 1922–1924.

Minneapolis Redjackets

NFL team, 1929, 1930.

Minnesota Vikings

NFL team, 1961 to present; won Central Division championship (Western Conference), 1968, 1969; won Western Conference championship, 1969; won NFL championship, 1969; won Central Division championship (National Conference), 1970, 1971, 1973, 1974; won National Conference championship, 1973, 1974.

MLB

See middle linebacker.

Moore, Lenny

Hall of Fame, 1975.

A multi-talented speedster, 6-foot-2, 198 pounds, Lenny Moore was the No. 1 draft choice of the Baltimore Colts in 1956 following an outstanding college career at Penn State. He lived up to expectations, indeed, exceeded them, winning Rookie-of-the-Year honors, the beginning of a glittering 12-year career with the team, which included two championship seasons, 1958 and 1959.

Since Moore could both catch passes and run with the ball, his talents meshed perfectly with those of Johnny Unitas. Lenny divided his playing time between halfback and flanker during the first five years of his career, then became a full-time running back. Statistically, he ranks among the leaders in several different categories. The 113 touchdowns he scored put him right behind Jim Brown in that department. Moore was named the Colts' promotional director in 1975.

Morrall, Earl

Most Valuable Player, 1968.

"You ask me what it takes to be No. 1? I think it's the same for a whole career or just one season," Earl Morrall once said. "And I can wrap

Morrall

it up in one word—dedication—working every day as if the whole game depended on you, even when you know you're not going to start.''

That was the philosophy that guided quarterback Earl Morrall through a 19-year career with six different teams, a career with more ups and downs than a busy elevator. Never once in those years did Morrall give up on himself. Whenever the opportunity presented itself, he was ready.

Deft, quick, and clever as a ball-handler, and guileful as a play-caller, Morrall began his career with the San Francisco 49ers in 1956. The next year he was with the Pittsburgh Steelers, and then it was on to the Detroit Lions. He spent seven seasons in Detroit before being dealt to the New York Giants.

When, in 1968, the Giants sent Morrall to the Baltimore Colts, Earl was regarded as journeyman quarterback, efficient but not spectacular. The press was forever calling him a ''crewcut veteran.'' Don Shula, coach of the Colts, wanted Morrall to backup Johnny Unitas.

Unitas' arm went bad and Earl took over. All he did was quarterback the Colts to 14 wins in 15 games and a stunning 34–0 victory over the Browns in the Conference title game. This was an ''up'' period for Earl. A ''down'' period quickly followed—Super Bowl III. Earl failed to see wide receiver Jimmy Orr open in the end zone, and the Jets were upset winners. ''I blew it,'' said Morrall.

Morrall played sparingly the next two seasons. Then in January, 1971, Unitas was injured just before halftime in Super Bowl V, with the Colts trailing the Cowboys. In stepped Morrall once more, taking the Colts to a 16–13 win.

The next year Earl went back to being No. 2 behind Johnny Unitas. When the season was over, Don Shula, who had switched to the Miami Dolphins, obtained Earl for the $100 waiver fee. It was one of Shula's smartest moves. When Bob Griese's ankle was broken in the fifth game of the season, in came Earl. ''Let's keep it together,'' he said in the huddle. ''Let's keep it moving.''

The Dolphins kept it moving all right. They didn't lose a game that season, becoming the first team to go undefeated since the Chicago Bears compiled an 11–0 record in 1942.

The next year Earl was back to playing the role of an understudy. Bob Griese directed the team in all but one game.

Through his long career, Morrall was called such names as "Bullpen Boy," "Super-Sub," "Mr. Inconsistent," and even "Old Rag Arm." It's true that no quarterback was No. 2 for so long a period. Morrall's consolation was that he got to be No. 1 once in a while.

Motley, Marion

Hall of Fame, 1968.

During the years that the Cleveland Browns were the dominant team in pro football, first in the All-America Football Conference and later in the National League, Marion Motley, a 238-pound fullback with a sprinter's speed, furnished the team's running attack. That's not all he did. He pass-blocked for Otto Graham—"I doubt anybody ever knocked him off his feet," Graham once said—and he darted to the outside to grab Graham's quick flares. He also backed up the line on defense.

Motley was never publicized very much, however. The headlines went to Graham and to coach Paul Brown. Even Graham's pass receivers—Mac Speedie and Dante Lavelli—were better known than Motley.

The countless records that Motley set were all wiped out by Jim Brown, who broke in with the Browns two years after Motley retired. Yet if Motley had been used in the same way Brown was, things might have been different.

"I had four plays and that was all," Motley said. "An old, ordinary end run—no wide running play—a buck up the middle, a trap, and a sideline screen pass.

Motley

179

"I'd carry the ball eight or nine times a game, and inwardly I always had the feeling I should have carried the ball more. But Paul Brown was a winner and didn't need any advice from me."

In spite of the limited manner in which he was used, Motley was the all-time AAFC rushing leader. By 1950, the year the Browns were taken into the NFL, Motley was 30 and his knees had gone bad. But he managed to lead the league in rushing that year and won All-Pro recognition.

One of the nicest tributes ever paid Motley came from Paul Zimmerman, one of pro football's most respected writers. When Zimmerman was writing his best-selling book, *A Thinking Man's Guide to Pro Football*, he decided to do a chapter on the greatest player he had ever seen. "There was no question in my mind," said Zimmerman. "He stood alone—Marion Motley."

mousetrap

See trap.

move list

There are several methods clubs use to hold onto players who are not on the active roster. The taxi squad is one such device. The move list is another.

When put on the move list, a player is being "moved" from the active roster to the reserve list, to the taxi squad, that is. But during this interim period, other clubs are not permitted to claim him. He can remain on the move list for seven games, after which the club must either activate him, put him on waivers, or use another of its "moves." A club is permitted twelve such moves each season.

moving pocket

A term made popular during the early 1970s by Hank Stram, coach of the Kansas City Chiefs, to describe rollout movement on the part of the Chiefs' quarterback, Len Dawson. One advantage of the moving pocket, according to Stram, was that it forced the pass rushers to hesitate until they knew which side of the field Dawson was going to sprint for. In addition, it enabled Dawson to neutralize the charge of the opposition's best rusher; when he wanted to, he simply rolled to the opposite side of the field. "It also provides the linemen with a blocking angle on the opposing pass rushers," said Stram, "and it's always easier to block a man on an angle, rather than head on."

muffed ball

The muffed ball looks like a fumble but it's not. A muff occurs when a player makes an unsuccessful attempt to catch or otherwise recover a loose ball. One type of muff occurs when a player is attempting to catch a punt or field-goal try and lets the ball slip through his hands. It's not classified as a fumble because he never actually had possession of the ball.

Why bother to distinguish one from the other? Because when the opposition recovers a muffed

muffed ball

181

ball, the ball is dead and can't be advanced. It's different with a fumble, of course.

multiple foul

Two or more fouls by the same team on the same down.

multiple offense

A type of attack which utilizes an assortment of offensive formations in any given game. The idea is to keep the defense guessing. The Dallas Cowboys and the Kansas City Chiefs are the two teams usually associated with a multiple offense.

Nagurski, Bronko

Hall of Fame, 1963.

The story is apocryphal, but it makes a point. After Bronko Nagurski had become a star fullback at the University of Minnesota, his coach, Doc Spears, was often asked how he happened to find the Bronk.

"I was driving past a farm one day," Spears would say, "when I noticed this big, strong farmboy plowing a field. I stopped to ask directions. The boy pointed—with his plow. That's how I found Bronko."

His enormous strength helped to make Nagurski the legendary figure he is today. And his size, too. He was 6-foot-2 and weighed 230. While these statistics would scarcely make him the equal of Larry Csonka, in the 1930s, when Nagurski was battering opposing lines for the Chicago Bears, to be 6-foot-2, 230 was to be huge. Red Grange, by comparison, weighed about 180 pounds. Linemen who exceeded 200 pounds, while not exactly rare, were not common. The Eagles had an end who weighed 160. The point is that Nagurski was a big man, a very big man, in what was then essentially a small man's game.

Salaries were likewise minuscule in those days. Nagurski's first contract with the Bears paid him $5,000 a year for two years. He later took up professional wrestling to supplement his income as a player.

Nagurski played a total of nine years for the Bears, and in six of those years he won All-NFL honors. How many yards he gained during his career is anyone's guess. The statistics that are available credit him with 4,301 yards, but keeping records was a haphazard business in those days.

Nagurski

183

The only thing the press wanted to know was who won and who lost, and sometimes they weren't very interested in that.

While Nagurski's name may not be found in any of the record books, there is plenty of testimony available from those who played against him and those who watched him play that gives evidence as to just how unstoppable he was. James T. Gallagher, a Chicago sportswriter, summed up a Nagurski performance in these words: "Those who were unlucky got in his way. Those who were lucky got out of it. The only thing that could stop him was a brick wall."

Namath, Joe

Most Valuable Player, Super Bowl III (1969).

Up until that January afternoon in 1969 when his sharp passing produced a stunning upset for the New York Jets over the Baltimore Colts in Super Bowl III, Joe Namath was regarded as something of a clown. Sure, he was held in awe for the strength and accuracy of his right arm, his fast drop-back, and his ability to release the ball within a millisecond or two.

Namath

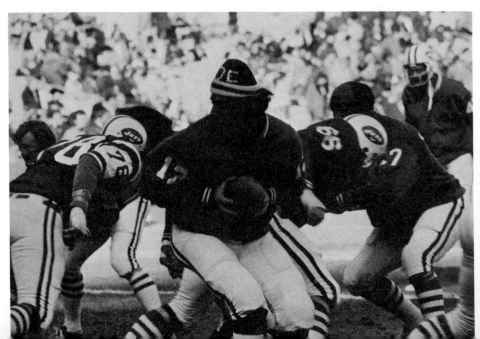

And he had won some statistical renown. He had thrown for a total of 4,007 yards in 1967, becoming the first quarterback in history to gain more than 4,000 yards passing. He led the American League in completions that year (with 491) and was second in touchdown passes (with 26).

It was for what he did off the field that he earned his clownish image. Tall, 6-foot-1, 190 pounds, with a hawkish nose, he had black, carefully combed hair that dropped over his collar. This in a time when a big percentage of the players wore crewcuts. He promoted the idea that he was a live one, that he liked girls, liked them very much, and that he also liked big cars, and Johnny Walker Red.

Once, following a game in which the Jets were beaten by Houston, 24–0, Namath was asked why his team failed to score. "Booze and broads," he replied in his best put-on fashion.

The next day newspapers everywhere declared that partying was ruining the Jets. "I don't deny that I said that," Namath stated later in the week. "But I sure was putting the guy on. We came ready to play. We just got beat."

Namath guided the Jets to the American League championship in 1968, beating the Oakland Raiders in the playoff game to win the right to meet the Colts in the Super Bowl. Baltimore had won 13 of 14 league games that year, and their fierce defensive unit had shut out four opponents. But this meant nothing to Namath. "We're going to beat the Colts on Sunday; I *guarantee* it," he told luncheon guests upon receiving an award from the Miami Touchdown Club a few days before the game.

Namath was as perfect as a quarterback can be that day, first using running back Matt Snell to loosen up things, then hitting wide receiver George Sauer time after time on quick turn-ins. He frequently changed plays and snap counts at the line of scrimmage, and constantly varied the length and cadence of his snap counts. Clive Rush, the Jets' offensive coach, watched Namath's performance from an observation post high above the field. At halftime he told Namath, "Do things just the way you did in the first half. Don't change a thing." Namath didn't change. The Jets won, 16–7.

When the final gun sounded, Namath ran from the field with one hand aloft, the index finger pointing to the sky. The Jets were No. 1, he was saying.

In the years that followed, Namath himself was frequently described as being No. 1, the best quarterback in the league in terms of his ability to move his team. He had some exceptional days. Early in the season of 1972, facing the Colts, he shredded Baltimore's highly regarded zone defense with long, looping passes and quick, short ones. He threw for six touchdowns and 496 yards that afternoon. Later in the season he put on another spectacular aerial show against the Oakland Raiders, what has been called one of the greatest performances by a quarterback ever. "He was like a magician out there," said an Oakland player. "He was unreal."

There were plenty of dismal days, too. Because of bad knees, he was unable to duck pass rushes and blitzes, and was injured several times as a result. For this, and other reasons, he missed big chunks of the seasons of 1970, 1971, and 1973.

Not everyone agrees that Namath is the greatest thing since city water. Interviewed by *Pro* magazine in 1974, writer Tex Maule echoed the opinion of some observers when he said, "You can't rank him [Namath] with the Van Brocklins, Starrs, and others because he hasn't played that well. He's had only one great year in his career. He hasn't done a damn thing since and he didn't do much before."

What must be taken as the majority view was once expressed by Jerome Barkum, a wide receiver for the Jets. One afternoon in 1974, a vintage year for Namath, during a game in which he was completing passes all over the place, Barkum spoke to him on the sidelines, "You are," he said, "the hottest thing since fire."

National Football Conference

One of the two conferences of the National Football League, consisting of the Eastern, Central, and Western Divisions. The other is the American Football Conference. Conference champions meet in the Super Bowl.

National Football League

410 Park Ave., New York, N.Y. 10022.

National Football League

While the National League's official record manual lists the first professional football games as having been played on August 31, 1895, between the Latrobe, Pennsylvania, YMCA team and a team from nearby Jeannette, Pennsylvania, it wasn't until 1920 that the first organized league was formed. In September of that year, representatives of 11 teams gathered at Ralph Hays's Hupmobile showroom in Canton, Ohio—Hays managed the Canton team, the Bulldogs—and formed the American Professional Football Association. Two years later the Association was renamed the National Football League.

But it was a "league" in only the loosest sense of the word. Franchises skipped from city to city, or would play one year and melt away the next. Games were scheduled whenever and wherever teams thought they could draw a crowd. And the league was hardly "national" in its appeal. Interest in the game was limited to western Pennsylvania, the adjacent region of Ohio, that is, Akron, Canton, and Massillon, and western New York State, Rochester, and Syracuse.

The game took an important step forward in 1925 when Red Grange signed with the Chicago Bears. A college star at Illinois, Grange's popularity rivaled that of Babe Ruth or Jack Dempsey, and when he and the Bears barnstormed the country, crowds flocked to see them, and pro football earned headlines for the first time.

During the depression years of the early 1930s, the number of NFL teams dropped sharply, from 22 in 1926 to less than half that number in 1931. Several changes were introduced to perk up the sport. The league was split into two divisions in 1933, Eastern and Western, and the winners of each met in a playoff for what was frequently called the world championship. The first of these, played on December 17, 1933, saw the Chicago Bears defeat the New York Giants, 23–21.

A change in the rules also helped. Passing was legalized from anywhere behind the line of scrimmage; previously the passer had to be at least five yards behind the line.

During World War II, the military draft took so many first-line players that the NFL considered shutting down. But most teams held on, and at the war's end, with the economy booming, the league enjoyed palmy days. In 1946, the average attendance per game exceeded 30,000 for the first time.

Through the years, the NFL frequently had competition to think about. As early as 1926, a rival league, known as the American Football League, sought to establish itself, but it lasted only one year. A more determined effort was launched in 1946 when the All-America Football Conference came into existence. The two leagues competed bitterly until 1949 when a merger agreement was reached, the NFL dictating the terms. Three AAFC teams—the Cleveland Browns, Baltimore Colts, and San Francisco 49ers—became NFL members as a result.

The 1950s were a time of growth and prosperity for the National League, although there were one or two weak franchises. Games were televised nationally for the first time, and owners began to receive substantial payments from the networks for the sale of game rights.

When another American Football League began operations in 1960, it hurt. Joe Namath of the New York Jets and other AFL stars began stealing headlines, fans, and even television revenues. A merger was the only solution. It came about in 1966.

The agreement gave rise to the American Football Conference and National Football Conference, the winners of which meet in the Super Bowl each January. Pro football continued to flourish in the years that followed the merger, with attendance increasing year by year, reaching an average of 58,000 per game in 1973.

But 1974 was a troubled year. The first formal players' strike was a wrenching experience. The World Football League offered competition, driving players' salaries to record heights. Attendance decreased and television ratings slipped. While there were a few worried faces, no one was thinking of handing back his franchise.

National Football League Players Association

1300 Connecticut Ave., N.W., Suit 408, Washington, D.C. 20036.

A certified union, the only one made up of professional athletes, the National Football League Players Association was founded on January 8, 1970, out of a merger of the AFL Players Association and the NFL Players Association.

National Football League
Players Association

The organization is governed by a board of player-representatives made up of one representative from each NFL team. The board elects the organization's president and executive committee, and passes regulations establishing organization policy.

Through a player strike called in the summer of 1974, the NFLPA sought to obtain several "freedom" issues from the NFL owners, including the right of veterans to veto a trade, the elimination of fines as a method of enforcing discipline, the use of an impartial arbitrator in the settlement of player-owner grievances, and a modification of the clubs' right to draft players. After 59 days, the strike collapsed without the organization having achieved its goals.

189

Neale, Earle (Greasy)

Hall of Fame, 1969.

Neale

As coach of the Philadelphia Eagles from 1941 to 1950, Greasy Neale led the team to a division title in 1947 and the NFL championship in 1948 and 1949. Never before and never since have the Eagles enjoyed so much success. And for this, Neale won admission to the Hall of Fame.

But Greasy Neale had several other careers before he ever became a pro coach. He played football with Jim Thorpe long before the National League had ever been thought of. He was an outfielder for the World Champion Cincinnati Reds in 1919. He coached the Washington and Jefferson team which held mighty California to a scoreless tie in the 1922 Rose Bowl. Neale was backfield coach at Yale when Alexis Thompson, the Eagles' owner, asked him to take over the team.

From the very beginning, Neale was recognized for his skill as an innovator. He studied the T-formation plays that the Chicago Bears had used in their 73–0 win over the Redskins in the 1940 NFL title game, and improved upon them. Neale pioneered the use of the fullback as a blocker. Eagle plays of this type, with the halfback slanting either inside or outside a defensive end, gave other coaches sleepless nights.

To throttle down the attack of enemy teams that used the T, Neale introduced the 7–4 defense. Two specialists, stationed about where the outside linebackers are positioned today, would "chug" the ends, prevent them from breaking downfield, while the defensive line—the Eagles' "Suicide Seven"— would proceed to wreck the play. "Neale," George Halas once said, "contrived the only defense which semi-effectively stopped the T."

The team that Neale took over in 1940 was a helpless one. They had won only one game the season before, and their No. 1 and No. 2 draft choices had been traded away. But Neale soon had the team winning, and by 1945 they were challenging for the title. Their Eastern Division championship in 1947 was the first in the club's history.

After winning the NFL title in 1948 and 1949, the Eagles slumped to a 6–6 record. That winter Greasy was vacationing in Florida when he received a telegram from Jim Clark, then the Eagles' owner, that said: "You will be paid the one year remaining on your contract, but you are no longer coach of the Eagles."

So ended the career of one of the game's most colorful figures. In the seasons that followed, the Eagles once again fell upon evil days. Except for one brief spurt in 1960, they have never attained the eminence they enjoyed under Greasy Neale.

neutral zone

The area between the offensive and defensive lines of scrimmage. It is the length of the ball in width.

Nevers, Ernie

Hall of Fame, 1963.

On Thanksgiving Day, 1929, the Chicago Cardinals upset their crosstown rivals, the Bears, 40–6. While it was surprising that the Cards could beat the Bears, much less trounce them, what's remarkable about the game was that one man, Ernie Nevers, scored every Cardinal point.

Nevers's six touchdowns and four extra points won him a prominent place in the NFL record manual. The feat is all the more outstanding when you consider that football was a low-scoring game in those days, and it was not uncommon for one team to defeat another by 6–0 or 9–0 or thereabouts. Forty points was almost unheard of.

Nevers, once described by Pop Warner, his coach at Stanford, as "the football player without a fault," did all the Cardinals' punting, passing, and placekicking, almost all of its ball-carrying,

Nevers

and returned punts and kickoffs. He was team captain, called the signals, and later was the team's coach. There is no truth to the story that he sold programs in the stands at halftime.

An All American and a Rose Bowl hero at Stanford, Nevers signed with the Duluth Eskimos in 1926, getting a princely salary for the day, $25,000. "But I made one mistake," Nevers said, "I forgot to ask how long the season was going to be."

It was a very serious mistake. Renamed the Ernie Nevers Eskimos, the team played all its games on the road, leaving Duluth in September and not returning until January. In that time, the Eskimos played 29 games—19 in league competition, ten exhibitions—and traveled 17,000 miles.

The squad consisted of only 13 players. Ole Haugsrud, the owner, and Dewey Scanlon, the coach, used to don uniforms and warm up with the team so that the crowd wouldn't get the idea that the Eskimos were undermanned.

They really weren't undermanned because they had Nevers, and he was indestructible. He missed only 27 minutes of those 29 games.

Nevers was also a professional baseball player, a pitcher for the St. Louis Browns, in 1926–1928. He sat out the 1928 football season, returning to the game in 1929 as a player-coach.

The year 1931 was Nevers' last as a player. The Duluth franchise had been shifted to Chicago and renamed the Cardinals. Ernie's body was so battered by this time that he used to have to arrive at the ballpark early in order to get all his taping done before kickoff. The frugal Cardinal management was unwilling to supply him with all the adhesive tape he needed, so sometimes Nevers had to use black electrician's tape.

That season the Cards played 19 games, and Nevers played every minute of every one. Not even the fans show that much dedication today.

Newark (New Jersey) Bears

AFL team, 1926.

Newark (New Jersey) Tornadoes

NFL team, 1930.

New England Patriots

NFL team, 1971 to present.

New Orleans Saints

NFL team, 1967 to present.

New York Bulldogs

NFL team, 1949.

New York Giants

NFL team, 1925 to present; won Eastern Division championship, 1933, 1935, 1938, 1939, 1941, 1944, 1946; won Eastern Conference championship, 1956, 1958, 1959, 1961, 1962–1964; won NFL championship, 1927, 1934; 1938, 1956.

√**New York Jets**

AFL team, 1963–1969; won Eastern Division championship, 1968, 1969; won AFL championship, 1968; won Super Bowl III (1969). NFL team, 1970 to present.

New York Stars

NFL team, 1974; franchise shifted to Charlotte, North Carolina, during 1974 season.

New York Titans

AFL team, 1960–1962; franchise taken over by league during 1962 season.

193

New York Yankees

AFL team, 1926. NFL team, 1927, 1928. AAFC team, 1946–1949; won Eastern Division championship, 1946, 1947.

New York Yanks

AFL team, 1936, 1937, 1940. NFL team, 1950, 1951.

NFC

See National Football Conference.

NFL

See National Football League.

NFLPA

See National Football League Players Association.

nickel defense

A type of zone coverage used when the offense is believed to be certain to pass. It derives its name from the fact that "five" deep defensive backs are employed. There are four linemen and two linebackers.

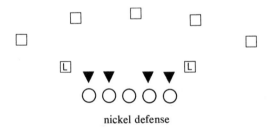

nickel defense

Nomellini, Leo

Hall of Fame, 1969.

If the National League kept records for durability, they'd probably all belong to Leo Nomellini, a two-way tackle with the San Francisco 49ers from 1950–1963. During those 14 seasons, Nomellini, who was nicknamed "The Lion," took part in 174 consecutive regular-season games and, counting preseason games and his ten Pro-Bowl appearances, he played in a total of 266 contests.

Nomellini

There are players who have participated in more games, but they're mostly kickers, and their total playing time doesn't amount to a full hour for an entire season. Nomellini, in the early stages of his career, played 60 minutes of every game, and until the day he quit always had a willingness to do so.

But the muscular Nomellini, who was 6-foot-3, 260 pounds, didn't win Hall-of-Fame recognition purely on the basis of his staying power. An alert, aggressive performer, he once took a ball almost off of Sammy Baugh's foot as Baugh was about to punt, and he carried it over the goal line for a touchdown. In a game against the Colts in 1957, Nomellini blocked a field-goal and try-for-point attempt to put the 49ers in a playoff with the Lions for the Western Conference title.

Born in Lucca, Italy, and brought to the United States as an infant, Nomellini had to forego high school to help support his family. The first football game he ever saw, he played in—as a Marine at Cherry Point, North Carolina, during World War II. He later earned All-America honors at Minnesota. He was the 49ers' No. 1 draft choice in 1950.

Nomellini could never fully explain his remarkable endurance record. His excellent physical condition was surely one reason. Even in the latter stages of his career, he reported to training camp in better condition than teammates five to ten years younger.

no-show, n.

When, in 1973, Congress passed a bill prohibiting the National Football League from blacking out games sold out 48 hours ahead of time, home games were televised for the first time in years. This situation gave rise to the no-show, a fan holding a ticket for a sold-out game who, because of unpleasant weather, adverse temperatures, or both, preferred to watch the game on home television.

numbering system

The assigning of numbers according to a player's position. In the NFL, numbers are assigned on this basis:

1–19: quarterbacks and kickers
20–49: running backs and defensive backs
50–59: centers and linebackers
60–79: defensive linemen and offensive linemen (except centers)
80–89: wide receivers and tight ends

There are many exceptions, however. Little was done to enforce use of the formula until 1972, and players active before that date are still permitted to use numbers they were originally assigned.

O

Oakland Raiders

AFL team, 1960–1969; won Western Division championship, 1967–1969; won AFL championship, 1967. NFL team, 1970 to present; won Western Division championship (American Conference), 1970, 1972–1974.

odd-man line

A variation of the basic 4–3 defensive alignment in which a defensive tackle lines up head-to-head with the center. The middle linebacker fills the gap.

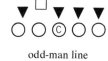

odd-man line

offense, n.

The team in possession of the ball. The term also refers to any effort on the part of that team to gain yards or score.

offensive guard

"When you play guard," Dick Bestwick, offensive line coach at Georgia Tech, used to tell football candidates, "it's because you're not smart enough to be a quarterback, not fast enough to be a halfback, not rugged enough to be a fullback, not big enough to be a tackle, and don't have the hands to be an end." That kind of thinking has gone the way of the drop kick. Guards today have such a variety of tasks to perform that the position demands a player of highly developed skills.

197

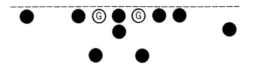

offensive guard

The guards have to be able to drive straight ahead, creating running room for the ball carrier on slants and dives. The man the guard is charging into is usually bigger than he is and about as quick. On sweeps, the guard must pull from the line to lead the interference. To O. J. Simpson, Reggie McKenzie is the most valuable player on the Buffalo Bills. Reggie McKenzie is a pulling guard.

Offensive guards also pass-block, their toughest assignment. Pass-blocking means standing your ground for three or four seconds while you are pummeled by a defensive end or tackle, a player who is usually bigger and stronger.

"My No. 1 weapon is my head," Dave Herman, a standout guard for the New York Jets, once said. Herman's neck measured 18½ inches. His hat size was 7⅞. Quite a weapon.

offensive holding

Illegal use of the hands when blocking a defensive player. The penalty is 15 yards.

offensive tackle

Rayfield Wright. Winston Hill. George Kunz. Ron Yary. If you know who these players were and the teams they played for (respectively, the Cowboys, Jets, Colts, and Vikings), consider yourself a fan of All-Pro caliber.

Wright, Hill, Kunz, and Yary represented the cream of the NFL's offensive tackles during the early to mid-1970s. But like virtually all other offensive tackles, they worked in relative obscurity. The guards pull on sweeps, and television broadcast-

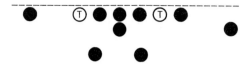

offensive tackle

ers cite their value, and they get their pictures in the paper for clearing the way for the likes of O. J. Simpson. Centers, since they are the ones who put the ball in play, get some recognition, too. But if you're an offensive tackle, it's not likely that anyone will ever know your name.

Being unheard of is only part of it. The tackles are usually set opposite the defensive ends, the biggest, toughest players on the defensive team. On pass plays, the end charges headlong into the tackle, smashing his helmet with an open hand, ramming him with his massive shoulder, even grabbing his jersey in an attempt to throw him to one side. The tackle can only bull and butt to counter the charge. On running plays, however, the tackle gets to fire out at the opposition. Running plays are fun.

The requirements for the job are good size and plenty of height, some speed and some quickness. And a touch of masochism.

official

Any one of the members of the six-man team charged with the responsibility of regulating play and enforcing the rules. Officials include the referee, umpire, head linesman, back judge, field judge, and line judge.

In total, there are approximately 100 officials employed by the National Football League, and they are paid approximately $350 for each of the dozen or so games they work during the season. Each summer they must attend a week-long clinic, at the end of which they are given a six-hour written examination. During the season, their work is evaluated by means of game films which are

199

screened by Art McNally, the NFL's supervisor of officials, and his staff. Coaches are also permitted to appraise officials' work.

offsetting penalties

This situation occurs when both teams are guilty of rule infractions on the same play. The penalties cancel out one another.

offside

When any part of a player's body is beyond the line of scrimmage at the time the ball is snapped, he is said to be offside. The penalty is five yards.

Sometimes the offside rule is confused with "encroachment." But the latter has to do with one player making contact with another *before* the ball is snapped.

"Offside" also refers to the side of the field away from the flow of the play. For example, a player on that side of the field may be described as an offside guard, or offside tackle, etc.

off tackle

In the offensive line, the area just to the outside of the tackle positions. A running play, for example, will be described as an off-tackle slant.

OG

See offensive guard.

onside

The side of the field to which a play is run. A player on that side may be described as an onside tackle, or onside guard, etc.

onside kick

A short kickoff by means of which the kicking team hopes to gain possession of the ball. The rules say that the kickoff must travel only ten yards, and that it can be recovered by either team. In the late stages of a game in which it's trailing, a team will seek to take advantage of this rule, kicking the ball just beyond the minimum distance, and scrambling forward in an effort to recover it. If the team fails, it's calamitous, for the opposition is almost certain to have the ball near midfield.

In actuality, all kickoffs are onside kicks, the term "onside" referring to the area of the field to which the play is directed. But the term "onside kick" is almost always applied only in the limited sense.

Oorang Indians (Marion, Ohio)

NFL team, 1922, 1923.

open field

That area of the field beyond the line of scrimmage.

option block

A type of block in which an offensive lineman drives a defensive player in whatever direction the defender wants to go, that is, along the path of least resistance. The ball carrier, watching carefully, cuts in the direction opposite.

The option block is different from the more traditional type of shoulder block, in which the offensive man is assigned to move the defensive player in a particular direction. As this suggests, option blocks are simpler to execute, yet they're more effective.

201

option clause

A player has a choice of either signing his contract or not signing it. Should he not sign, he receives a letter stating that the club intends to exercise its option on the player's services for an additional year, without a contract and at not less than 90 percent of his then current salary. The paragraph that spells this out in the Standard Player Contract is known as the option clause. In the May following the option year, the player becomes a free agent.

The NFL owners believe that the option clause is as necessary to football as turnstiles and ticket takers, and that without it there would be chaos. The wealthier owners, it's said, such as Lamar Hunt and Clint Murchison, would wind up with all the best players. There'd be no competition. But the National Football League Players Association believes the clause should be abolished, and that the game would be the better for it.

The idea that the rich teams would buy up all the best talent has been called the Dynasty Theory by Ed Garvey, Executive Director of the NFLPA. "To accept the Dynasty Theory," he said, "you also have to accept the idea that these guys [the owners], are purely sportsmen, that they're in football because they love the game. They're not, of course; they're businessmen. They're in it for a profit. They're not going to do anything that would destroy the competitive balance of the league and thereby jeopardize profits.

"Suppose that the option clause was abolished, and Lamar Hunt went out and hired Joe Namath, agreeing to pay him, say, $300,000 or $400,000. Is he then going to try to get Sonny Jurgensen? Or Roman Gabriel? Nonsense."

A survey among members of the Players Association showed that 31 percent of those polled were in favor of complete elimination of the option clause, while 62 percent wanted the clause "changed to allow more freedom to the players." The remaining seven percent were satisfied with the option clause as it exists.

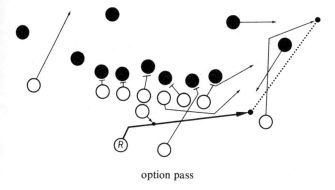

option pass

option pass

A play in which a running back has the choice of carrying the ball or passing it. The play begins as a sweep, the back running parallel to the line of scrimmage after taking the quarterback's handoff. As he reaches the point where he is to turn downfield, he pauses momentarily to check the defensive coverage. If the deep defensive backs are darting forward to play the run, the back passes (as shown here), but if the defensive men are dropping off to cover the receivers, he continues running.

option run

Any running play in which the ball carrier reads the blocking and picks whatever opening develops. This is in contrast to the more traditional method in which the runner hits into a designated hole.

Orange (New Jersey) Tornadoes

NFL team, 1929.

OT

See offensive tackle.

out end

The wide receiver set to the side opposite the tight end; the split end.

outlet

The pass receiver, usually a running back, who gets the pass when the other receivers are covered or in the case of a strong pass rush. *See* safety valve.

out of bounds

The football is out of bounds whenever it touches or crosses a sideline or endline. The same holds true for any player.

outside

In the case of the offensive line, the area between the sidelines and each of the tackle positions.

outside linebacker

Either of the two linebackers who is stationed three to four yards behind the line of scrimmage and just to the outside of either of the defensive ends. *See* linebacker.

overshift

Any defensive alignment in which players are shifted from their normal positions to the strong side in order to counter offensive strength.

Owen, Steve

Hall of Fame, 1966.

As head coach of the New York Giants for 22 years beginning in 1932, Steve Owen won a reputation as an innovator. Also as a winner. In those 22 years, the Giants won eight division and two league titles.

From Oklahoma, Owen was a cowhand in his youth, although he also found time to play some football at Phillips University in Enid, Oklahoma. After he had been in New York for a couple of decades or so, Frank Graham said of him: "If you had never met him, you might think he had just checked his horse at the station in Enid, and expected to go back and claim it any day."

A beefy tackle for the Kansas City Cowboys in 1924 and 1925, Owen was, by his own definition, a "smash-and-shove player." His smashing and shoving made a vivid impression on the Giants, and they purchased his contract from the Cowboys for $500. "I had seen fat hogs go for more than they paid for me," Owen said, "but in those days, a fat hog was a lot more valuable than a fat tackle."

Extremely popular with his teammates and highly thought of by Giant owner Tim Mara, Owen was named co-coach of the team in 1931, collaborating with quarterback Benny Friedman. The next year Owen was put in sole charge.

The A formation was one of Owen's first innovations. Most teams of the day used the single wing. In this formation, the line was overbalanced to one side and the backfield men were deployed to that side.

The A formation was different in that the backfield was set to the other side, to the weak side. The A carried the Giants to the NFL championship in 1938 and to the Eastern Division crown the next year.

Other coaches switched over to the T, but not Owen. He stayed with the A formation until 1949,

Owen

205

and that year brought in Allie Sherman to give the Giants T power, with Charlie Conerly doing the quarterbacking.

Pro football of this period was dominated by the Cleveland Browns, but Owen developed a method for smothering the Cleveland attack. He assigned his tackles and guards to rush the passer, while the center jammed the middle. The ends would slide back to defend the short-pass areas. There were four deep defenders. This came to be known as the umbrella defense because the alignment of the backs resembled the shape of an open umbrella. With minor variations, the umbrella became the 4–3 defense of the 1960s.

The Giants enjoyed splendid success with the umbrella at first, but eventually other teams learned to poke big holes in it. When it came time for Owen to make changes, he was reluctant to do so.

The 1953 season was his last as head coach of the New York team. He coached in the Canadian Football League for several years, returning to the Giants as a scout in 1963. He died a year later.

"Every team strives to do today what Steve was doing twenty years ago," said George Halas not long after Owen's death. "He taught us all plenty."

P

See punter.

Page, Alan

Most Valuable Player, 1971.

When they start giving out Most Valuable Player awards to defensive tackles, anything can happen. But in Alan Page's case, while it may have represented a breakthrough, it was never regarded as surprising.

Take what happened in a game against the Lions in 1971. Page, with his strength, finesse, and incredible quickness, was the dominant figure on four consecutive plays. On first down, he flattened quarterback Greg Landry for a nine-yard loss. When the Lions tried a sweep, Page hit running back Altie Taylor for a four-yard loss. On third down, Landry dropped back to pass. Page forced him out of the pocket and chased him down. Landry managed to gain two yards, making it fourth and 11. To cap his performance, Page surged in to block Earl Weaver's punt.

Page, who is 6-foot-4, 248 pounds, began doing things like that for the Vikings beginning in 1967. The year before he had graduated from Notre Dame, playing defensive end on an undefeated Irish squad. When he joined the Vikes, coach Bud Grant switched him to tackle. He had to work hard to learn the new blocking assignments, but by midseason he was a starter. Up until that time, no rookie had ever broken into the Vikings' starting lineup.

Page has been described as the best pro lineman there is in causing "hurries," a term coined by

Page

207

Bud Grant. A hurry occurs when a lineman makes the quarterback throw the ball before he really wants to. "Sometimes," says Grant, "a hurry is better than a sack."

Page has also gained renown for recovering fumbles. One season he recovered seven, a feat that won him a place in the NFL record manual. But he says he derives his greatest satisfaction from causing fumbles. It was Page who jolted Terry Metcalf in an NFC playoff game in 1974, causing the Cardinal star to drop the ball. Nate Wright turned the miscue into a Viking touchdown.

Once Page had won starting status with the Vikings, his next goal was to become All Pro. It took him two years.

In 1970 he achieved another ambition when he was named Defensive Player of the Year in the National Conference. The next season he won the league's MVP award.

"I enjoyed winning the award," he said, "because it showed that the press and the fans are finally realizing that runners and quarterbacks are not the only reason games are won and lost."

Parker, Clarence (Ace)

Hall of Fame, 1972.

When the Brooklyn Dodgers entered the NFL in 1930 the owners of the club sought to establish a rivalry with the New York Giants, a Dodger-Giant baseball rivalry being a very profitable item.

But it never happened. Whenever the football Giants played the football Dodgers, apathy ran rampant. The Giants were simply too good. In the first 20 meetings of the two teams, the Dodgers lost 19 times.

Ace Parker turned things around. As the Dodger quarterback, beginning in 1937, he steered the team to three successive wins over the uppity Giants, and even got the team to finish second in its division.

Parker called the signals on offense, threw passes, and carried the ball. On defense, he played safety. Records for the season of 1938 reveal that in the 11 games the Dodgers played, Parker spent a total of four minutes on the bench, surely one reason he was named Player of the Year.

The military claimed Parker's services from 1942–1944. Brooklyn struggled without him, using over-age players and others otherwise not susceptible to the draft. Attendance kept dropping and in 1943 the club was forced to surrender to the bill collectors.

When Parker returned from the service, he signed with the Boston Yanks for a year, played about "three minutes," and the following year switched to the New York Yankees in the All-America Football Conference. Directing a single-wing attack, he led the Yankees to a 10-3-1 record and the Eastern Conference title. They gave the Cleveland Browns a scare in the playoff but eventually the Browns won. In those days, the Browns always won. The season was Parker's last in pro football.

Sammy Baugh, Sid Luckman, and Don Hutson are usually rated as the most noted players of the 1940s. Not in the borough of Brooklyn, however. There Ace Parker's was the biggest "name" of all.

Clarence (Ace) Parker

Parker, Jim

Hall of Fame, 1973.

For eleven seasons with the Baltimore Colts beginning in 1957, big, quick Jim Parker used his 6-foot-3, 275-pound frame to pass-block for Johnny Unitas and create running room for such backs as swift Lenny Moore and, later, Tom Matte. He was the first "pure" offensive lineman to win Hall-of-Fame recognition. Previous enshrinees played offense *and* defense.

"Just keep 'em away from John." That's how coach Weeb Ewbank summed up Parker's responsibilities when he arrived at his first training camp in the summer of 1957. "That was the big rule," Parker said. "If we kept 'em away from John, we all ate well."

Parker served as Unitas's protector, first as a tackle, later as a guard. He won All-Pro honors four times in each position, a remarkable achievement.

As a tackle, Parker usually blocked the defensive end. At guard, he was assigned the bigger, stronger defensive tackle. "That's the one thing I liked about playing guard," Parker once observed. "The tackles were bigger and usually not as agile as the ends. I liked the big guys. Speed boys gave me trouble."

When a knee injury he had suffered failed to respond to treatment, Parker stepped down as a player. His election to the Hall of Fame came in the very first year he was eligible for the honor.

parlay card

Parlay cards, also known as pool cards, are distributed each week during the football season in high schools, on college campuses, in office buildings and factories. It's said that they have a higher total circulation than all the nation's daily newspapers combined.

Each card lists 20 or so college games and about ten pro games, each with a point-spread. The bettor attempts to select the winning team in a minimum of three contests, and returns to the seller a numbered stub indicating his selections and the amount of his wager. With most cards, if any one of the bettor's selections loses or just equals the spread—ties it—he loses his wager. If all his choices beat the spread, he is paid at the odds listed on the reverse side of the card.

The point-spreads listed in parlay cards are different from those used by bookmakers, who take bets on single games. They are different because they are usually fixed at the most frequent margins of victory—3, 4, 6, 7, 13, 14, 20, and 21 points.

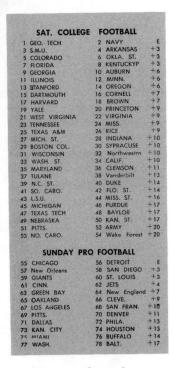

parlay card

SAT. COLLEGE FOOTBALL

1 GEO. TECH	2 NAVY	E
3 S.M.U.	4 ARKANSAS	+3
5 COLORADO	6 OKLA. ST.	+3
7 FLORIDA	8 KENTUCKYP	+3
9 GEORGIA	10 AUBURN	+6
11 ILLINOIS	12 MINN.	+6
13 STANFORD	14 OREGON	+6
15 DARTMOUTH	16 CORNELL	+7
17 HARVARD	18 BROWN	+7
19 YALE	20 PRINCETON	+9
21 WEST VIRGINIA	22 VIRGINIA	+9
23 TENNESSEE	24 MISS.	+9
25 TEXAS A&M	26 RICE	+9
27 MICH. ST.	28 INDIANA	+10
29 BOSTON COL.	30 SYPRACUSE	+10
31 WISCONSIN	32 Northwestrn	+10
33 WASH. ST.	34 CALIF.	+10
35 MARYLAND	36 CLEMSON	+11
37 TULANE	38 Vanderbilt	+13
39 N.C. ST.	40 DUKE	+14
41 SO. CARO.	42 FLO. ST.	+14
43 L.S.U.	44 MISS. ST.	+16
45 MICHIGAN	46 PURDUE	+17
47 TEXAS TECH	48 BAYLOR	+17
49 NEBRASKA	50 KAN. ST.	+17
51 PITTS.	52 ARMY	+20
53 NO. CARO.	54 Wake Forest	+20

SUNDAY PRO FOOTBALL

55 CHICAGO	56 DETROIT	E
57 New Orleans	58 SAN DIEGO	+3
59 GIANTS	60 ST. LOUIS	+3
61 CINN.	62 JETS	+4
63 GREEN BAY	64 New England	+7
65 OAKLAND	66 CLEVE.	+9
67 LOS ANGELES	68 SAN FRAN.	+10
69 PITTS.	70 DENVER	+11
71 DALLAS	72 PHILA.	+13
73 KAN. CITY	74 HOUSTON	+13
75 MIAMI	76 BUFFALO	+14
77 WASH.	78 BALT.	+17

The reason for this is to increase the likelihood of ties, which adds to the seller's advantage.

If the bettor is successful in picking the outcome of three games, that is, if he beats the spread on each, he is usually paid at the rate of four-to-one. The payoff for picking four winners is ten-to-one; five winners, fifteen-to-one, etc.

In any case, the odds are atrocious. This chart shows the enormous advantage the seller has:

Number of Games Played	Payoff on $1	Odds Against Winning	Percentage Retained by Operator
3 out of 3	$4	8–1	50%
4 out of 4	$10	16–1	37.5%
5 out of 5	$15	32–1	43%
6 out of 6	$25	65–1	61%
7 out of 7	$50	128–1	61%
8 out of 8	$100	256–1	61%
10 out of 10	$250	1,024–1	80%
12 out of 12	$500	4,096–1	80%
15 out of 15	$2,000	32,768–1	90%
16 out of 16	$5,000	65,536–1	88%

As the chart indicates, the bettor's best—or least worst—strategy is to pick four games. In such a case, the seller retains "only" 37½ percent of the handle.

But the chances of winning are even less than the chart indicates because the effect of ties is not considered. Most sellers consider a tie to be a losing pick. Approximately one of every 20 games selected ends in a tie. This means that of every 100 bettors selecting four teams, 20 lose because of the tie factor, and half of all ten-team bettors lose because one of their selections involves a tie.

The pool-card seller never has to worry about laying-off bets. Whether a game might be fixed or not doesn't interest him. He knows that even if his bettors know in advance the outcome of one game, the odds would still be with him, except in the case of those who picked four games.

Law-enforcement officials, and bookies, too, regard parlay-card selling as a petty business, but, in total, it is anything but. According to a study of sports betting conducted for the Fund for the City of New York, more than $25 million is bet annually in New York City on football pools, and another $10 million on baseball and basketball pools. Operators keep as much as $28 million of the total, the study reported. The Boston *Globe* has estimated that football cards in the Greater Boston area gross more than $2 million per week during the season.

The volume is undoubtedly higher than these or other estimates. Any person with a sixth-grade education and a talent for efficiency and salesmanship can establish and operate a football pool. Because the bets are small—"The odds are so lousy that no one bets more than a couple of bucks," says a New York bookie—and risks low, the operator needs no great initial capital outlay or tie-ins with other operators. Some police officials, however, believe that organized crime has a hand in pool-card selling.

Despite the volume, parlay cards are regarded by both bookies and police as the lowliest form of gambling. No first-class bookie would think of handling pool cards, and police look upon sellers with such disdain they don't even bother to harass them, much less arrest them. The people who play parlay cards are suckers, they figure.

pass

See forward pass.

pass defense

See zone defense, man-to-man defense.

pass interference

Illegal interference with a player's opportunity to catch a forward pass or make an interception. On any pass play, both the offensive and defensive players have an equal right to the path of the ball. Bodily contact, however severe, is not interference, says the rulebook, as long as the player is making "a bona fide . . . attempt to catch or bat the ball."

The penalty for defensive interference is an automatic first down at the point where the infraction occurred. For offensive pass interference, the penalty is 15 yards from the line of scrimmage.

pass pattern

The term used to describe the running or faking done by a receiver as he attempts to get free for a pass. The term can also be applied in a collective sense to the different pass routes run by two or more receivers.

pass route

The path taken by a receiver as he attempts to get free for a forward pass.

pass rush

The all-out charge by the defensive line in an attempt to sack the quarterback.

pass rush

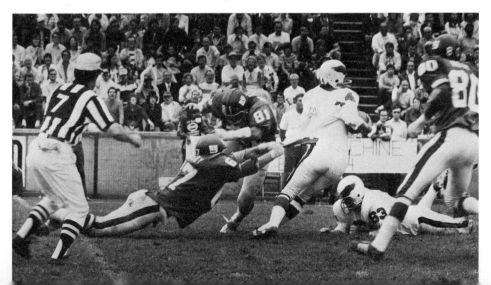

PAT (point after touchdown)

See try-for-point.

√**penalty**

A punishment, handicap, or loss of advantage imposed upon a team for a rule infraction. The various penalties, along with the infractions that cause them, are listed below:

Five Yards
   crawling
   defensive holding or illegal use of hands, including chucking
   delay of game
   encroachment
   too many timeouts
   false start
   illegal formation
   illegal shift
   illegal motion
   illegal substitution
   kickoff out of bounds
   invalid fair-catch signal
   more than 11 players on the field
   fewer than seven players on the offensive line at the snap
   offside
   failure to pause one second after shift or huddle
   running into kicker (also automatic first down)
   more than one man in motion at the snap
   facemasking
   player out of bounds at snap

Ten Yards
   offensive pass interference
   illegal player downfield

Fifteen Yards
   clipping
   fair-catch interference
   illegal batting, kicking, or punching a loose ball

illegal crackback block
offensive pass interference
piling on (also automatic first down)
roughing the passer (also automatic first down)
roughing the kicker (also automatic first down)
unnecessary roughness (if by defense, also automatic first down)
unsportsmanlike conduct
delay of game at start of half
holding, illegal use of hands, or tripping on offense

Loss of Down (No Yardage)
  second forward pass behind the line of scrimmage
  forward pass strikes ground, goal post, goal post
    crossbar, or goes out of bounds
  forward pass is first touched by an eligible re-
    ceiver who has gone out of bounds and re-
    turned
  forward pass is touched or caught by a second
    eligible receiver before being touched by the
    defense
  forward pass accidentally touches ineligible re-
    ceiver on or behind the line of scrimmage

Five Yards and Loss of Down
  forward pass thrown from beyond the line of
    scrimmage

Fifteen Yards and Loss of Down
  forward pass intentionally touched by an in-
    eligible receiver on, behind, or beyond the line
    of scrimmage
  intentional grounding of a forward pass

Suspension from Game and Five Yards
  illegal equipment (player, when legally equipped,
    may return after one down)

Disqualification and Fifteen Yards
  flagrant roughing of the kicker or passer
  striking an opponent with one's fist, or striking
    an opponent on the head or neck with one's
    forearm, elbow, or hands

215

kicking or kneeing an opponent

entering a game a second time with illegal equipment

any palpably unfair act (the distance of the penalty is determined by the referee after consultation with the other officials)

Touchdown

a palpably unfair act that deprives the opposition of the opportunity to score a touchdown

penalty marker

The handerchief-size yellow flag carried by officials and thrown to the ground to indicate a rule violation; also called a flag.

period

One of the four 15-minute segments of a game; a quarter.

Perry, Joe

Hall of Fame, 1969.

If the NFL record manual had a category, "Running Backs, Most Durable," Joe Perry's name would be pre-eminent. In a vocation where five or six years of playing time is considered excellent, Perry's career with the 49ers and Colts spanned 16 seasons.

During his playing days, however, Perry was much more renowned for his speed than his durability. They called him "The Jet."

He first came to the attention of the 49ers during World War II when he was stationed at the Alameda Naval Air Station, across the Bay from San Francisco. He played for the base team which was coached by John Woudenberg, a tackle for the 49ers. Woudenberg kept telling San Francisco

Perry

coach Buck Shaw about Perry. "Whenever we need a touchdown," Woudenberg said, "we hand Perry the football, point him in the right direction, then step aside."

When Shaw went over to Alameda to watch Perry, he found that Woudenberg's appraisal wasn't far from the truth. The 49ers signed him as soon as he was discharged.

Perry was the AAFC's rushing leader in 1949, and he led the NFL in rushing in 1953 and 1954 with 1,018 and 1,049 yards, respectively. Running backs today break the 1,000-yard mark with some degree of regularity. But in Perry's time, with teams playing only 12 games a season, almost no one did. Perry, in fact, was only the fourth man in NFL history to exceed 1,000 yards.

Toward the end of his career, Perry was dealt to the Baltimore Colts. There, despite his 34 years and a bad knee, he continued to excel. He was the Colts' No. 1 fullback in 1961, gaining 675 yards.

Once, in looking back over his career, Perry lamented the fact that he had never played on a championship team. "In 1954, 1955, and 1956, we had the offense to do it," he said, "but we couldn't stop anyone on defense. And we were too thin. When someone got injured there was no one to go in.

"The closest we came to a championship was in 1957, when we tied the Detroit Lions and then lost in the playoff. We were leading, 27–7, and I was already counting my coin, but they came back to beat us, 31–27.

"Man, I cried for a week after that, and I wasn't the only one.

"And then the Lions beat Cleveland, 56–14, for the title. Don't you know, we could have creamed Cleveland, too?"

personal foul

Instances of illegal hitting are often classified as personal fouls. Unnecessary roughness, clipping,

217

piling on, kicking, punching, or running into the passer or kicker—each of these is a personal foul. The penalty for a personal foul is 15 yards.

Philadelphia Bell

WFL team, 1974, 1975.

Philadelphia Eagles

NFL team, 1933 to present; merged with Pittsburgh Steelers during 1943 and operated as Phil-Pitt; won Eastern Division championship, 1947–1949; won Eastern Conference championship, 1960; won NFL championship, 1948, 1949, 1960.

Philadelphia Quakers

AFL team, 1926; won AFL championship, 1926.

Pihos, Pete

Hall of Fame, 1970.

He wasn't fast and he wasn't especially elusive, but it didn't matter. In the years that Pete Pihos played for the Philadelphia Eagles, he was one of the best pass receivers in the business.

A college star at Indiana, indeed, an All American at two positions, end and fullback, Pihos was drafted on the second round by the Eagles in 1947. Square-jawed and powerfully built, he helped spark the Eagles to three consecutive division championships and to the NFL title twice.

Pihos was 6-feet tall and weighed 205. A sports columnist of his day once commented that, "He was the sort of guy you'd expect to buy a piano and promptly carry it home."

He caught passes something like a piano-mover, outwrestling the defensive players for the throw. If

Pihos

a defensive man went for the ball at the same time Pihos did, he could expect an elbow in the belly or to be butted on the chin by his helmet.

Short passes, often quick hooks, were his forte. He led the league in receiving for three consecutive years beginning in 1953 and won All-Pro honors six times. When he retired in 1955, he held almost all of the Philadelphia pass-receiving records.

"He was the greatest third-down receiver I ever saw," Vince McNally, general manager of the Eagles, once said. "He was a great tackler, too. But his greatest asset was his aggressiveness. Every week he came to play."

piling on

Falling upon or throwing oneself upon a downed ball carrier after the whistle has sounded. In the days of mass play, piling on was one of the game's leading features. Today it's illegal, and the penalty is 15 yards.

pinch, n.

A double-team block.

pit, n.

The collision zone between the charging offensive and defensive lines.

pit

pitchout

pitch, pitchout, n.

A short, soft backfield toss that travels laterally or slightly backwards. Usually it's the quarterback who pitches to one of the running backs.

Pittsburgh Americans

AFL team, 1936, 1937.

Pittsburgh Pirates

NFL team, 1933–1938; team renamed Steelers following 1938 season.

Pittsburgh Steelers

NFL team, 1939 to present; merged with Philadelphia Eagles during 1943 season and operated as Phil-Pitt; merged with Chicago Cardinals during 1944 season and operated as Card-Pitt; won Cen-

tral Division championship (American Conference), 1972, 1974; won American Conference
championship, 1974; won Super Bowl IX (1975). 1979

placekick, n.

A play in which the ball is kicked from a fixed
position on the ground. In the case of a field-goal
or try-for-point attempt, the ball is held by a teammate. When kicking off (at the beginning of a half
or following a field goal or touchdown), the ball
may be placed on a kicking tee.

placekicker

See kicker.

placement

A placekick.

play, n.

The action between two downs.

play-action pass

A pass play in which the quarterback first fakes a
handoff to a running back. At the same time the offensive line fires out as if blocking for a run. The
idea is to get the linebackers to "freeze," to hold
them in tight. Meanwhile, receivers circle into the
short zones, and the quarterback straightens up
and fires to one of them.

playbook

A team's formations, plays, and the terminology
it uses are set down in minute detail in its play-

book, a copy of which is issued to each player. There are separate playbooks for the offensive and defensive teams.

Usually the playbook takes the form of a spiral-bound, three-hole notebook. When a coach discusses a particular play or formation at training camp, he distributes printed diagrams of it, and the players put it into their books. By the end of training camp, the book may contain 300 or more pages.

Much has been written about the secret nature of playbooks, perhaps too much. Teams are able to find out all they want to know about one another by studying game films. If a coach could know in advance which plays in the playbook a team was going to use against his team, it would be helpful. But the entire playbook would be a case of over-kill.

player selection meeting

See draft.

playoffs

See post-season playoffs.

plunge, n.

A quick thrust into the line by one of the running backs.

plunge

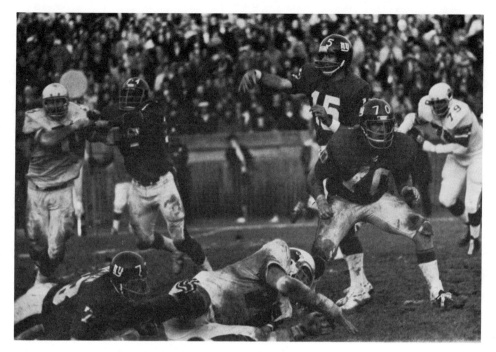

pocket

pocket

The protected area formed by the five interior
linemen in which the quarterback sets up to throw.
The offensive guards attempt to keep the defensive
tackles about at the line of scrimmage, while the
offensive tackles ride the defensive ends to the
outside. The center helps out one of the guards or
tackles or is assigned to pick up any blitzer. Sometimes the pocket is called the cup.

point after touchdown

See try-for-point.

point-spread

In football betting (which is illegal, except in the
state of Nevada), the relative difference between
two teams, expressed in points. It is also known as
the line.

223

The point-spread works like this: If the Colts are listed as nine-point favorites over the Eagles, Colt backers win only if their team wins by more than nine points. If the Colts should win by exactly nine points, it is a tie bet and the amount of the bet is returned. To avoid this situation, this lack of action, spreads are often quoted in half points.

What you have to bear in mind about the spread is that it is not necessarily an indication of how one team is going to perform against another. It's simply a market prediction which is meant to encourage betting action. The central banks that issue the spread are making a market, just the way Wall Street does in the case of an over-the-counter stock.

Most non-professional bettors fail to regard the line in this manner. They look upon it, instead, as a forecast of the game's outcome. Indeed, they believe in the line almost as if it were handed down by some deity.

The line comes out of Las Vegas. On Sunday night following the completion of the day's games, assorted bookies sit down and estimate point spreads for the following week. Some rely heavily on records and statistics. Others put the greatest emphasis on their own observations, what they see when watching games on television. They all take into consideration how the public backs certain teams. The Dolphins and the Steelers, for example, are glamour teams and have been excessively popular among non-pro bettors in recent seasons.

The following day—Monday—these bookies offer their opinions to as many as a dozen pro bettors. In so doing, they establish what is known as the early line, or the outlaw line. If the early line lists the Cowboys as 11-point favorites over the Saints, the bookies have to be prepared to accept bets—usually of a few thousand dollars—on either side.

Should bets pour in on one side more heavily than on the other, the bookies adjust the spread, but it's invariably a slight adjustment. A half a point is normal. As the process continues, the spreads level off. The result is the "official line," which is offered to the public on Tuesday morning.

Bob Martin, a top-level Las Vegas bookmaker who handles bets for what he refers to as the gambling fraternity, that is, professional gamblers, says that he starts working immediately after the games on Sunday and stays at it until sunup on Monday to get his line ready. "I have no 'plants' around the country feeding me information," he says. "I read key newspapers from various sections and look for such things as dissension and injuries."

His efforts are meant to produce what he calls the "right" price, which he defines as a point spread that will attract an equal number of people betting on each team. It's Martin's quotations that are distributed by the Associated Press and United Press International, and which probably appear on the sports page of your local newspaper.

The line that comes out of Las Vegas early in the week gets adjusted locally. Hometown sentiment is one thing that causes adjustment. Fans—*real* fans—much prefer to bet with the hometown team than against it. To bookies, fan loyalty usually translates into ½ point. If Cleveland is favored by 7½ points over New Orleans in a neutral city such as New York, then the price is likely to be 8 points in Cleveland and 7 points in New Orleans.

Reports of injuries also can affect the spread. Through the years, the nation's gamblers and bookmakers have manifested much more concern over Joe Namath's gimpy legs than the medical profession ever has. Every ache and pain, every minor twinge, is important.

In an effort to prevent skullduggery, i.e., a betting coup based on secret information, the NFL requires all coaches to report injuries received by players in each game. Early each week during the season, an injury list is compiled, and it is released to the media on Tuesday.

In theory, this sounds fine. In practice, it's not

225

so fine. The problem is that the average coach has no great desire to inform an opponent as to just how his team stacks up physically. Reporting every injury and having the information released to the press and television does nothing to help a team. Some coaches have refused to report injuries, while others are purposely vague in their reports.

But it's not injuries, reports of injuries, nor home-town sentiment that affects the spread the most. It's money. "It's supply and demand," says one bookie. "When you get a certain amount bet on one side of a game, you adjust the spread to draw more money to the other side."

Poly-Turf

See synthetic turf.

pool card

See parlay card.

Portland Storm

WFL team, 1974, 1975.

Portsmouth (Ohio) Spartans

NFL team, 1930–1933; franchise transferred to Detroit following 1933 season.

possession

A rulebook term that refers to a player who holds and controls the ball for sufficient time to "perform an act common to the game."

post pattern

A pass route in which the receiver races straight downfield then veers toward the center of the field and the goalpost, the "post."

post pattern

post-season game

Any one of the series of several games that follow the regular season, and which are played to determine the NFL champion team. These include conference championships themselves and, ultimately, the Super Bowl.

post-season playoffs

Any one of the games following the regular season and leading to the Super Bowl. In the first stage, the divisional playoffs, the winners of each division (Eastern, Central, and Western) of each conference (American and National), and the non-winning team with the best won-lost record in each conference, compete to determine which teams will compete in the conference championship games. The winners of the conference championships meet in the Super Bowl.

Pottsville (Pennsylvania) Maroons

NFL team, 1925–1928.

power I

A variation of the T formation in which the fullback and halfback line up directly behind the quarterback, while a third running back, also regarded as a halfback, lines up behind the offensive tackle on what would normally be the weak side.

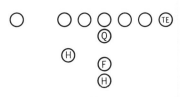

power I

power play

Any running play where the blocking is concentrated at a specific point.

power sweep

See sweep.

preseason game

In baseball, they're called exhibition games. They're the games that are played before the beginning of the regular season.

prevent defense

Any defensive alignment meant to stop—"prevent"—the completion of a long pass. Sometimes it involves a change in personnel, with extra cornerbacks or safeties going into the game in place of a lineman and one of the linebackers. Other times it merely involves a change in deployment, with the deep defensive backs lining up deeper than usual and dropping back quickly as soon as the quarterback sets up to throw.

The prevent defense is usually seen in the closing minutes of a half. The team in possession is trailing and is seeking desperately to catch up or go ahead, using passes almost exclusively.

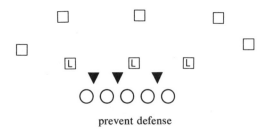

prevent defense

prevent zone

A type of zone defense used by a team when the opposition is deemed certain to pass. It sometimes involves the use of a three-man front, three linebackers, and five deep defensive backs. The nickel defense and the 53 (which *see*) are other types of prevent defenses.

primary receiver

On a pass pattern, the player first designated to receive the ball.

Pro Bowl

The annual Pro Bowl game matches all-star teams of the American and National Conferences. Usually played the week after the Super Bowl, it brings down the curtain on the pro football season. The contest was first played in January, 1951.

Professional Football Hall of Fame

2121 Harrison Ave., N.W., Canton, Ohio 44708

The Professional Football Hall of Fame is located in Canton, Ohio, site of the organizational meeting in 1920 which led to the formation of the National Football League. A modern three-building complex, the first building of which was dedicated in 1963, the Hall of Fame houses several exhibition areas, a motion picture theatre, a research library, plus two enshrinement halls containing bronze busts of all members.

Several new members are elected each year by a 27-man selection board which includes at least one sports writer from each of the NFL's cities. A player must be retired for five years before he can

229

Professional Football Hall of Fame

be considered for membership, but there is no such requirement in the case of a coach, owner, or league official. As of 1975, membership in the Hall of Fame totaled 85.

Enrichment ceremonies are held annually at the Hall of Fame, usually on the last Saturday in July. The Hall of Fame is open to visitors every day of the year. There is a modest admission charge.

Pro Football Writers Association

c/o Dick Connor, Secretary-treasurer, Denver *Post,* Denver, Colorado 80201.

An organization of approximately 250 newspaper, wire service, and magazine writers who cover professional football on a regular basis. Founded in 1963, the organization holds its annual meeting in conjunction with the Super Bowl.

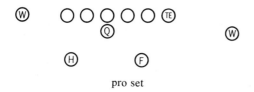

pro set

pro set

The most frequently used variation of the T formation. The fullback lines up on the same side as the tight end, the halfback on the other side.

Providence Steamrollers

NFL team, 1925–1931; won NFL championship, 1928.

pull

Action on the part of an offensive lineman, usually a guard, wherein he steps back from the line, then quickly turns and moves laterally to trap block or lead the interference on a sweep.

pump, v.

To fake a throw. As the quarterback sets up to pass, he sometimes will look at a receiver, cock his arm, then whip it forward—but not release the ball. The purpose is to get a linebacker or defensive back to look or move in the direction of the receiver. If that happens, the quarterback is likely to throw in the opposite direction.

punt, n.

A kick from scrimmage, with the ball being dropped and kicked before it reaches the ground.

Punts usually occur on fourth-down situations wherein the team in possession does not want to risk trying for a first down and is too far away from the opponent's end line to attempt a field goal.

If the punted ball goes untouched, it is dead where it stops and belongs to the defending team. The punting team, however, can "down" the ball anywhere simply by touching it.

If the punted ball goes over a sideline, possession goes over to the defending team at the point where the ball went out of bounds. If the defending team touches and does not control the punt, it becomes a free ball and can be recovered by either team. When a punted ball goes into the end zone, it's a touchback and the ball is brought out to the 20-yard line.

punter

"I try to put everything I can get into every kick—my knees, my hips, everything," the Chiefs' Jerrel Wilson, one of the best punters of recent years, once said. "I really try to hit the ball, really try to bust it."

"Busting" the ball, sending it high and far, is really the essence of the job. And getting height is just as important as getting distance. A kick may travel 55 to 60 yards and have the fans gasping, but unless it stays aloft for at least four seconds there can be trouble. The kickoff coverage unit has to have sufficient time to get downfield. Otherwise, a long runback can result. "Those frozen ropes," Kansas City coach Hank Stram once observed, "can really kill you."

The punted ball comes off the instep to rotate on its longitudinal axis; it spirals. End-over-end punts are for amateurs.

Once he gets the kick away, the punter becomes a safetyman, a tackle on the punt-coverage squad. How do punters tackle? Without enthusiasm.

punter

punt return

The runback of a punt.

pursuit

Persistent and aggressive movement on the part of
the defensive team in chasing down the ball carrier.

233

Q

QB

See quarterback.

QUADRA

One of the NFL's three basic scouting combines, the others being BLESTO-VIII and CEPO. The QUADRA teams—the Dallas Cowboys, Los Angeles Rams, San Francisco 49ers, and San Diego Chargers—collect and exchange information on talented college players.

quarter, n.

One of the four 15-minute periods that constitute a game; a period.

quarterback

About the quarterback, this must be said at once: He is the most important man on the field. He has to be able to throw the ball accurately at distances of up to 50 yards, and he has to know how to hand off smartly. He must be a tactician, knowing all of his team's plays and having the ability to decide which ones will work against the defenses he faces. He has to be durable.

But that's only part of it. When Harland Svare was coaching the San Diego Chargers several years ago, he hired Dr. Arnold J. Mandell, M.D., Chairman of the Department of Psychiatry at the University of California, San Diego, to study the attitudes and behavior of his team in an effort to develop a winning edge. Dr. Mandell observed the

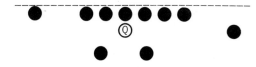

quarterback

Charger squad at team meetings, in the locker room, at practice sessions, on the sidelines during games, and conducted more than 200 interviews with team members. He later published some of his findings in an article in *Saturday Review/World*.

The "major determinant" in becoming a successful quarterback, Dr. Mandell found, was self-confidence, a self-confidence he described as ". . . a super arrogance." Said Dr. Mandell: "To stand there to the last millisecond, waiting for your receiver to reach the place the ball is supposed to go while you are being rushed by mammoth defensive linemen—that takes sheer courage." Surely, Dr. Mandell's findings go a long way toward explaining the success of quarterbacks such as Joe Namath and Sonny Jurgensen, two of the most gifted passers of recent times.

All of this should not imply that a quarterback can do it alone. Not at all. He needs linemen who will give him a couple of seconds to set up and throw. He needs a strong running game to keep the defense off balance. He needs fast, sure-handed receivers. And he needs a defense that can keep the opposition from scoring and get him the ball once in a while. Gather these elements, add a bold quarterback, and you're likely to have a championship team.

quarterback draw

A running play that looks initially like a pass, with the quarterback dropping back a few steps and the offensive linemen pass-blocking instead of firing out, the idea being to "draw" the defensive linemen in. But it's not a pass. The quarterback

235

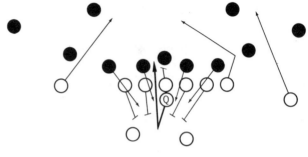

quarterback draw

keeps the ball and, with the center providing interference, charges straight ahead.

quarterback sneak

An offensive play in which the quarterback takes
the center's snap, tucks the ball to his belly, and
hits into the line, the center and the guards
blocking for him. The quarterback sneak is sometimes used in situations where a yard or less is
needed for a first down. Using wedge blocking, the
offensive linemen can usually move back the defense the needed distance. Another advantage of
the quarterback sneak is that there is no handoff
involved, which lessens the chance of fumble.

quick kick

A surprise punt. The quick kick usually comes on
third down and is executed from a conventional offensive alignment. Since the defense is not expecting a punt and is not deployed to return it,
the ball usually rolls dead deep in the receiving
team's territory—which is the purpose of the play.

quick opener

A running play in which the quarterback hands off
to a running back who plunges straight ahead and
into an opening created by the offensive linemen.

Racine (Wisconsin) Legions

NFL team, 1922–1924, 1926.

Ray, Hugh (Shorty)

Hall of Fame, 1966.

Membership in pro football's Hall of Fame is pretty much limited to former players, and founders of some of the NFL's more prestigious franchises. One exception is Hugh (Shorty) Ray, who served the league as supervisor of officials beginning in 1938.

In seeking to make football more efficient, Ray charted games, making slide-rule calculations and taking stopwatch observations by the hundreds. It was Shorty Ray who first noted that the total amount of actual playing time in a game amounts to only about 13 minutes.

Ray established the practice of visiting training camps to explain the rules to players and coaches, and he was the first to give written tests to officials. "At one time, officials couldn't pass a written test on the rules," Ray once said, "not even with a rulebook at their elbow. Well, now they score 95 percent or better, and they don't need the rulebook."

Football safety was another topic that interested him. Mark Duncan, who later was to succeed Ray as supervisor of officials, once remarked, "Ray's idea of a big afternoon was to see everyone leave the field without limping." Ray died in 1956.

RB

See running back.

ready list

A selection of plays, often numbering between 20 and 30, culled from a team's playbook to be used against a particular opponent. The ready list is an integral part of the game plan.

receiver

See wide receiver.

red dog

A term made popular during the 1960s to describe the headlong charge across the line of one or more linebackers in an effort to sack the quarterback; that is, a blitz.

The term "red dog" dates to 1949. In a game between the Chicago Bears and Chicago Cardinals that season, the Bears' Ed (Catfish) Cody, a fullback playing linebacker for the first time, charged into the offensive backfield and spilled the quarterback 13 times. "He looked like a 'mad dog' coming through there," said one of the Bear coaches.

In time, every team began shooting linebackers. The term "dog" remained as a code word. With some teams, "white dog" meant one linebacker charged; "blue dog," two linebackers charged, and "red dog" meant all three came crashing through.

red formation

A variation of the T formation in which the fullback lines up on the same side of the formation as the tight end. *See* pro set.

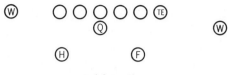

red formation

Reeves, Dan

Hall of Fame, 1967.

The National Football League was in existence for a very long time before it became truly national. Not until 1946, the year that Dan Reeves moved his Cleveland Rams to Los Angeles, did pro football begin to have significance for the entire country.

It took vision on Reeves's part to make the move. Also a few dollars. When he announced his intention of shifting operations to the West Coast, some of his fellow owners reacted as if their teams were going to have to cross the Rockies in covered wagons. Only when Reeves offered to pay visiting teams as much as $5,000 over the existing guarantees was he permitted to make the switch.

Reeves, who died in 1971, was a pioneer owner in other respects. When, in 1946, he signed UCLA halfback Kenny Washington to a Ram contract, he opened modern pro football to blacks. Reeves's experimental telecasts of Ram home games in 1950 led the NFL to adopt its "blackout" policy, considered a vital factor in sport's mushrooming growth of the 1960s. And it was Reeves who was the first to demonstrate the value of sophisticated scouting methods. All of these are notable contributions, but it's for changing the map of pro sports that Reeves is remembered first.

referee

The official who is in control of the game; the final authority on all interpretations of the rules.

referee

The quarterback is the referee's responsibility on individual plays, and he watches the snap and the movement of the deep backs for possible infractions. On running plays, he stays with the quarterback after the handoff to be certain he's not the victim of a late hit. He then hurries downfield, watching the runner as he goes. When the runner is brought down, the referee, after checking with either the line judge or head linesman, indicates the forward point of the ball. .

On pass plays, after checking the blocking in the line, the referee shifts his attention to the quarterback. As soon as the ball is released, he shouts, "Gone!" This helps the umpire to determine whether any offensive linemen strayed downfield too early. It also serves to notify the defensive linemen or blitzers that any contact with the quarterback may be construed as a late hit.

On kicking plays, the referee focuses his attention on the kicker, ruling on any possible roughing-the-kicker foul.

regular season

The NFL's 14-week, 182-game schedule that is sandwiched between preseason games and post-season playoffs.

release, v.

To free oneself of an opponent in order to perform another assignment. For example, a tight end will sometimes brush block a defensive player, then release and head downfield for a pass.

reserve squad

See taxi squad.

return, n.

A runback of a kick, a punt, or an intercepted pass.

return kick, n.

A play in which the ball, after having been recovered by the opposition, is kicked back without an intervening play from scrimmage. While permitted under the rules, return kicks are virtually nonexistent in modern football.

reverse, n.

A play in which a running back slants in one direction, then hands or passes the ball to a teammate heading in the opposite direction. The teammate can be the other running back, the tight end, or a wide receiver. The ball carrier usually heads for the outside, although the play can also be run off tackle.

241

Robustelli, Andy

Hall of Fame, 1971.

Robustelli

Up until fairly recent times, few defensive players were recognized for their skills as such. Mostly everyone played "both ways," and if you happened to be an offensive star, defense was a chore you put up with. All of this began to change in 1949 with the adoption of the unlimited substitution.

Andy Robustelli, a defensive end who began his career with the Los Angeles Rams in 1951, was one of the first players to demonstrate that playing defense could be just as much of an art as throwing a pass or catching it. He played for the Rams for five seasons before being traded to the New York Giants in 1956. While there, his coach, Allie Sherman, once said of him: "Watch Andy on the field, and you'll be studying a real master. Terrific speed of mind, hands, and feet make him the best. But he also has extra determination, a burning desire to excel."

Robustelli played in six championship games for the Giants, was the team's defensive captain for six years and was an All-NFL selection for nine of his 14 years.

Despite all of this, Robustelli came close to not playing professional football at all. He starred in high school football in Stamford, Connecticut, his hometown, and then, after a short Navy hitch, went on to Arnold College in Milford, Connecticut. You don't hear about Arnold College any more because it's been absorbed by the University of Bridgeport, and you hardly ever heard about it in Robustelli's day because it was so small. While there, he won Little All-America honors as an end, an offensive end, a pass receiver, that is. A scout for the Rams happened to see Robustelli perform and was ready to send an enthusiastic report to Los Angeles, but during the game Andy broke a leg.

The Rams decided to take a chance anyway, and drafted him in the 19th round, which really isn't taking much of a chance. The only "bonus" he received was air fare to the West Coast. His starting salary as a rookie was set at $4,250.

For months, Robustelli and his wife weighed the advantages and disadvantages of a pro career against those of a high school coaching job he had been offered. Once he made his decision to report to the Rams, he had reasons to doubt whether it was the right one. Two of them were Tom Fears and Elroy (Crazylegs) Hirsch, both of whom were to land in the Hall of Fame by virtue of their ability to catch passes. Robustelli didn't even bother to unpack during his first two weeks at camp.

Ram coach Joe Stydahar got Robustelli to quit thinking about becoming a receiver and concentrate on the defensive side of the game. In the first Ram scrimmage that summer, Robustelli smothered passers, flattened ball carriers, and left blockers sprawled all over the place. Afterward, Stydahar told him to unpack.

Despite his rookie status, Robustelli won a starting role with the Rams that year, one in which they won the NFL championship. The only problem was that Robustelli longed to play nearer his home, and eventually that longing prompted a trade between the Rams and the Giants.

Robustelli retired as a player after the 1964 season. But ten years later the Giants called him back to serve as the club's director of operations.

Rochester (New York) Jeffersons

APFA team, 1920, 1921. NFL team, 1922–1925.

Rochester (New York) Tigers

AFL team, 1936, 1937.

Rock Island (Illinois) Independents

APFA team, 1920, 1921. NFL team, 1922–1925. AFL team, 1926.

rodmen

rodmen

The two members of the chain crew who handle the poles linking the ten yards of chain used to indicate a first down.

roll out, n.

Lateral movement on the part of the quarterback before passing.

roll-out pass

A pass play in which the quarterback first sprints to either the left or right before passing. The roll-out pass puts the outside linebacker under extreme pressure. If he darts forward in an effort to deck the quarterback, the quarterback flips the ball over his head. If the linebacker drops off to cover the receiver, the quarterback can keep the ball and run with it.

roll out

rookie

A first-year player.

Rooney, Art

Hall of Fame, 1964.

It was 1933 when Art Rooney was awarded the Pittsburgh Steeler franchise in the National Football League. It cost him $2,500.

The team was not the most important of his interests. Horses were—breeding them, racing them, betting on them. Through these and other enterprises, he became a millionaire.

All the while, the Steelers were becoming more and more noteworthy for their lack of on-the-field success. Except for the expansion clubs, the Steelers remained the only team that never won so much as a division championship. Each year it was a struggle just to finish at .500, and they did not do that very often.

245

This did not seem to bother Rooney too much. The team was his hobby, the payroll crammed with his cronies. The coaches were his pals. The Steeler offices, his club.

Stockily built, with iron-gray hair, and a cigar shoved in the corner of his mouth, Rooney had an engaging manner and usually could be found wearing a grin. But deep down, all that losing hurt.

During the 1960s, Rooney turned the operation of the Steelers over to his son, Dan. The Steelers began to win, capturing a division title in 1972 and getting as far as the AFC title game. They were a playoff team again in 1973.

A year later they won everything—division, conference, Super Bowl. And Art Rooney, at 74, was there to see it.

roster

Officially known as the active roster, this refers to a club's list of 40 players eligible to play. Taxi-squad members and those on the injured reserve or move lists are not considered members of the active roster. (During 1974, because of disruptions caused by the players' strike, rosters were increased in size to 47 regulars, and the use of the taxi squad was eliminated.)

While the composition of rosters varies from team to team, the variations are slight. Many squads are put together in this fashion:

8 offensive linemen (3 tackles, 3 guards, 2 centers)
5 receivers (3 wide receivers, 2 tight ends)
5 running backs (3 halfbacks, 2 fullbacks)
2 quarterbacks
6 defensive linemen (3 ends, 3 tackles)
6 linebackers (4 outside linebackers, 2 middle linebackers)
3 cornerbacks
3 safeties
1 punter
1 kicker

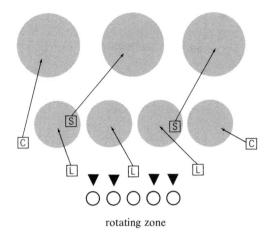

rotating zone

rotating zone

A type of zone pass coverage in which there are four short zones and three deep. At the ball's snap, each member of the defensive secondary darts toward his assigned coverage area, slanting in either clockwise direction (as shown here) or counterclockwise. Either way, they're said to be "rotating."

rouge

In Canadian football, a term that refers to the one point that the kicking team receives when a punt or missed field goal goes beyond the deadline (the end line), or when a punt or missed field goal is recovered by a defensive player who is then tackled in the end zone.

roughing the kicker

Because he's extremely vulnerable back there, the kicker is protected by certain safeguards set down in the rulebook. If, after he's punted the ball away, an opposition player runs into him, the penalty is five yards. If the enemy player runs into him in a

247

violent manner—if the kicker is "roughed," in other words—the penalty is 15 yards. In either case, the offense is awarded an automatic first down, which is much more hurtful than the penalty yardage. But no punishment is to be meted out in cases where contact is caused "by the kicker's own motion," the rulebook states.

roughing the passer

The quarterback is fair game—until the ball has left his hands. If a member of the defensive team then comes in contact with the quarterback, and the contact is not simply a result of his momentum, it can result in an automatic first down for the offense, plus a 15-yard penalty for the defense.

Rozelle, Pete

Pete Rozelle began calling the plays for the National Football League in January, 1960. He was 33 then. Detractors called him "the boy commissioner."

A "boy commissioner," apparently, was just what the National League needed. Under Rozelle's direction, what had been a merely popular sport became a national obsession.

Tall and lean, with deep lines furrowing his usually tanned face, Rozelle is known to be smart and hard working, warm and witty. He is an organizer, a planner, and, most of all, a diplomat.

You can measure what he achieved in terms of the league's lucrative television contracts, which he negotiated, or by attendance figures. He saw regular-season attendance rise from 3.1 million in 1960 to 10.7 million in 1973. A good number of teams had been added, of course, but average attendance per game increased from 40,000 to 58,000 during the same period.

At the time Rozelle was voted into the commissioner's job, he was general manager of the Los

Rozelle

Angeles Rams. Before that, he spent two years in the Navy, then attended Compton Junior College, then the University of San Francisco, where he became sports information director after graduation. He became publicity director of the Rams in 1952, left the team three years later to do private public relations, then returned to the club in 1957 as general manager.

When Commissioner Bert Bell died in 1959, the NFL owners met the following January to choose a successor. Marshall Leahy, the league attorney, and Austin Gunsel, the treasurer, were the leading candidates. After three days and 26 ballots, neither could gain the needed votes. The owners settled upon Rozelle as a compromise choice.

Rozelle has been applauded for his ability to urge ever-increasing amounts of money from the television networks. It may be his foremost achievement. But he would not have been so successful in this regard if he had not first been able to convince the owners to pool television receipts, so he could bargain for one and all at the same time.

This was not an easy matter, considering the differences involved. For example, the television rights to the Packers' games were worth little as compared to the Giants' rights. But no one has ever voiced regret at the compromise. The very first TV contract that Rozelle negotiated brought the Giants $325,000 more than they had ever received before.

Rozelle got all three major networks involved in the bidding for television rights, then managed to get a law enacted to make it legal. It's Public Law 87-331, which was introduced by Representative Emanuel Celler, passed by the House and Senate, and signed into being by President Kennedy. Rozelle was also the man responsible for night football telecasts in prime time. He bears no responsibility for Howard Cosell, however.

Also high on Rozelle's list of achievements is the amalgamation of the rival American League into the NFL. That happened in 1966, and gave rise to the Super Bowl, biggest of all sports extravaganzas. Once the merger was approved, Rozelle followed up by getting congressional action to make the merger exempt from antitrust prosecution.

A close observer of Rozelle, quoted in *The National Observer,* once described his style in these words: "He'll get an idea and talk casually with several others about it. As the talk goes on, pretty soon they start feeling as if it's their idea. Eventually, one of them will spring it at a meeting and Pete will sit there and say, 'Gee, that's a splendid idea that John has.' He doesn't care who gets the credit as long as the job gets done."

Rozelle also presided over the organization of NFL Properties, Inc., which controls merchandise licensing for the clubs. Their enterprises range from 12-page advertisements in *Sports Illustrated* down to those football dolls with the heads that wobble.

While he's famous for his skill as a negotiator and conciliator, Rozelle can be tough when he has to be. He suspended Detroit star Alex Karras and Green Bay idol Paul Hornung for a year for betting. He got Joe Namath to relinquish his ownership in a restaurant said to be frequented by

persons of "undesirable background and talents."
He suspended the Rams' Lance Rentzel and fined
the San Diego Chargers in drug cases.

Coaches have not escaped his discipline. When
Otto Graham was coaching the Washington Redskins, he was once guilty of criticizing game officials, a league no-no. Rozelle called him to confirm it, then fined him. "You can't do that,"
Graham protested. "I just did," said Rozelle, and
hung up the phone.

As pro football entered the decade of the 1970s,
new problems loomed, many of them created by
the sport's success. Congress enacted legislation in
1973 that served to lift the NFL's blackout of
home games in home markets. In turn, this led to
an increasing number of "no shows," a "no
show" being a fan who, after buying a ticket for a
game, fails to attend it, preferring to watch on
home television.

The players' strike in 1974, during which time
Rozelle's office itself was made an issue, pointed
up the increased demand on the part of the players
for a larger share of the pie.

The owners felt they knew how to deal with
these and other problems. In the spring of 1974,
they voted to give Rozelle a new contract, one that
would keep him in office at least until December,
1982.

Rozelle rule

The Rozelle rule, so-named because it was first in-
voked by NFL Commissioner Pete Rozelle, involved athletes who played out their option with
one team so they could be free to negotiate with
another. In cases where the two teams involved
could not agree upon a price, the commissioner
unilaterally fixed the amount of compensation to
be paid to the club that lost the player. The compensation usually took the form of draft choices or
players.

The National Football League Players Associa-

251

tion said that the Rozelle rule inhibited teams from signing free agents, since club owners never knew what draft choices or players Rozelle might take from them to compensate the other team. The organization brought legal action challenging the rule.

runback, n.

Any return of a punt, kickoff, missed field goal, or intercepted pass.

running back, n.

For the first 50 or so years of its existence, the National Football League referred to all offensive

runback

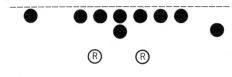

running back

backs who carried the ball as either halfbacks or fullbacks. Not any more. Now they're all running backs.

Still, the distinction remains, and most coaches and players recognize it. There's an analogous situation in baseball. The second baseman and shortstop are both infielders, but individually there are important differences between the two.

The halfback is usually the faster of the two running backs, with obvious ability as an open-field runner. He is also one of the team's better pass catchers. He usually lines up on the weak side (because there are already two receivers on the other side, a wide receiver and the tight end). Swift, sleek O. J. Simpson of the Buffalo Bills was the classic example of the modern halfback.

The fullback has two basic roles. First, he's the power man, the ball carrier who's called upon to get the tough yards inside. Second, he's a blocker, that is, he must have the ability to help spring loose the halfback. Think of a contemporary fullback, and you think of Larry Csonka, big— 6-foot-3, 240 pounds—strong, and unstoppable.

Virtually all running backs have good size, weighing in at from 225 to 235 pounds. But there are always exceptions, "little" men who achieve success by virtue of their quickness and elusiveness. The most notable examples are the Cards' Terry Metcalf (5-foot-10, 185 pounds) and the Patriots' Mack Herron (5-foot-5, 170 pounds).

Through the years there have been few changes in the running game. Success has always depended on the ability of the offensive linemen to create an opening and the skill and power of the ball carrier to hit into that opening to break a tackle. The "run to daylight" philosophy espoused by Vince Lombardi during the 1960s increased the runner's choices, but there still had to be a hole created *somewhere,* and the need for quickness and strength did not change.

The cause of the running back was aided somewhat shortly before the 1972 season opened, when the rulemakers decreed that the hashmarks were to be moved closer to the center of the field, three yards, one foot, and nine inches closer. This meant that when the ball was placed on a hashmark, the field no longer had a "short side" to it. A sweep or any other play to the outside could be run in either direction. Before the change, the defensive team simply reinforced the wide side, and waited.

The first year that the new rule was in effect was a vintage one for running backs. Indeed, it has been called The Year of the Running Back. Ten runners—six in the American Football Conference, four in the National—rushed for 1,000 yards or more. It was the most 1,000-yard performances in any single NFL season.

While the rulemakers may have made it somewhat easier to gain yardage, they have done nothing to reduce the fearful hazards of being a running back. There are more perils to the job than any other. Evidence is the NFL's weekly injury list, which always abounds with the names of runners.

Most running backs don't expect their careers to last any more than five or six seasons. "One of the things that make a short career," O. J. Simpson once said, "is the type of defensive players you meet—bigger and more aggressive each year. They know how to hit players around the knees, not high. Consequently, there are more knee injuries."

The best tipoff that the running back's job is the toughest of all comes from a quick scanning of the team rosters. Forty-year-old quarterbacks are not altogether rare. Packer wide receiver Max McGee was a Super Bowl hero at 35, and Jim Otto, after 15 years as the Raiders' starting center, was still making All-Pro teams.

But to be a running back and to be 31 or 32 is to be at the end of your career. And by the time you're 35, you're almost certain to be getting your football on television.

run pass, n.

See option pass.

rushing

Running with the ball on a play from scrimmage.

S

S

See safety.

sack, v.

To tackle or otherwise dump the quarterback for a loss while he is attempting to pass.

safety (in scoring)

A term that refers to the two points awarded a team that forces the opposition to down the ball behind its goal line. For example, a ball carrier retreats into his own end zone and is tackled there; the opposition gets two points. Or a player in at-

sack

tempting to recover a punt accidentally kicks the ball into his own end zone where a teammate falls on it. This, too, is a safety; two points for the opposition.

Sometimes the rule regarding the scoring of safeties seems confusing. A player, for instance, will be tackled in his own end zone after intercepting a pass. But that's ruled a touchback, not a safety, and no points are recorded for either team.

How do you tell one from the other? It's a question of which team started the play. In order for a safety to be declared, the team scored upon must be the team that put the ball in play.

The term "safety" predates pro football, going back to a period before the system of downs had been established. A team could retain possession of the ball all day long, as long as they didn't kick it away or lose it by fumbling. Any time a team had possession dangerously close to its own goal line, players could retreat to the "safety" of the end zone. Instead of being assessed points or losing possession, the team was awarded the ball on its 25-yard line.

safety (position)

When the front four fails to put forth a strong pass rush, when the linebackers are lax in covering the short zones, and when the receiver outraces the cornerback—then it's all up to one of the safeties. If he makes the play, fine; it he doesn't, it's usually disaster.

While the safety's prime responsibility is to throttle the pass, he also must be ready to stop running plays, surging forward to halt the ball carrier as fast as possible. Since the runner is likely to outweigh the safety by 30 or 40 pounds, you can judge that it is not a job for those of limited courage, and going one-on-one with the likes of Larry Csonka borders on the suicidal.

There's some confusion as to how each of the safeties is to be designated. Since most teams are

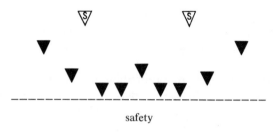

safety

right-handed, the tight end lines up on the right side, and that becomes the strong side. The safety that covers him is known as the strong safety, although he may also be known as the tight safety or simply the left safety. It depends on the team.

The safety on the other side, because he doesn't have to cover anyone man-to-man, is sometimes called the free safety. He may also be referred to as the right safety or weak safety.

When the offensive team lines up with the tight end on the left side, the free safety becomes the tight safety. Some teams adjust by flip-flopping the safeties, that is, having them exchange playing positions. The same man is "free" all the time, while the other always covers the tight end. Other teams simply assign their safeties to play a particular side of the field no matter what type of formation the offense employs.

During the 1960s the free safety was much freer than he is nowadays. He'd read the quarterback and play the ball. For this reason, free safeties were almost always the interception leaders. But as pass defenses became more zone oriented, the freedom of the free safety diminished. Like everyone else in the defensive backfield, he was given a zone and made to cover it.

Good speed—the ability to cover 40 yards in 4.7 to 4.8 seconds—is one of the chief requisites for playing safety. Of course, speed isn't everything. Like all defensive players, safeties must know the opposition, know what the team is likely to do from particular formations, and know the specialties of each of the players.

The safety also has to be aware of what his teammates are doing or going to do. For instance,

258

if a safety knows that he's going to be getting help inside, he can play the receiver tight to the outside.

The biggest play for a safety is the interception. It doesn't happen very often; five or six interceptions in a season is considered very good. In one recent year, Dick Anderson of the Dolphins, considered by many to be the standout safety of the mid-1970s, led the NFL with eight.

While interceptions represent ecstasy, they don't make up for those moments when the safety permits himself to get beaten. There, in full view of the spectators and uncounted television viewers, he's totally victimized, and the mistake is quickly documented by the scoreboard. "You want to crawl into a hole or something" is how the moment is usually described.

safety blitz

A defensive maneuver by one of the safeties in which he barrels through the line in an attempt to sack the quarterback or make him hurry the throw. One or more of the linebackers may also blitz in.

Defensive coach Chuck Drulis of the St. Louis Cardinals is credited with developing the safety blitz during the mid-1960s. On some blitzes, the Cards not only sent their free safety, Larry Wilson, charging in, but all three linebackers as well.

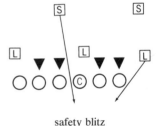

safety blitz

safety valve

A short, often laterally directed pass to a running back, thrown when the quarterback is unable to spot a receiver downfield and is being pressured by the defense.

St. Louis Browns

NFL team, 1923.

259

safety valve

St. Louis Cardinals

NFL team, 1960 to present; won Eastern Division championship (National Conference), 1974.

St. Louis Gunners

NFL team, 1934.

Sam

With some teams, the term used to identify the strong-side linebacker.

San Diego Chargers

AFL team, 1961–1969; won Western Division championship, 1961, 1963–1965; won AFL championship, 1963. NFL team, 1970 to present.

San Francisco 49ers

AAFC team, 1946–1949. NFL team, 1950 to present; won Western Division championship (National Conference), 1970, 1971.

Sarah

With some teams, the term used to identify the strong-side linebacker.

Schmidt, Joe

Hall of Fame, 1973.

The Detroit Lions were very rich in talent in 1952, a year they won the NFL title. The following summer when linebacker Joe Schmidt, a seventh-round draft choice from the University of Pittsburgh, showed up at training camp, scarcely anyone took notice.

Schmidt himself had little confidence. Not big—6-feet tall, 215 pounds—he was awed by the size of the Detroit players. "What am I doing here?" he kept asking himself.

One day before an exhibition game with the Buffalo Bills, an assistant coach told Schmidt his opportunity had arrived. "You're gonna play the whole game," he said. "You're gonna sink or swim."

Schmidt thought he passed the test, but nobody said anything to him. Lion rookies were treated like outcasts in those days. Not long before the season opened, the club traded away Dick Flanagan, a veteran linebacker. That's when Schmidt began to realize he had a chance of making the team.

Schmidt went on to spend 13 seasons with the Lions. He was an All-NFL selection eight times, and his teammates voted him the Most-Valuable-Lion award four times. The Lions won the NFL title in 1952 and again in 1957.

261

Schmidt

This was all very nice, but Schmidt's most memorable experiences in pro football date to his rookie season. "That first year, making the team, playing with a championship ball club—that was my biggest thrill," he says.

Schmidt, who played left linebacker at first and was later moved to the middle, was quick and agile, but his greatest talent was his ability to diagnose plays in the blink of an eye. "He had an uncanny ability to read the play and move to it," Mike Pyle, a one-time center for the Bears, once said. "You couldn't get to him to block him. A guy like Ray Nitschke would lay back there waiting to belt you. Not Schmidt. He'd be gone."

After his career as a player had ended, Schmidt was head coach of the Lions for six seasons beginning in 1967. It was a forgettable experience. Once, in attempting to explain the frustrations of coaching, he said, "I expected everyone to be like me. I guess," he added, "that was a mistake."

scissors

A blocking maneuver by two adjacent members of the offensive line whose paths crisscross as they fire out at the opposition.

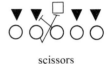

scissors

Scott, Jake

Most Valuable Player, Super Bowl VII (1973).

Jake Scott, a free safety for the Miami Dolphins, won the outstanding player award in Super Bowl VII for his two key interceptions, each off of quarterback Billy Kilmer, each halting a Redskin scoring threat.

A relatively obscure player at the time, Scott had a year of competition in Canada before joining the Dolphins in 1970. He played his college football at the University of Georgia. Besides playing safety, Scott was the Dolphins' punt return specialist. He was a member of the American Conference Pro Bowl squad in 1971 and 1972.

Scott

At the luncheon honoring him as the Super Bowl's MVP, Scott was presented with an automobile by *Sport* magazine. "I'm going to have a second set of keys made," he said, "and give them to Manny Fernandez." Fernandez, a defensive tackle for the Dolphins, was a vital factor in the team's victory, intimidating the Redskins throughout the afternoon and making 11 individual tackles.

Then Scott thought for a minute. "I'm going to have a third set made, too," he said. "I'm giving those to Billy Kilmer."

263

scout, n.

An employee of a team or group of teams, paid to gather information on talented college players.

scouting combine

An association of teams united to collect, analyze, and disseminate information on talented college players to members. There are three NFL scouting combines: BLESTO-VIII, CEPO, and QUADRA.

scramble

Evasive movement by the quarterback to avoid the defensive rush.

scramble

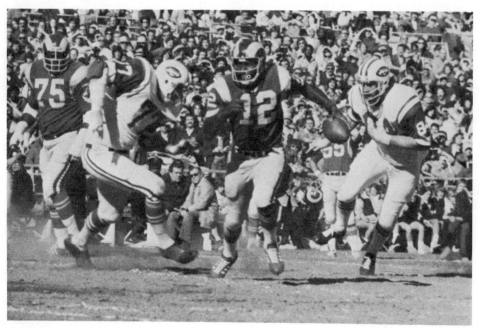

screen pass

A pass play in which three or more linemen, after making their initial blocks, slant to one side of the field to form a blocking wall—a "screen"—for a running back who takes a short, soft throw from the quarterback.

The success of the screen pass depends on the acting ability of the quarterback. He has to keep retreating straight back, making the defensive players believe they have beaten the offense. Often the screen pass is used to thwart a team that has been rushing the passer successfully.

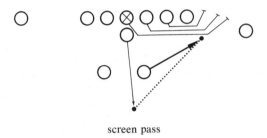

screen pass

scrimmage

An offensive play, a down; also, a practice session under game conditions.

scrimmage line

See line of scrimmage.

seam

In the zone pass defense, the gap or opening between two coverage zones.

secondary, n.

The defensive backfield—the two cornerbacks and the two safeties.

series

A succession of offensive plays.

set, n.

A formation.

setback, n.

Any running back who lines up behind the quarterback. In the normal pro alignment, there are two setbacks, the halfback and the fullback.

setbacks

Sherman, Allie

Coach of the Year, 1961, 1962.

Rosey Brown. Andy Robustelli. Sam Huff. Jim Patton. Alex Webster. Jim Katcavage. Y. A. Tittle. Del Shofner. Erich Barnes. Those were the stars of the New York Giants during the early 1960s when the team rolled to three straight conference titles. Allie Sherman was their coach.

Sherman had been first hired by the Giants in 1949 to help convert quarterback Charlie Conerly, a college tailback, into a T-formation quarterback. Sherman was 28 then, not long out of Brooklyn College where, as a left-handed quarterback, he had first learned the T. Smallish—5-foot-10, 160 pounds—he signed with the Eagles after graduation and there devoted most of his energies to helping Earl (Greasy) Neale learn the intricacies of T-formation football. It was Neale who recommended him to the Giants. Sherman became offensive coach in 1959 and succeeded Jim Lee Howell as head coach in 1961.

Sherman bolstered the team with trades that brought in Y. A. Tittle, defensive back Erich Barnes, and end Del Shofner. These, plus Sherman's ability as a strategist, helped the Giants to achieve an era of greatness, however brief.

The team nosedived in 1964, winning only two games. In 1966, they won only half that number. Sherman was fired two years later.

Some people said that his trading policies eventually ruined the team. Others said he was no longer able to motivate the players. Still others claimed he was sacrificed to mask mistakes on a higher level. Whatever the reason, many people agreed that Allie Sherman would be back one day.

Sherman

shift

The movement of two or more offensive players at the same time before the snap. Usually the term is applied to running backs who, for example, may shift from the I formation to the pro set as the quarterback calls signals.

shoot the gap

To charge from a position in the defensive backfield across the line of scrimmage through a hole created by offensive blocking. Linebackers also shoot the gap.

shotgun formation

Popularized by the San Francisco 49ers during the 1960s, the shotgun is primarily a passing formation in which the quarterback stands five to seven yards in back of the center, and takes a direct snap from him.

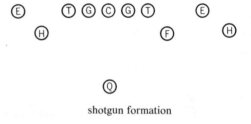

shotgun formation

shovel pass

A soft, underhand, backward pass usually from the quarterback to a running back cutting to the outside.

Shreveport (Louisiana) Steamboat

WFL team, 1974 (franchise transferred to Shreveport from Houston in midseason), 1975.

Shula, Don

Coach of the Year, 1964, 1966–1968, 1972.

Don Shula was no magician or miracle worker, as he was sometimes called, although his record suggests that he was. Five times he was named the NFL's coach of the year. He was the first coach in pro history to win 100 games in the span of only ten years.

One season—1972—his Dolphins were 17–0, an unprecedented feat. He made a habit of leading teams to the Super Bowl, and twice the Dolphins won there.

A stocky, sometimes chunky figure, almost 6-feet tall, Shula never coached a losing team. In 1970, he took a Dolphin squad that had lost 10 of 14 games the previous season, and turned things completely around, winning 10 of 14.

Shula

What was his secret? There was none, really. Shula's teams played sound, well-disciplined football. A mistake was a rarity. When he coached the Baltimore Colts, as he did from 1963–1969, he had Johnny Unitas, and his teams featured the pass. When he took over the Dolphins, Larry Csonka and Jim Kiick were on hand, so Miami always relied upon the run.

shovel pass

A cover story in *Time* magazine in 1972 hailed Shula as having ". . . perhaps the soundest, best organized, technical mind in pro football today." That was part of it, of course. But mostly it was an innate desire, indeed, an obsession, to achieve perfection, or at least approach it.

"I'm about as subtle as a punch in the mouth," Shula once said. "I'm just a guy who rolls up his sleeves and goes to work. I don't have peace of mind until I know I've given the game everything I can. If you allow yourself to settle for anything less than No. 1, you're cheating yourself."

sideline

The boundary line that marks the outside edges of the playing field. The sideline itself is out of bounds.

sideline

sideline and go

A pass route in which the receiver first runs toward the sideline, then breaks straight downfield.

sideline pass

A pass pattern in which the receiver breaks downfield, then cuts sharply for the sideline. Proper timing is essential, with the quarterback anticipating the receiver's route and releasing the ball toward the sideline before the receiver reaches it.

sideline and go

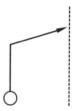

sideline pass

Simpson, O. J.

Most Valuable Player, 1973.

Jim Brown was always thought of as the king, the greatest running back of all time. He was, until 1973, the year that O. J. Simpson began to challenge Brown's preeminence.

That was the year that O. J. (for Orenthal James) twisted, darted, and juked his way into the NFL record manual and, equally important, helped to give his team, the Buffalo Bills, their first winning season in seven years.

These are the records that O. J. set in 1973:

Most yards gained rushing, season—2,003
Most yards gained rushing, game—250
Most rushing attempts, season—332
Most rushing attempts, game—39
Most games, 200 or more yards rushing, season—3
Most games, 100 or more yards rushing, season—11

Simpson, who graduated from USC in 1968, came into pro football as one of the most highly regarded prospects of all time. He had good size—6-foot-1, 212 pounds. He was quick and very fast—9.3 for 100 yards. He had starred in the Rose

Simpson

Bowl, was *Sport* magazine's "Man of the Year," and winner of the Heisman Trophy. So the kind of year he had in 1973 was really no surprise. What was surprising was that it took so long to achieve it.

The first years in Buffalo were cruel. There was a dearth of talent, and the quality players who were on hand were usually sidelined by injuries. Coach John Rauch had O. J. catching passes and returning kicks. He also had him carrying the ball, but not very often. The Bills won a total of eight games in O. J.'s first three years with the team. O. J. has referred to this period as "a helluva grind."

Then, in 1971, Lou Saban became the Buffalo coach, and he began at once to bolster the offensive line, obtaining such players as guards Reggie McKenzie and Joe DeLamielleure. He restyled the team's attack so that O. J. became the featured performer. It didn't take O. J. long to begin living up to his college press notices.

"I don't feel I have to challenge tacklers," O. J. once told Buffalo newspaperman Larry Felser. "There's no compulsion on my part to run over people, like Csonka or Larry Brown.

"I run a lot by instinct and how much I can see when I'm through the hole. Gale Sayers and Hugh McElhenny were the kind or runners who went round the tackler, and I've always patterned myself after them."

The season of 1974 was another outstanding one for O. J., or The Juice, as he came to be known. He rushed for 1,125 yards, and the Bills landed a spot in the championship playoffs, but they lost to the Steelers in the opening round.

For a time that season, O. J. had the Bills dreaming Super Bowl. There's nothing wrong with that. When an O. J. Simpson is in your lineup, you can dream any dream you want.

single-wing formation

An offensive formation in which a halfback acts as a wingback, that is, he is stationed outside either the right or left end. The ball is snapped back four or five yards to either the fullback or tailback. The fourth back, set behind the strong-side guard, is known as the blocking back.

The single wing was in use in the 1920s and 1930s and even predates pro football itself by a couple of decades. Plays develop slowly when the single wing is used, and thus the passing game is less effective than when the T formation is in use.

single-wing formation

slant, n.

A running play in which the ball carrier approaches the line of scrimmage at an angle, then veers into the hole.

slant route

A pass pattern in which the receiver runs diagonally from his position at the line of scrimmage, slanting either toward the sideline or over the middle.

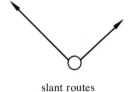

slant routes

slot, n.

A gap created in the offensive line outside one of the tackle positions. A fourth receiver, frequently a running back, usually lines up in the slot.

slotback, n.

A player who lines up in the slot.

slot formation

Any one of several passing formations in which a player who is to act as a fourth receiver is positioned in a gap on either one of the flanks of the offensive line. In one frequently used variation, a

273

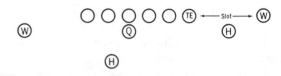

slot formation

running back lines up in the gap between the tight end and the wide receiver on the right.

slot-I

A variation of the T formation in which a wide receiver is the slot man. The backs line up in an I arrangement.

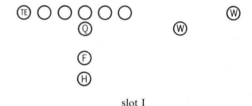

slot I

snap, n.

Every play from scrimmage begins with the snap, the passing of the football from the center to the quarterback.

snap count

The number, announced by the quarterback in the huddle, on which the ball is to be snapped. "On three," the quarterback may say, in which case he wants to get the ball on the third "Hut."

snapper, snapper-back

Terms, now virtually obsolete, used to describe the center, the player who puts the ball in play from scrimmage.

snap

Southern California Sun

WFL team, 1974, 1975.

spearing

An attempt by one player to hurt or injure another by lunging at him helmet first. If judged deliberate by an official, spearing can result in a 15-yard penalty.

special teams

The term "special teams" is one used by coaches and television broadcasters. They also call them kicking teams, specialty teams and, simply, "teams." But to most players the only thing special about them is their injury rate, which is six or seven times that recorded for ordinary plays from scrimmage. To the players, the special teams are known as suicide squads.

The reason that special-team assignments are so perilous is easy to understand. On some of them,

275

opposing players line up 20 or 30 yards apart, and when the whistle blows they come careening toward each other under a full head of steam. It's a demolition derby. It takes a good size and speed to be a member of a special team, but most of all it takes temerity, a word the dictionary defines as "foolish boldness, recklessness, rashness."

There are nine special teams, each with a different set of responsibilities:

1. punting and covering punts
2. punt returns
3. punt blocking
4. kickoffs and kickoff coverage
5. kickoff returns
6. onside kickoffs
7. recovering onside kickoffs
8. field goals and try-for-point conversions
9. blocking field goals and try-for-point conversions

Up until fairly recent times, special teams were staffed by players who were considered somewhat dispensable, that is, raw rookies and soon-to-retire veterans. Those days have gone the way of the leather helmet. Anywhere from 30 to 35 members of the squad will have special-team assignments, and a good number of these players will be first-stringers.

Different special teams require players of different skills. Speedsters are needed to block punts. Open-field blockers staff the team when a long punt return is sought. Sure-handed players are employed when a team expects an onside kick.

Naturally, responsibilities overlap. Take, for example, the case of Ted Vactor, who played for the Washington Redskins for five years beginning in 1969. While Vactor was listed on the Redskins' roster as cornerback, he seldom played that position. He was a special-team specialist, playing left end on the punting unit, right safety on punt returns, inside the left end on kickoffs, and on the wide side against field goals. He also served as the deep receiver on kickoff returns. Vactor should have gotten an award for surviving.

Paul Brown, when he coached the Cleveland Browns, is credited with being the first to recognize the importance of special teams, and he organized individual practice sessions for them. Don Shula carried such recognition a step farther, appointing the NFL's first special teams' captain, Alex Hawkins. Hawkins' nickname was evidence of the relative obscurity in which special-team players perform. He was known as "Captain Who?"

George Allen of the Washington Redskins added several refinements to the coaching of special teams. He was the first to hire an assistant to coach them on an exclusive basis, a policy many NFL teams now follow. Allen believed that special teams were crucial to the Redskins' success. "Football is one third offense, one third defense, and one third kicking," he once said. Allen's emphasis on special teams is apparent to visitors to Redskins Park, Washington's seven-acre practice complex located about 30 miles west of the Capitol. Among the many meeting rooms, one is marked "Special Teams."

spike, v.

To slam the ball to the turf after scoring a touchdown.

split, n.

The spacing between offensive linemen. A team will occasionally split players in an effort to create gaps in the defensive line for their runners. Other times it's done to give linemen more favorable blocking angles.

split end

The wide receiver who lines up on the side of the formation away from the tight end, and who is

277

split end

"split" six or seven yards from the tackle. The position is also called spread end, wide end, and weak-side end.

split-T formation

A variation of the standard-T formation popularized during the 1950s, the split T was characterized by wide gaps between the members of the offensive line, as much as three yards between the ends and tackles, two yards between the tackles and guards, and one yard between the guards and center.

spotter

The member of the radio or television broadcast team who identifies players for the play-by-play man.

spread formation

A variation of the T formation in which the halfback and fullback are set very wide, outside the tackle positions. The idea is to enable them to get downfield quickly as pass receivers.

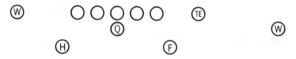

spread formation

square-in, n.

A pass pattern in which the receiver sprints straight downfield, then breaks at a 90-degree angle over the middle.

square-out, n.

A pass pattern in which the receiver sprints straight downfield, then breaks at a 90-degree angle toward the near sideline.

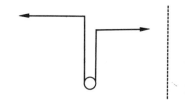

square in, square out

squib kick

A kickoff in which the ball is laid on its side, not placed on a kicking tee, the idea being to produce a

squib kick

279

short kick that will bounce crazily, allowing the kicking team an opportunity to recover it. *See* onside kick.

SS

See strong-side safety.

Stabler, Ken

Most Valuable Player, 1974.

Stabler

A brash left-hander, with long hair and the nickname, the Snake, Ken Stabler was named pro football's most valuable player in his first full year as starting quarterback for the Oakland Raiders. What he did that year was pilot the Oakland team to a division title, completing 57.4 percent of his passes, then past the Dolphins in the opening round of the playoffs, eliminating the Super Bowl champions on a touchdown pass in the final minute of play. A week later, however, the Raiders were turned back by the Steelers in the AFC title game.

Although the 1974 season was the first in which he started every game, Stabler was no newcomer to the Raiders. Far from it. A graduate of Alabama where he learned his football under Bear Bryant, Stabler was the Raiders' No. 2 draft choice in 1968 and a member of the taxi squad that season. He dropped out of football the next year because of personal problems, mostly marital.

He returned to the Raiders in 1970 to spend that season and most of the next two watching from the bench. The Raiders had Daryle Lamonica, the so-called Mad Bomber, to do their quarterbacking, and George Blanda to back him up.

As zone defenses became more efficient, Lamonica's effectiveness diminished. But Stabler showed he could beat the zone with his deft short passes, his ability to roll out, and his willingness to tuck the ball to his belly and run with it. "He's mobile. He doesn't stick to a pattern," Gene Up-shaw, the Raiders' All-Pro guard, said of him. "He's here; he's there. He's a snake, man."

Stabler won the Oakland starting job from Lamonica in 1973, taking over in the season's third game and starting all the others. The Raiders won their division title and Stabler wound up with 163 completions in 260 attempts, giving him a glittering 62.7 percentage, best in the league.

"Stabler's shown he can produce," said George Blanda. "There's no stopping him now."

stack defense

Any defensive alignment in which one or more of the linebackers plays directly in back of a lineman. As the play develops, the stacked linebackers wheel out of their concealed position, targeting on the ball carrier.

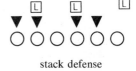

stack defense

stack-I

A variation of the T formation in which the tight end, fullback, and halfback line up directly behind the quarterback.

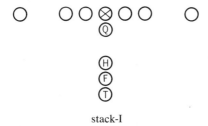

stack-I

Starr, Bart

Most Valuable Player, 1966; Super Bowl I (1967), II (1968).

Quietly, deliberately, seldom with any fanfare, Bart Starr quarterbacked the Green Bay Packers to NFL championships in 1961, 1962, 1965, 1966, and

281

Starr

1967, and to victories in Super Bowls I and II. During most of these years, Starr was taken for granted, and frequently he was overshadowed by his more flamboyant teammates—Paul Hornung, Jim Taylor, Ray Nitschke, and Willie Davis.

Bart's self-effacing manner was one of the reasons for this. If he completed an important pass, he gave credit to the receiver. When he scored the game-winning touchdown in the NFL championship in 1967, making a bold, last-second decision to keep the ball himself, the guard who blocked for him—Jerry Kramer—received much more acclaim than Bart ever did.

It's different nowadays. Starr has come to be regarded for what he was—an inspiring leader, intelligent, and capable of doing everything well. The enormous contribution he made to Green Bay's long string of successes is now fully realized.

As a passer, Starr came as close to being perfect as any quarterback ever. During 1964 and 1965, he threw a record 294 consecutive passes without one being intercepted. He also owns all-time record for passing efficiency, with a 57.4 completion percentage.

Starr was also a clever tactician, probing and picking at the opposition until he found a weakness. When the Packers faced the Kansas City Chiefs in Super Bowl I, Starr determined in the first period that the Chiefs' cornerbacks, Fred Williamson and Willie Mitchell, were vulnerable. In the second quarter, he began to make use of this knowledge, assigning Max McGee and Carroll Dale to run quick square-outs in front of Williamson and Mitchell. When the two cornermen adjusted, Starr sent McGee and Dale deep. The Packers led, 14–10, at halftime, and in the third period the Chiefs collapsed. "Starr was the biggest single difference between the two teams," said Kansas City coach Hank Stram after the game.

Starr came to the Packers in 1956, a 17th-round draft pick from the University of Alabama. He was shuttled in and out of the lineup for two seasons. When Vince Lombardi took over the team in 1959, Starr failed to impress him until the last few games of the season. He became Lombardi's No. 1 quarterback the following year.

"Everything I am as a man and a football player I owe to Vince Lombardi," Bart declared in an article in *Sport* magazine in 1970. "He is the man who taught me everything I know about football, about leadership, about life.

"He took a kid and made a man out of him, with his example, with his faith. Maybe I could have done it myself. Maybe."

Arm miseries began to bother Bart in 1967 and eventually forced his retirement. The 1971 season was his last as a player, but he remained with the team as an assistant coach for a year, then gave up football entirely to pursue his lucrative business enterprises, which included a promotional agency in Green Bay and two automobile dealerships in Alabama.

Late in 1974, when the Packers offered him a three-year contract as coach and general manager,

283

Bart quickly accepted. Whatever he achieves as a coach, it will be difficult for him to surpass his achievements as a player. In the decade that pro football became the nation's No. 1 sport, Bart Starr was the No. 1 quarterback.

Staten Island (New York) Stapletons

NFL team, 1929–1932.

Statue of Liberty play

A popular play of the 1920s and 1930s, the Statue of Liberty was a fake pass, the quarterback dropping back, cocking his arm. A receiver or backfield man would dart behind the quarterback and snatch the ball from his upraised hand, then scamper around an end. The end-around play that teams use today is similar.

Staubach, Roger

Most Valuable Player, Super Bowl VI (1972).

Staubach

During the late 1960s and early 1970s, the Dallas Cowboys were often tagged as "next year's champions." They were always the team that was supposed to win—but never did. Year in and year out, they would find some way to lose the championship.

Then along came Roger Staubach. In his first season as the Cowboys' starting quarterback, he guided the team to ten straight victories and into the Super Bowl, where they faced the Miami Dolphins. Roger was slick that afternoon, keeping the offense rolling by converting third-down plays with his crisp passes. In total, he completed 12 of 19 passes for 119 yards and two touchdowns, leading the Cowboys to their first Super Bowl win.

Most observers hailed Roger, not so much for his technical skills, but for his ability as a leader.

"Roger Staubach has true leadership," said Tex Schramm, president and general manager of the Dallas team. "The other players see it and respect it. It's just there—self-assurance, confidence, maturity—whatever it is that defines leadership."

Some of these qualities may have stemmed from Staubach's military training. After graduating from the Naval Academy, he spent four years in the Navy. He was a 27-year-old rookie when he first reported to the Cowboys in 1969.

He led the NFL in passing in 1971 and again in 1973. He missed most of the 1972 season with a shoulder injury.

Off the field, Staubach is known to be a deeply religious and private man, and he makes frequent appearances for worthy causes. He, his wife, and three daughters live in a modest ranch-style brick house in a Dallas suburb. His tastes are simple. After the Cowboys won the Super Bowl—and Staubach had received his $25,000 check—he permitted himself the luxury of having an extension telephone installed in his office-den.

Stautner, Ernie

Hall of Fame, 1969.

When Earl Morrall, who later was to win distinction with the Colts and Dolphins, quarterbacked the Pittsburgh Steelers in 1957 and 1958, he got to know Ernie Stautner, the Steelers' All-Pro tackle.

"I remember a game against the Browns," Morrall once recalled, "in which we were getting pounded, 45–10. It was late in the fourth quarter, and most of us had one eye on the clock, hoping we'd soon be able to escape from public view.

"Not Stautner. He wouldn't quit. It was as if it were a crucial game and the score close.

"Not long before it ended, he stormed through the line to trap the Cleveland quarterback in the end zone, dragging him to the ground for a safety. That made the score, 45–12. I've always thought those

Stautner

two points should have gone to Stautner personally."

Tenacity was only one of the many championship qualities Stautner displayed in his 14 years with the lowly Steelers. He had good quickness and was exceptionally strong. He also had a weapon he called the hammer head.

At the ball's snap, he'd drive the heel of his left hand straight at the nose of the player opposite him. "Many's the time," he once said, "my hand was cut and the base of the palm black and blue after a game. I had to start wearing a piece of padding."

Right after he struck out with the left hand, he followed with a hand slap with his right hand. "You should put a helmet on sometime and see how it feels when it's hit. The reverberations are really something."

It *must* have been effective. Stautner was an All-Pro choice nine times.

After he retired as a player, Stautner decided to teach tackling. He joined the coaching staff of the Dallas Cowboys in 1966 and became defensive coordinator. The Cowboys' "Doomsday Defense" began to assert itself almost from the day Stautner arrived. It was the hammer head, no doubt.

stick-um

stick-um

The stick cream or liquid that pass receivers apply to their fingers to help them hold onto the ball.

strong dog

A blitz by the strong-side linebacker.

Strong, Ken

Hall of Fame, 1967.

Ken Strong is usually remembered by fans of the New York Giants for his skill as a punter and placekicker. But he also carried the ball; indeed, he was one of the outstanding running backs of the 1930s. When Grantland Rice once described the Giants' running attack as being "led by a runaway buffalo, using the speed of a deer," it was Strong he was talking about.

After an outstanding college career at NYU—he was the nation's leading scorer as a senior—Strong signed, not with the Giants, who failed to bid high enough, but with the Stapleton (Staten Island) Stapes, an NFL franchise from 1929 to 1932. Not until the Stapes folded did Strong join the Giants.

His all-around talents helped to transform the team. The Giants finished with a 4–6–2 record in 1932. The following year, however, Strong's first with the team, they won the Eastern Division title, but lost to the Bears in the championship playoff.

The next season they won the division championship again and once more faced the Bears for the league title. Strong calls the game the "greatest" of his career. The Giants, trailing, 10–3, at halftime, switched from cleats to basketball shoes in an effort to get better footing on the frozen field.

The change benefited Strong more than anyone. He raced for two touchdowns in the fourth

Strong

287

quarter, one of them on a 42-yard run, and, switching back to conventional footwear, booted two field goals and three extra points. New York won easily, 30–13. Hundreds of fans poured from the stands at the end of the game, and surrounded Strong, yelling, cheering, and clapping him on the back. The New York *Post* noted: "The only time that Strong was stopped all day was by the crowd at the end of the game."

As a boy growing up in West Haven, Connecticut, Strong learned the art of drop-kicking by booting the ball over low-slung telephone wires. He learned placekicking at NYU. He led the NFL in field goals in 1933 and again in 1944.

Strong was also an excellent punter. This is how he once described his punting style. "I'd stand flat-footed, and if the snap looked good I'd draw my left foot back a bit, then step out on my right, hop on my left, and kick. Just one-and-one-half steps."

Strong did his punting, kicking, and running for the New York Yanks of the American Football League in 1936 and 1939, following a salary dispute with the Maras. He returned to the Giants in 1939, then retired—for the first time. When the Giants were struck with a shortage of playing talent during World War II, they asked Strong to return, and he did.

When Strong retired for keeps in 1947, he held most of the Giants' kicking records. He stayed on as the team's coach. Don Chandler, one of Strong's protegés, became the player who broke his records.

strong side

The side of the ball on which the greater number of offensive or defensive players line up. The right side is usually the strong side because the tight end lines up on that side. The other side is known as the weak side.

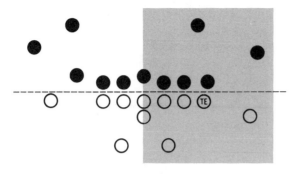

strong side

strong-side safety

The safety who covers the tight end; usually the left safety. *See* safety.

stunting

Swerving, looping, or crisscrossing by defensive linemen and linebackers, before the ball's snap, in an effort to confuse the offense.

stutter steps

Quick, short, choppy steps taken by a ball carrier to avoid being tackled, or by a receiver to confuse the defenseman covering.

Stydahar, Joe

Hall of Fame, 1967.

A fearsome tackle for the Chicago Bears during their years of glory in the late 1930s and early to mid-1940s, Joe Stydahar stood 6-foot-4 and weighed 240 pounds. Statistics like that aren't imposing by today's standards, but they were in those days. Indeed, Stydahar was sometimes called "Jumbo Joe."

289

Stydahar did not win distinction by virtue of his size, however. The fact is that he was a bruiser.

After he retired as a player, Stydahar coached, first for the Los Angeles Rams, then the Chicago Cardinals, and, last, the Bears. In Stydahar's first season as the Rams' head coach, the team absorbed a 49–14 thrashing at the hands of the Philadelphia Eagles. Afterward, Stydahar was livid. "No wonder you guys get licked," he roared, "every guy on this team has still got all his own teeth."

To Stydahar, toothlessness was a sign of competence, if not excellence. "When you charge, you have to keep your head up," he once said. "Sure you lose a lot of teeth, but you make a lot of tackles."

Stydahar was elected to membership in the Hall of Fame in 1967. He undoubtedly received the news of his election with a grin, a toothless grin, to be sure.

submarine

A type of defensive charge in which the lineman keeps low to the ground to avoid being tackled. It is normally used in short yardage or goal-line situations when the ball carrier is expected to be hitting into the middle of the line.

substitute, n.

A player who enters the game in place of another.

substitution, n.

Relieving one player or a group of players for another. Unlimited substitution is permitted in pro football. However, players are permitted to enter and leave the field only when the ball is dead.

sudden death

Tie games are decided in accordance with the NFL's sudden-death rule. In the case of post-season games, including the conference championships and the Super Bowl, an additional period is scheduled, and the rule states that the first team to score is the winner. The game cannot end in a tie.

In the case of preseason and regular-season games, the same is true—the first team that scores wins. However, the amount of overtime play is limited to 15 minutes. Thus, if neither team should score in the extra period, the game ends in a tie.

suicide squads

See special teams.

Super Bowl

The National League's annual championship game which matches the titleholders of the American Conference and the National Conference. The first Super Bowl was played at the Los Angeles Coliseum on January 15, 1967.

The Super Bowl came into existence through the merger agreement between the American League and National League hammered out in 1966. In the first four Super Bowls, the AFL champion met the NFL champion, with each league winning twice. When the merger agreement became final in 1970, with the AFL teams being absorbed by the National League, Super Bowl rivalry continued, but under the NFL banner.

Lamar Hunt, owner of the Kansas City Chiefs, suggested the name Super Bowl. Before it was so named, it was referred to in league meetings as the "Final Game" or the "Big One." Harry Wismer, who owned the AFL's New York Titans, wanted to call it the "Golden Game."

Super Bowl

Hunt had given his daughter some "silly putty" to play with as a toy. Because of the enormous resiliency of the doughlike substance, the little girl called it a super ball. Hunt says that he had the term "super ball" in his subconscious when he suggested Super Bowl.

At first, some league officials were less than enthusiastic about the name. The program for the first AFL-NFL championship game did not use the term, billing the contest as the "World Championship Game." But sportswriters and broadcasters used the term so extensively that the league adopted it officially. In time, the term was sanctified by the use of Roman numerals to designate each game in the continuing series.

Super Bowl Trophy

See Vince Lombardi Trophy.

Susie

With some teams, the term used to identify the
strong-side linebacker.

sweep

A type of running play, made popular during the
Vince Lombardi era of the Green Bay Packers, in
which the ball carrier runs wide to the outside
behind the blocking of two or more linemen.

The halfback is normally the ball carrier. The
fullback cuts down the defensive end. Both guards
pull to lead the interference. After taking the handoff, the ball carrier has to belly-back to allow the
pulling linemen to get out in front of him.

"It began to be a part of me, this sweep," Lombardi said in *Run to Daylight,* "during my days at
Fordham. I was impressed playing against the
single-wing sweep the way those Pittsburgh teams
of Jock Sutherland ran it. Lombardi admitted that
the Green Bay sweep had "a lot" of those Sutherland qualities, including the same guard-pulling
techniques and the same ball-carrier cutback feature. "There's nothing spectacular about it," said
Lombardi. "It's just a yard gainer."

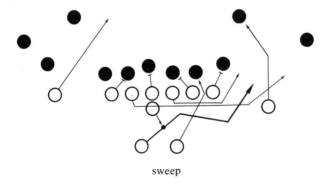

sweep

swing pass

See flare pass.

synthetic turf

synthetic turf

Up until 1966, football was played exclusively on grass. That year synthetic fields began to go down like supermarket parking lots. By the mid-1970s, about half of all stadiums that offered pro football were equipped with synthetic fields.

There are three types: AstroTurf, Tartan Turf, and Poly-Turf. AstroTurf, a product of the Monsanto Chemical Corporation, has a bristlelike surface made of nylon. American Biltrite's Poly-Turf is similar in appearance, though manufactured of polypropylene. Tartan Turf, from the Minnesota Mining and Manufacturing Company, looks and feels like a carpet of padded nylon nap. In each case, the synthetic surface is anchored to a layer of

294

foam rubber which is supported by layers of asphaltic concrete, crushed stone, and soil.

Players are in fairly unanimous agreement about artificial turf: They don't like it. In 1972, the National Football League Players Association demanded a moratorium on synthetic turf installations. In a survey taken by the Association, 85 percent of the players who responded said that they preferred to play on natural grass.

One complaint has to do with heat, with surface temperatures reaching as much as 30 degrees higher than in the case of grass. Lack of traction can be another frustration. But the greatest problem has to do with injuries. In the minds of many players, synthetic turf and getting hurt are closely linked.

However, a study prepared for the National Football League, the results of which were published in 1973, claimed there was "no difference between artificial and natural turf in an analysis of major injuries, but that artificial turf has a poorer safety record when minor injuries are included."

The debate continues. Obviously, the topic deserves more thorough study.

tackle, n.

See defensive tackle, offensive tackle.

tackle, v.

The act of bringing a ball carrier to the ground.

tackle-eligible formation

A seldom seen offensive formation in which a tackle is positioned at one end of the line, and thus becomes eligible to receive a forward pass.

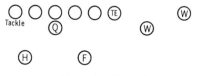

tackle-eligible formation

tailback

In the old single-wing formation, the back who was positioned the greatest distance from the line of scrimmage, and usually the back who received the snap from center. Today the term refers to the offensive player deepest in the formation.

Tartan Turf

See synthetic turf.

taxi squad

Officially known as the future list or reserve squad, the term "taxi squad" refers to the small group of players, usually seven, under contract to the team but not on the active roster. These players practice with the team but are not permitted to suit up for games. A member of the taxi squad may be activated during the season, in which case he becomes a full-fledged member of the team.

"Cab squad," "band squad," and "ghost squad" are other terms that have been used to describe these players, but taxi squad is the name used most frequently. The term originated with the Cleveland Browns of the All-America Football Conference in the late 1940s. The club was owned by Arthur (Mickey) McBride, a well-to-do businessman, with large real estate holdings in the Midwest, a radio station, a race wire syndicate, and taxicab companies in Cleveland, Akron, and Canton.

A team was allowed to carry only 33 players in those days, but McBride hit upon the idea of hanging onto players who were cut from the squad by putting them to work as cab drivers. While league rules prohibited the practice, no one ever told McBride to stop.

Today, the taxi squad is much the same, except that it's legal, and players don't have to drive cabs. Usually the squad includes a quarterback, a running back, a wide receiver, an offensive lineman, a defensive lineman, and a defensive back.

Taylor, Jim

Most Valuable Player, 1962.

There's only one reason that Jim Taylor of the Green Bay Packers is not rated as *the* outstanding running back of the 1960s. The reason is Jim Brown. Indeed, if it were not for Brown, Taylor might be regarded as the outstanding ball carrier of all time.

Taylor really shouldn't be classified as a running back. The term is too generic. Taylor was a fullback. He was built like a fullback, with broad,

Taylor

well-muscled shoulders, and heavily muscled legs.
And he had the skills of a fullback, the ability to
start fast and find the hole quickly.

You could also tell Taylor was a fullback by his
attitude. He was about as subtle as mugging,
smashing into the line when the hole failed to
open, using his body as a battering ram. When hit,
he simply refused to stop.

"I love the game," Taylor once said. "I love the
contact. I like to hit a man. It's not that I want to
hurt anybody—I don't. But . . ."

A college star at LSU, Taylor played for Green
Bay for three years before he became well known
as a pro. An injury put him out of action for most
of 1959, but the following season he rushed for
1,101 yards, beating the Packer team record.

The next year he was even better, gaining 1,307
yards, the most any player had ever gained in a
season—except Jimmy Brown.

Taylor's biggest year was 1962. He won the
rushing title that Jim Brown had claimed for five

consecutive years, carrying 272 times for 1,474 yards. In the title game that year, the Packers vs. the Giants, Taylor butted heads with New York linebacker Sam Huff throughout most of the afternoon, yet still gained almost as much yardage as the entire Giant team. The Packers won, 16–7.

Taylor didn't appreciate the fact that his skills and accomplishments were always being compared to those of Jim Brown. He felt that most people making the comparison overlooked the fact that he was a complete ballplayer, one with the ability to carry the ball, catch passes, and block. Taylor felt that Brown was less than complete because Brown was seldom called upon to block. "When I block, Lombardi makes me get down on all fours in a crab block," Taylor once said. "Every bit of yourself has to get around the guy you're blocking. Jim Brown never heard of the crab block. It's all news to him."

Injuries hindered Taylor in the final years of his career, yet in key games he always managed to put on a vintage performance. When the Packers played the Browns in the NFL title game in 1965, it was Taylor's punishing runs that kept Green Bay drives going and enabled the Pack to control the ball. He was named the game's Most Valuable Player.

When Taylor was unable to win a salary increase he felt he deserved, he played out his option in 1966. Vince Lombardi, feeling betrayed, banished him to New Orleans. There Taylor played his final season.

Jim Taylor's name is prominent in the NFL record manual in these categories: most yards gained, lifetime; most rushing attempts, lifetime; most touchdowns, rushing, lifetime; and most seasons 1,000 or more yards, rushing. In each case, however, Taylor is No. 2 on the list. You know who the No. 1 man is.

TE

See tight end.

tee

See kicking tee.

T formation

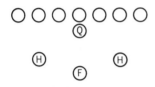

T formation

When a team breaks from the huddle and comes up to the line of scrimmage, the quarterback takes up a position directly behind the center, and he receives the snap from between the center's legs. This is the essential ingredient of the T formation.

Once he's got the ball, the quarterback can either hand off to a running back or pedal back and pass. He can even run himself.

Before the T, teams used the single-wing formation or one of its several variations, and the ball had to be snapped back four or five yards. Plays were slow in developing as a result.

But with the T, a running back could be moving at full speed, or close to it, at the time he received the handoff, which makes for obvious advantages. A team could also fake more when using the T. Overall, it provides for a much more rounded attack.

Another benefit of the T is that it enables the center to block. With the single wing, the center had to put his head down and peer through his legs toward the target, the back who was to get the ball. This meant he was always being clobbered by the defense. But with the T, the center merely has to hand the ball back. Thus, he can keep his head up, driving forward as he snaps.

The T is not perfect. It lacks the power of the single wing in short yardage situations. Another drawback is that it takes a highly skilled quarterback to make the T go. Besides leadership qualities, he has to be a deft ball handler and have exceptional talents as a passer.

While the T formation is often identified as a post World War II innovation, it is much older than that. George Halas's Chicago Bears used the T in December, 1940, when they destroyed the Washington Redskins in the NFL championship, 73–0. In the weeks that followed, Halas was inundated with requests for films of the game. The swing to the T was on.

Actually, Halas had been using T-formation plays for years, but scarcely anyone noticed. As early as 1920, the Bears employed an offensive formation which was known as the "loose T" in which the ends were split and the halfbacks positioned two or three steps outside the fullback.

The Bears added the man-in-motion concept to the basic T in 1931, with the quarterback pitching to the motion man or throwing him a pass. Another wrinkle was added in 1940, the year of the Bears' playoff win. They spread the left end wide, then sent a man in motion to the right. They would then send the play in the direction opposite, to the left, an innovation that has been credited to Clark Shaughnessy, who served as an assistant to Halas.

But Halas wasn't the man who invented the T. He merely revived it.

Amos Alonza Stagg, the football patriarch who died in 1965 at the age of 103, and who served as head coach at the University of Chicago for 41 years, and at the University of the Pacific for 15 years after that, once said that he was using the T as early as 1894, instructing his quarterback to take the ball from the center in about the same way Bob Griese does today. As for the man-in-motion idea, Stagg said that in 1898 he was using a "flyer," a man who ran parallel to the line of scrimmage to receive a backward pass. (The forward pass was yet to be legalized.)

In the T formation of the 1940s, the fullback lined up a few yards behind the quarterback, while the two halfbacks were set to the outside, approximately in back of the tackles. This version of the T gave way to the standard pro set (which *see*) and its countless variations: the double-wing, triple-wing, red, blue, brown, green, spread-I, slot-I, power-I, and stack-I formations.

Thorpe, Jim

Hall of Fame, 1963.

Thorpe

In his book, *Pro Football's Hall of Fame,* Arthur Daley recalled the first formal meeting of the selection committee to pick the charter members of the Hall of Fame. One of the younger members of the panel, impressed by the skills of modern players, had difficulty putting Thorpe in perspective, so he sought the opinion of Jimmy Conzelman, the only selector who had actually played pro ball against Thorpe.

Said Conzelman: "Jim Thorpe could have made any team in the National Football League today. What's more, he would have been the best player on that team. I might also add that he would have been the best player in the entire league."

Conzelman must have been convincing, because Thorpe was named a charter member of the Hall of Fame, one of the countless tributes he received. When, in 1950, the Associated Press polled the nation's sportswriters to determine the "Football Player of the Half Century," Thorpe was the choice.

Anyone who saw Thorpe play speaks of him the way Conzelmen did. So enthusiastic are the comments, in fact, that it's difficult to separate the fact from the fiction. Thorpe is football's answer to Abner Doubleday, or is it Paul Bunyan?

It's said that Thorpe's punts averaged 80 yards and, with a new ball, he could boom a kick from one end zone to the other. It's claimed he could sprint the length of the field in ten seconds fully uniformed.

Many legends concern his skill as a ball carrier. He was said to be capable of either blasting over tacklers or faking them silly. "Give him the ball and he'd run through a whole team," Indian Joe Guyon, one of Thorpe's teammates, once said.

In Thorpe's final college season, his team, the Carlisle Indians, played Army. The New York *Times,* noting Thorpe's recent Olympic triumphs, described him as "the athletic marvel of the age."

"At times the game itself was almost forgotten while the spectators gazed on Thorpe, the individual, to wonder at his prowess," the *Times* continued. "He simply ran wild, while the Cadets tried in vain to stop his progress. It was like trying to stop a shadow."

Words like "peerless" and "undaunted" were always being used to describe Thorpe. He was forever "astonishing" coaches or making them "goggle-eyed." His "instincts were flawless" was another typical comment.

While much that has been written about Thorpe and his skills may have been embroidered or magnified, there is no denying the fact that in the early days of the pro game he was its dominant figure. People flocked to see him.

He played for an assortment of teams, selling his talents to the highest bidder. His first pro team was the Canton Bulldogs. He signed with them in 1915.

"Some of my business advisers frankly predicted that I was leading the Bulldogs into bankruptcy by paying Jim the enormous sum of $250 a game," Jim Cusack, owner of the Canton team, once commented. "But the deal paid off beyond my greatest expectations. Jim was an attraction as well as a player, and whereas our paid attendance averaged around 1,200 before we took him on, we filled the Massillon and Canton parks for the next two games—6,000 for the first and 8,000 for the second. All the fans wanted to see the big Indian in action."

Thorpe continued as a drawing card for the Bulldogs for several years. When representatives of the most noted teams of the day met in Canton in 1920 to reorganize the American Professional Football Association, the league that later became the NFL, Thorpe, in recognition of his popularity, was elected president.

Thorpe continued playing for another ten years, toiling for such teams as the Oorang Indians and the Rock Island Independents. He signed with the New York Giants in 1925, his contract calling for him to be paid $200 whenever he played a complete half. The next season he was back with the Bulldogs in Canton.

On November 30, 1929, the Associated Press carried this story: "Chicago—The Chicago Bears routed their ancient rivals, the Chicago Cardinals, 34–0, in the annual Thanksgiving Day game at Wrigley Field today. Jim Thorpe played a few minutes for the Cardinals, but was unable to get anywhere. In his forties and musclebound, Thorpe was a mere shadow of his former self."

Thorpe's final years were troubled. He settled in California and worked part-time as a motion picture extra and as an adviser on football shorts. But he had problems, not the least of which was a fondness for alcohol. "What did Thorpe drink?" one of his teammates was once asked. "Anything he could get his hands on," was the answer.

One wire service reported him to be digging ditches and penniless. Another told how he was hauled into court and fined for drunk driving. He went through a couple of divorces. In 1953, he died of a heart attack at his trailer home in Lomita, California.

three-point stance

The set position most players use as the quarterback calls signals. The words "three-point" refer

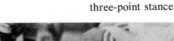

three-point stance

304

to the player's two legs and one hand which are in contact with the ground.

In assuming a three-point stance, the player spreads his feet about shoulder-width apart, then, bending at the knees, leans forward, placing one hand to the ground. Not only does the three-point stance permit a player to move quickly to either side or straight ahead, it's an advantageous position from which to launch a block.

throwing underneath

A method of attacking the zone pass defense in which the quarterback sends one or both of the running backs into the short-pass area just beyond the line of scrimmage. Since the linebackers are dropping back to protect their coverage zones, the quarterback is said to be throwing ''underneath'' the linebackers.

tight end

Most pass receivers don't like to catch the ball over the middle, because it usually means that they're going to be hit by at least two defensive players. Yet over the middle is where the tight end catches most of his passes, which gives you some idea of the qualifications necessary for the job. Bigness and toughness are surely two of them, although not necessarily in that order.

Catching passes constitutes only about half of what the tight end does. He also has to block; indeed, in this regard the tight end is vital to the team's running game. He has to cut down the

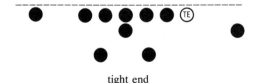

tight end

middle linebacker on plays up the middle and dart over and pinch the outside linebacker to the inside on sweeps to the right. Other times the defensive end is the man he must block.

To accomplish these duties, the tight end has to have the size and strength of a lineman and also be about as fast and agile as a wide receiver. It's almost like being two players at once.

The tight end's position is so named because he lines up "tight" next to the tackle, usually on the right side. In short-yardage situations close to the goal line, a team will occasionally use a double tight-end formation, with one tight end positioned on the right side, and the second, replacing a wide receiver, set to the left.

While most tight ends run short routes and are adept at catching passes in heavy traffic, a sprinkling have exceptional speed and are used on deep routes. Raymond Chester of the Colts and Richard Caster of the Jets are two who fall into this category. Maybe they're trend-setters.

tight safety

The safety who covers the tight end, usually the left safety. *See* safety.

time-out

Any interval during the game when play is not legally in progress and the official clock is stopped. Automatic timeouts occur:

following a touchdown or field goal
during a try-for-point attempt
when the ball goes out of bounds
when a receiver makes a fair catch
at the end of a down when a foul occurs
when the line judge signals there are two minutes remaining in a half
at the end of a period
following a change in possession
when a kicked ball is illegally touched

In addition, each team is allowed three 1½-minute time-outs each half. The referee can also allow a timeout of two minutes duration when a player is injured, and of three minutes duration for equipment repair.

Tittle, Y. A.

Most Valuable Player, 1963; Hall of Fame, 1970.

It didn't end in storybook fashion for tall, bald Y. A. Tittle. As quarterback for the New York Giants, he guided the team to the Eastern Conference title in 1963. They then faced the Bears for the NFL crown.

The Giants led, 10–7, late in the second quarter when Y. A. drifted back to throw. In blitzed Chicago linebacker Larry Morris to slam him to the ground. Pain shot through Tittle's left leg, and he knew instantly that the knee had been seriously damaged.

They taped the knee at halftime and filled it with pain-killing drugs. But when he tried to throw, he couldn't plant his left leg properly. Five of his six passes were intercepted. The Bears won, 14–10.

Tittle

In the game's closing minutes, Tittle sat on the bench, a blue Giant parka over his shoulders. His head was bowed and he wept. It wasn't the agonizing pain. It was the knowledge that another championship opportunity had slipped away.

Tittle had brought the Giants into the championship playoff in 1961 and 1962, only to be defeated by the Green Bay Packers both times. In 1964, injuries, retirements, and some trades that didn't work out very well ruined their chances, and the next year Y. A. retired.

While Y. A. may not have won an NFL championship, it's about the only thing he failed to win. His 17-year career began in 1948 when he won Rookie-of-the-Year honors with the Baltimore Colts, who were then members of the All-America Football Conference. Before that, Y. A. starred at Louisiana State University.

He was born in Marshall, Texas, in 1926. His father, a postman, named him Yelverton because it was a family name, and Abraham because he wanted something biblical. But he was always called. "Y. A."

"Kids in my part of Texas would rather play football than eat," he once said. "Sammy Baugh was our idol, and we all spent hours pitching footballs through old tires hung from tree limbs the way we had seen Baugh do it in the newsreels."

In Tittle's third year with the Colts, the team folded and the players were parceled out to the other NFL teams. Y. A. ended up with the San Francisco 49ers. There he stayed for ten seasons.

His years in San Francisco were often frustrating ones. In 1957 the team finished the season in a tie for first place in the Western Division with the Detroit Lions. In the playoff, the 49ers led, 24–7, at halftime, Y. A. having passed for two touchdowns.

The third quarter began with Tittle marching the team downfield once more. But the Lions' defense stiffened and the 49ers were stopped. When the Lions took over the ball, quarterback Tobin Rote was unstoppable with his passes, and the Lions ended up winning.

A young man named John Brodie came upon the scene that year, and it wasn't long before the 49ers began grooming him as Y. A.'s successor. Three years later Y. A. was in New York, beginning all over at 35.

Charlie Conerly was the New York quarterback at the time, and he had been so for 14 years. He was deeply esteemed by his teammates, who looked upon Tittle as an intruder. But little by little, Y. A. won over the Giants, and in 1960 he was given command of the team. When he began to make the Giants win, fans in San Francisco hung banners in the stands that read BRING BACK TITTLE and WE WUZ ROBBED.

Statistically and esthetically, Tittle ranks as one of the finest passers of all time. His execution of the screen pass was marvelous to behold; he was both bold and deft with it.

Tittle has a handsome Rookie-of-the-Year plaque and a towering MVP trophy. He has all the baubles that go with being named to the Hall of Fame. But the chances are good he'd trade them all for a championship ring.

Toledo (Ohio) Maroons

NFL team, 1922, 1923.

touchback

When a team gains possession of the ball in the end zone it's defending on a play that begins with the other team causing the ball to cross the goal-line, a touchback is recorded. No points are scored on a touchback. The next play starts from the team's 20-yard line.

An exception to the rule occurs in the case of field goals attempted and missed from beyond the 20-yard line. In such cases, the defensive team takes possession at the line of scrimmage.

A touchback occurs in each one of these situations: when a kickoff is downed in the end zone, when a punt is downed in the end zone, and when a pass is intercepted in the end zone and the runner is tackled there.

touchdown

The six-point score earned by a team carrying the ball into or catching it in the opposing end zone. Scoring a touchdown also earns the team a try-for-point opportunity.

In the game's early days, the football had to be actually touched to the ground, but today's rule-book states that a touchdown is recorded whenever any part of the ball, legally in possession of a player, is carried on, over, or above the opponent's goal line.

In the World Football League, a touchdown earned seven points, not six, plus the right to try for an "action point." This is an eighth point a team can score by running or passing the ball into the end zone from the 2½ yard line. There was no placekicking for the extra point in the WFL.

Trafton, George

Hall of Fame, 1964.

Trafton

In his playing days with the Chicago Bears from 1920–1933, George Trafton epitomized the team— tough, durable, and out to win in any manner deemed necessary.

Trafton was the Bears' center; he was, in fact, *the* center of professional football in those days, winning All-Pro honors eight times.

In photos of the Bear team taken in the 1920s, Trafton is usually pictured with his head cocked slightly to one side, and wearing a menacing expression. Red Grange once called him the "toughest, meanest, most ornery critter alive." Knute Rockne booted him out of Notre Dame for playing semipro football on Sundays. Many of the stories about Trafton confirm Red Grange's description of him. Once, in a game against the Cardinals, the opposition center kept whacking Trafton with his forearm. "What do you call that?" Trafton asked the center. "That's a Southern California arm block," the center said, grinning. "Don't you like it?"

On the next play, Trafton arranged for his two guards to step on the center's toes, pinning his feet to the ground. As the ball was snapped, Trafton took several steps backward, then charged forward, hitting the man full force with a savage cross-body block.

When the man came to, Trafton was standing over him. "That," he said, "was a Notre Dame drop kick."

For more or less than 20 years, Trafton was a part of the pro football scene, playing, scouting, or coaching. "He was the only guy I ever met who claimed he was the greatest at his position," Jimmy Conzelman once said. "Of course, he actually was."

trainer

It's been estimated that the average pro team uses up more then 500 miles of adhesive tape from the time training camp opens until the season ends. Since it's the trainer who uses it, the statistic gives you some idea of what the trainer does and how often he does it.

Actually, taping is only one of the trainer's many duties. As the member of the team's administrative staff whose overall responsibility is to assist the club physician in the conditioning and medical treatment of players, the trainer plays an important role in the team's success.

Among their duties, trainers wrap players' ankles before games and practice sessions, wrap or tape injured knees, wrists, and hands, and supervise the exercise and treatment program set down

trainer

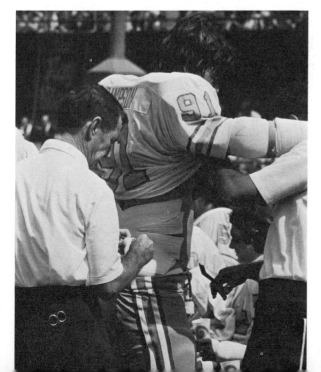

311

for injured players. In this regard, trainers massage injured muscles and administer diathermy treatment and whirlpool baths. When emergency treatment is necessary on the sidelines during a game, it's the trainer who gives it.

If trainers had a motto, it could be: "Get 'em ready! Keep 'em ready!"

trap, n.

A blocking maneuver by members of the offensive line, wherein one member of the unit pulls from his position within the line, allowing a defensive man to penetrate. A second offensive player, charging over from an unexpected direction, then blocks the defender. It's occasionally called a mousetrap.

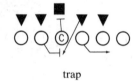

trap

tree

The various pass routes that can be run by a receiver as set down in a single diagram.

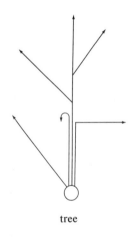

tree

triple-wing formation

A variation of the T formation in which the fullback takes a set position just off the line of scrimmage between the tight end and tackle. Three receivers can thus get downfield quickly from the strong side.

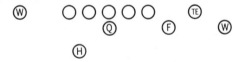

triple-wing formation

Trippi, Charlie

Hall of Fame, 1968.

Only once have the Cardinals won the NFL title,

and the year they did—1947—it was more Charlie Trippi's doing than anyone else's. A single-wing tailback from the University of Georgia, Trippi signed with the Cards in April of that year, becoming the final building block in the team's "dream backfield" assembled by owner Charlie Bidwill. It consisted of quarterback Paul Christman, fullback Pat Harder, with Marshall Goldberg and Trippi as the halfbacks.

The Cards, in Chicago then, beat the Bears on the last day of the season to win the Western Division title, then faced the Eagles at Comiskey Park for the NFL crown. Trippi never had a better day. About midway through the first quarter, he found daylight off tackle and broke into the open, racing 44 yards for the game's first touchdown.

In the third quarter, with the score 14–7 in the Cards' favor, Trippi returned a punt 75 yards for another touchdown. The Cards went on to win, 28–21. While Trippi set several records that afternoon, the fact that he gained a total of 206 yards was perhaps his most notable achievement. Only once in playoff history has the figure been exceeded.

Trippi

The Cards were back in the championship game the very next year, but this time they lost to the Eagles. Everything went downhill after that. Head coach Jimmy Conzelman decided to quit, and injuries and retirements hurt the team.

In desperate need of a quarterback, the Cards asked Trippi to take over the position in 1951. He did, but he was never much better than adequate. Another coaching change and front-office bickering wrecked the team. In 1953 the Cards managed to win only one game.

Through the years that followed their winning of the championship in 1947, tragedy seemed to stalk the Cards. Owner Bidwill died of pneumonia in 1947. Halfback Jeff Burkett was killed in an airplane crash. Tackle Stan Mauldin collapsed and died in the dressing room.

Trippi did not escape. During the 1955 season, he was cut down by a block from the blind side,

313

suffering a severe head injury. He was unconscious for hours while surgeons worked over him.

Trippi played a few games later in the season as a defensive back, but his years of hurtling into the line or through it were over. He retired at the end of the season.

try-for-point

The opportunity given a team which has scored a touchdown to add another point by successfully executing a single play from scrimmage. The ball is put in play from the two-yard line or any point beyond it.

In the NFL, the placekick is used almost exclusively to score the point. The ball must go over the crossbar and between the goal posts. The rules also permit the ball to be run or passed over the goal line.

Tunnell, Emlen

Hall of Fame, 1967.

One of the first players to enter the Hall of Fame purely on the basis of his defensive skills, Emlen Tunnell of the New York Giants set career records for interceptions (79), interception yardage (1,282), punt returns (258), and punt-return yardage (2,182). One season he gained more yards returning punts and kicks and intercepted passes than the total yardage gained by the Giant running backs.

From Garrett Hill, Pennsylvania, Tunnell played college football at Iowa. He was a single-wing tailback there, a position he hoped to play with New York. Unfortunately, he happened to join the Giants the same year as Charlie Conerly, also a tailback and one of the best in the business, and Conerly wasted no time in establishing himself as No. 1.

But Tunnell adjusted to playing defense quickly. "There's something about knifing in and bringing a guy down with a sharp tackle," he said, "that's more satisfying than a long run behind good blocking. Tackling is football, running is track."

Tunnell played on two conference championship teams in his years with the Giants. The 1956 team won the NFL title.

He was always a daring player, going for the interception whenever he sensed the opportunity. This free-wheeling style put him in conflict with Tom Landry when the latter became the team's defensive coach. Tunnell quit the Giants and signed on with the Packers at the invitation of Vince Lombardi. In Green Bay he played on two more conference championship teams, one of which—the 1961 team—won the NFL crown.

One day Tunnell was running wind sprints on the Green Bay practice field, when he tried a favorite exercise of his, leaping up to touch the goal post crossbar. But this time his fingers failed to make contact with the crossbar. He tried again with the same result. Tunnell then realized that his legs had lost their spring, and he decided to make the 1961 season his last.

He became a scout for the Giants and, later, the team's defensive backfield coach. He's now the Giants' assistant director of pro personnel.

Turner, Clyde (Bulldog)

Hall of Fame, 1966.

A big, beefy center, Bulldog Turner first won national acclaim as an All American at little Hardin-Simmons College in Abilene, Texas. The Detroit Lions made a determined effort to land him, but were outwitted by George Halas. Turner signed with the Bears in 1940 and bulwarked four championship teams, winning All-Pro honors six times.

Turner was a member of the Bear team that

Turner

overwhelmed the Redskins, 73–0, in the 1940 NFL championship. The Bears scored so frequently that afternoon and kicked so many extra points into the stands that the officials began to run out of footballs. In the fourth quarter, as the Bears were lining up for yet another try-for-point attempt, the player who was to hold the ball came in from the bench and instructed Turner to make a bad pass from center. "We're losing too many footballs," he said. "And we don't need to kick any more points."

"Go to hell!" Turner told him. "I'm not going to make a bad pass. I'm going to put the ball right into your hands." And that's exactly what he did.

Turner explained his thinking to Myron Cope in the book, *The Game That Was:* "The reason I wouldn't make a bad pass from center was I had never made a bad pass—not in all the time I played center. As a matter of fact, in my whole thirteen years of pro football I never made a bad pass."

If Turner merely passed the ball back well, it's not likely he would have won great renown. It also happened he was an outstanding defensive player, not only in backing up the line, but filling in as a tackle or a guard when needed. He was very agile for a big man and led the league in interceptions in 1942 with eight.

The interception that he remembers best occurred several years later. After picking off one of Sammy Baugh's passes on the Bear three-yard line, Turner began weaving his way downfield, picking up blocking as he went. As he crossed midfield, he could see that there was only one player between himself and the Bear end zone, and that was Baugh. The two men ran shoulder to shoulder for a while, and then Baugh made a leap, grabbing Turner about the head. Turner scarcely noticed. He simply carried Baugh across the goal line with him.

After retiring as a player in 1952, Turner was an assistant coach for the Bears. He gave that up in 1956 to return to his central Texas ranch.

turn-in, n.

A pass pattern in which the receiver veers over the middle.

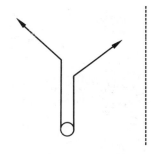

turn-out, n.

A pass pattern in which the receiver veers toward the sideline.

turn in, turn out

turnover, n.

Losing the ball by a fumble or interception.

turn the corner

On a sweep, the cut made by the ball carrier as he heads downfield.

two-minute warning

An official's verbal notification to the head coach that two minutes of playing time remain in the half. An automatic time-out occurs.

two-point option

In the American Football League, which operated from 1960–1969, a team scoring a touchdown had the option of trying for either one or two points. The ball was placed on the two-yard line. A team was awarded one point for a successful placekick, or two points for successfully running or passing the ball across the goal line. The two-point option is also used in college football.

317

two-point stance

two-point stance

A ready position in which a player crouches slightly, but without either hand in contact with the ground. Linebackers, defensive backs, and wide receivers usually employ the two-point stance.

umbrella defense

A defensive alignment introduced by coach Steve
Owen of the New York Giants in 1950, so called
because the deployment of the backs was said to
resemble an open umbrella. Sometimes it was referred to as the 6–1–4 defense.

The guards and tackles rushed the passer and
covered the run. The center, stationed a yard or
two off the line, played the fullback man-to-man.
The ends covered the short-pass zones. There
were four deep backs.

Tom Landry played cornerback on the Giant
team that year, and later, when he became the
Giants' defensive coach, he helped to convert the
6–1–4 to the 4–3–4, the three-linebacker defensive
alignment popular during the 1960s and 1970s.

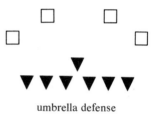

umbrella defense

umpire

The official who, on plays from scrimmage, lines
up in the middle of the defensive secondary. As
the ball is snapped, he checks interior linemen for
holding and supervises the short-pass area.

When a pass play does develop, the umpire
edges toward the line of scrimmage in order to en-
sure that the interior linemen do not stray downfield too early. On screen passes, he focuses his
attention on the receiver, seeing to it that the man
is permitted to run his pattern. It's also the umpire's responsibility to see to it that the players'
equipment conforms to the rules.

unbalanced line

An offensive alignment with more players positioned on one side of the center than the other.

unbalanced line

unit

A particular group of players, as in the case of a team's offensive unit, defensive unit, field-goal unit, kick-return unit, etc.

Unitas, Johnny

Most Valuable Player, 1964, 1967.

Unitas

"The most valuable thing I can say about playing quarterback and passing a football is that those acts involve no deep, dark mystery," wrote Johnny Unitas in an instructional article in *Sports Illustrated* in 1972. "The whole art, if I may call it that, is based on a few simple elements. Once certain principles are understood, the complexities unravel and the job becomes straightforward."

That's the way football was to Johnny Unitas—simple and uncomplicated. That's the way he was himself—direct and open. In his 18 years in the National League, he never once failed to display the dignity, dedication, and honesty that were so deeply ingrained in his character.

Voted the greatest quarterback in pro football's first 50 years, Unitas completed more passes for more yardage and more touchdowns than anyone else in the game's history. There was no one better at doing all the things a quarterback has to do.

The Unitas story is well known—how he was the quarterback that nobody wanted, playing sandlot football in Pittsburgh for $6 a game; how the Colts signed him in 1956 for the price of an 80-cent telephone call; how his first pass was intercepted and run back for a touchdown.

Two years later Unitas guided the Colts to the Western Conference championship. They then met the Giants for the NFL title. Decided in overtime, the game has been called the greatest in pro history.

Unitas was unchallenged as the game's hero. With 90 seconds to play, trailing, 17–14, the Colts were in possession on their own 14-yard line. Unitas then completed four passes, taking the team to the Giants' 20-yard line, whereupon Steve Myhra booted a field goal. In the overtime period, Unitas engineered an 80-yard drive for the winning touchdown.

On the final sequence of plays, everyone expected Unitas to keep the ball on the ground. But on second down, inside the Giant 10-yard line, he had tossed a soft pass to end Jim Mutscheller. Mutscheller was shoved out of bounds on the New York two-yard line.

"What if you had been intercepted?" Unitas was asked after the game. "I don't call pass plays expecting to be intercepted," he replied. "I never call any play I expect to fail."

Unitas had the Colts back in the championship game the very next season, and this time they buried the Giants, 31–16. The Colts went downhill after that, but began winning again in 1963. They captured the Western Conference championship in 1964, only to be upset by the Browns in the title match.

Unitas accepted defeat stoically. Injuries, too. These included broken ribs, torn knee cartilage, a punctured lung, and ripped ligaments in his throwing arm.

The last-named kept him on the sidelines during most of what was perhaps the gloomiest day of his career—the day the Jets upset the Colts, 16–7, in Super Bowl III. When it was over, a sports writer asked Unitas, "How good is Joe Namath?"

"Sixteen to seven," replied Unitas. "That's how good."

Unitas played his last game as a Colt on December 3, 1972. A dismal season with the San Diego Chargers followed. After that, he quit.

Writer Mickey Herskowitz once asked Unitas how he felt about retiring. "With me it has always been point blank—yes or no, can you or can't you," said Unitas. "I just couldn't play anymore. It was time to quit and get out. I was taking up someone else's time."

321

Unitas owns and operates a restaurant in Baltimore called The Golden Arm, another in central Florida, and has real estate interests in central Florida. He joined CBS Television as a sports broadcaster in 1974. His comments on pro football were unusual, unusual for the medium, that is, in that they were always characterized by honesty and candor. No one ever got any sham from Johnny Unitas.

Van Brocklin, Norm

Most Valuable Player, 1960; Hall of Fame, 1971.

In his 12-year career as a pro quarterback, nine with the Los Angeles Rams, three with the Philadelphia Eagles, volatile Norm Van Brocklin, the Flying Dutchman, built an impressive record, and when he was named to membership in the Hall of Fame in 1971 no one was surprised. He also had a 12-year career as a coach, but his record in that regard is not quite so glittering.

The problem may have been the very high standards that he applied to himself, both as a player and as a coach. Van Brocklin could not stand to lose.

In 1960, when Van Brocklin quarterbacked the Eagles to the Eastern Conference title, the team fought back to win eight games in the last quarter. He then steered the team, rated no better than mediocre by most observers, to a playoff win over the Green Bay Packers.

Van Brocklin led the NFL in passing three times—in 1950, 1952, and 1954. He was twice the league's leading punter. He played on two world-championship teams, three conference winners, one conference co-champion, and in nine Pro Bowl games.

Van Brocklin

One of Van Brocklin's most notable accomplishments as a player came in 1951. One September afternoon against the New York Yankees at the Polo Grounds, he threw passes that totaled a record 554 yards. That same year he helped to guide the Rams to the NFL championship, flinging a 73-yard touchdown pass to Tom Fears in the final quarter to produce the victory.

From the time of his All-America days at the University of Oregon, Van Brocklin's style was to get into the pocket and stay there no matter what. His comment, "I only run out of sheer terror," became a classic.

When Van Brocklin embarked on a coaching career in 1961, taking over the Minnesota Vikings in their first year of operation, this credo made for conflict, for the team's quarterback happened to be rambling, scrambling Fran Tarkenton. The friction that developed between the two eventually caused Tarkenton to quit. Shortly after, Van Brocklin announced his own resignation. Had the Vikings been winners, undoubtedly the relationship between the two men would have been an amiable one.

Two years later, during the 1968 season, Van Brocklin was named coach of the Atlanta Falcons, and he quickly made the young team competitive. The Falcons narrowly missed the playoffs in 1973 and were picked as a playoff contender the next year.

But it never happened. Weakened by trades that were said to have been made out of Van Brocklin's vindictiveness (he traded away the team's player representative on the first day of the players' strike), the Falcons lost one game after another. Van Brocklin was dismissed before the season ended.

The year had to be one of the most frustrating of his career. At a routine news conference following one of the Falcons' worst defeats, a writer asked Van Brocklin whether he was still a fighter, as he insisted that he always had been.

Van Brocklin answered by challenging the writer to a fight, and then he extended the invitation to the other writers, photographers, and broadcasters who happened to be in attendance. You'd have to say he made his point.

Van Buren, Steve

Hall of Fame, 1965.

As part of the build-up surrounding the team's silver-anniversary celebration in 1957, the Philadelphia Eagles selected the "greatest player" in the team's history. It was an easy choice to make—Steve Van Buren.

During the years that Van Buren was at his peak as a running back, the Eagles were pro football's most powerful team. Van Buren led the league in rushing yardage for three consecutive seasons beginning in 1947 (the first player to do so), and the Eagles won the division championship each of those three years and captured the NFL title twice. Before the dawn of the Van Buren era, Philadelphia had never won anything.

Tall, slim, and well-muscled, Van Buren was one of the first running backs to combine power and speed. At Louisiana State University, he not only ran with the ball, but passed, punted, and placekicked. When Van Buren became an Eagle in 1944, coach Earle (Greasy) Neale decided to make a specialist out of him. Van Buren responded by leading the league in rushing during his rookie year.

Van Buren

Van Buren was always popular among his teammates and a favorite of the fans. In 1948, the Eagles played the Chicago Cardinals for the NFL championship. On the day of the game, one of the worst blizzards in Philadelphia history struck the city. Snow covered the field and drifted to mountainous heights along the sidelines. Neither team could generate a sustained attack.

Late in the third quarter, the game scoreless, the Eagles recovered a Cardinal fumble on the Chicago 17-yard line. Not long after, the quarter ended and the teams changed sides. Fullback Joe Muha tore through the middle of the line for three yards. Quarterback Tommy Thompson carried the ball to the Cards' five-yard line on a keeper. Then the fans began to chant, "Steve! Steve! Give it to Steve."

That's exactly what Thompson did. Van Buren bulled his way into the end zone for the game's only score.

Steve ended up the day with a total of 98 yards rushing. The Chicago *team* totaled only 96 yards.

In the championship game the next year, Van

325

Buren was just as sensational. He carried the ball 31 times, gaining a record 196 yards. No one has ever come close to equalling the figure.

Van Buren's career was cut short by an injury to his knee in which he sustained torn ligaments. They placed his leg in a cast. When it was removed, the knee had calcified and he could hardly bend his leg. It took months of treatment before he could use the leg again.

Jim Brown later eclipsed most of the records set by Van Buren. That hasn't made any difference to fans of the Eagles. In Philadelphia, Van Buren is still No. 1.

vig

In football betting, the difference between what you receive when you win and what you pay when you lose. For example, when you bet $100 and win, you receive $100. But if you lose, you pay $110. That $10 is the bookie's profit. It represents odds of 10 to 11, not an easy percentage to beat. It means that you have to chose right 55 percent of the time merely to keep even.

Or look at it like this: No matter which team wins, the bookie keeps $1 of each $22 bet. His commission, then, is 4.5 percent.

Bookies look upon themselves as businessmen, not gamblers, and because they do they do not expect their profits to be incidental or haphazard. They seek a guaranteed income. What bookies try to do is keep the action balanced, always taking the vig, which is short for "vigorish."

When imbalances occur, as they do inevitably, the bookie does the same thing any overstocked merchant does. He lowers the price or, more particularly, he adjusts the spread, making the less-bet team a more attractive "buy." The adjustment is slight, perhaps half a point.

Another way to keep the books in balance is to "lay off," to contact another bookmaker, one who has a greater volume of betting on the other side, and get him to take his coverage. But laying off is no easy matter. "The idea that all a bookmaker has to do is make a phone call to get things balanced out is a complete myth," says Ralph Salerno, a former member of the Central Intelligence Bureau of the New York City Police Department and later a consultant to the City's Off-Track Betting Corporation. "In any number of cases, I spoke with the arresting officers after a gambling raid, and I've asked them whether the books were in balance and the answer has always been 'No.' Bookmakers *attempt* to lay off, but their success in doing so is not nearly as high as generally believed."

When a bookmaker finds that it is impossible to lay off, he can make one of two choices: He can stop taking bets, in which case he risks alienating some of his customers, or he can gamble. Most choose the latter course.

Bookies *do* gamble. But their risks are small and short term. The bookie realizes that he risks ten of his dollars to win eleven of his customer's, a 12.1 percent advantage, sufficient to make him a winner over the long haul.

Vince Lombardi Trophy

The winning team in the Super Bowl receives this award, a sterling silver trophy in the form of a football mounted on a three-sided base. The Vince Lombardi Trophy was first presented following Super Bowl V, and, with the exception of the inscription, was the same as trophies awarded following the first four Super Bowl games.

Vince Lombardi Trophy

327

waivers

Dropping a player from a team, relinquishing all claim to him, is done by placing the man on waivers. He then may be claimed by another team. If no team claims him, the team that owns the player can, if it wants to, place him on its taxi squad.

When a claim is made, however, the team can withdraw the player's name from the waiver list. Usually some type of bargaining follows the entering of a claim. The team that owns the player may say, "If you're serious about this, we're going to withdraw his name." Or the team may suggest a trade. Or the team might say, "Let his name go through, and we'll give you a draft choice."

One of the great blunders involving waivers took place in 1962 when the San Diego Chargers put a young quarterback named Jack Kemp on injured waivers. Sid Gillman, the Charger coach at the time, figured no one would claim Kemp, and turned his attention to other things. But the Buffalo Bills did enter a claim and Gillman "forgot" to recall him. Kemp went on to lead the Bills to two AFL championships.

Besides the recallable waivers, there are also "injured waivers." An injured player is placed on this list so as to make available a place on the roster for a healthy player. Any other club is permitted to claim the injured player, but in so doing it assumes medical responsibility for his injury.

If no team claims him, he remains under contract to the waiving team and he continues to receive his salary and medical benefits. In the case of more than one claim, the player becomes the property of the team with the poorest won-lost record.

Wanda

With some teams, the term used to identify the weak-side linebacker.

Washington Redskins

NFL team, 1937 to present; won Eastern Division championship, 1937, 1940, 1942, 1943, 1945; won NFL championship, 1937, 1942; won Eastern Division championship (National Conference), 1972; won National Conference championship, 1972.

Waterfield, Bob

Hall of Fame, 1965.

"He's a specialist," said Jack Teele, an executive with the Los Angeles Rams. "But his specialty is everything." Of course, it was Bob Waterfield that Teele was describing. In an eight-year career with the Rams that began in 1945, Waterfield ranked as the best passer of the day, carried the ball whenever it was necessary, boomed punts 50 yards and more, and led the league in field goals three times.

Early in the season of 1948, the Rams faced the Eagles, a team that was to win the NFL title that year. Late in the third quarter, Philadelphia led, 28–0.

Suddenly Waterfield caught fire, passing for one touchdown, scoring a second himself. He threw for a third touchdown and set up a fourth with his passes. He also punted, intercepted a pass, recovered a fumble and booted four try-for-point attempts. The game ended in a tie, 28–28. "When the Eagles get back home," said a Philadelphia newsman, "they're never going to be able to explain what happened to them."

Waterfield was a star right from the beginning, leading the Rams to the NFL title as a rookie. When the season was over, owner Dan Reeves

Waterfield

quickly signed him to a three-year contract at $20,000 a year, making him one of the highest-paid players of the day.

In the years that followed, Waterfield helped to introduce a new word into football's lexicon—"bomb." Before Waterfield's time, teams often punted when faced with a third-down-and-long-yardage situation. Not Waterfield. He'd send his receivers sprinting downfield at full tilt, then drop back and uncork a long, long arching throw, leading the receiver with the ball, so that the man could catch it over his shoulder without breaking stride.

The Rams enjoyed many successful seasons in the years that Waterfield quarterbacked the team. They won the Western Division crown four times, and the NFL title twice. However, in his final years with the team, Waterfield often alternated with Norm Van Brocklin as the team's quarterback.

Waterfield tried coaching following his retirement as a player. After serving as an assistant coach for a while, he became head coach of the Rams in 1960. It was not a happy season. Poor trades had robbed the team of much of its talent and the Rams finished with a 1-12-1 record. That ended Waterfield's career as a coach. "He didn't resign," said Jim Murray of the Los Angeles *Times*. "He escaped."

weak side

The side of the ball on which the smaller number of offensive or defensive players line up. The left side is usually the weak side because the tight end lines up on the other side.

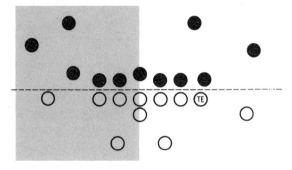

weak side

weak-side safety

The free safety; the safety who lines up on the side of the field away from the tight end. *See* safety.

wedge

On kickoffs, the four-man blocking unit that races upfield ahead of the return man. As the wedgemen watch the flight of the ball, they drop back to form a cone of protection for the return man. On a command of "Go!" from the wedge captain, they shoot upfield.

wedge-buster

On a kickoff, the member of the kicking team who is assigned to attack the wedge head-on while running full tilt. Once the wedge is destroyed, his teammates bring down the ball carrier.

WFL

See World Football League.

wide receiver

Any player who's assigned to catch passes must have speed and quickness. From football's earliest days, these have been basic requirements.

Nowadays it also takes the perception necessary to read the type of zone coverage being used against him, and the canniness to make the proper adjustment. For example, suppose a wide receiver cuts to the inside and a cornerback moves to cover him. Well, in certain types of zones, the receiver knows that the cornerback will stay with him for only a few strides, and that if he cuts this way or that he'll be in the open. He doesn't even have to put a "move" on the defender.

In the days of man-to-man coverage, a receiver was assigned a pass route in the huddle, and he stayed with it no matter what. Being a pass receiver is more creative today.

Up until fairly recent times, the wide receiver set to the left was known as the split end, while the wide receiver on the other side was termed the flanker or flanker back. There was never much difference between the two, however. With some teams, the split end was the bigger of the two, because he had more blocking to do than the flanker, the latter depending on the tight end to handle the linebacker on plays to the outside.

Also, since he lined up next to the tight end, the

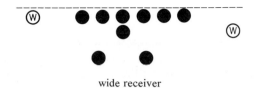

wide receiver

flanker was more likely to run a combination pattern. The split end was on his own. To a degree, these distinctions, however minute, have carried over to the present day.

It takes an enormous amount of concentration to be successful as a wide receiver. He has to be able to blot everything else out of his mind as he moves to make the catch. A distraction means a dropped football. When the prospective distraction is 6-foot-3, 230 pounds—as are most linebackers—you can understand why concentrating is no easy matter.

While some teams like to point out that their receivers are responsible for running scores of different patterns, the number can usually be reduced to only five or six. What varies is the distance of the route and the moves that accompany it.

Among the basic routes that receivers run are the sideline, which is self descriptive; the hook, in which the receiver stops, turns, and makes the catch; and the up or fly pattern, one in which the receiver breaks straight downfield.

There's also the corner pattern, wherein the receiver breaks downfield and slants to the outside, that is, toward the "corner" of the field. The post pattern is the reverse of this, the receiver breaking from the outside in the direction of the goalpost. Last, there's the square-in, the receiver cutting over the middle after a short downfield run.

wide side

In situations where the ball is placed on a hashmark, the wide side is the area between the ball and farthest sideline.

333

wild card

A term used in connection with the NFL's divisional playoff system, which involves the winners of each of the division titles (Eastern, Central, and Western) in each conference (American and National), plus the wild-card teams: the non-championship team in each conference with the best won-lost record.

Will

With some teams, the term used to identify the weak-side linebacker.

wingback

In the single-wing formation, any offensive back who lines up outside either of the end positions.

Winnie

With some teams, the term used to identify the weak-side linebacker.

wishbone

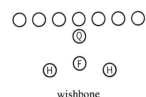

wishbone

A variation of the T formation in which the quarterback has several run-pitch-or-pass options on each play. It gets its name from the wishbone-shaped placing of the backs. The wishbone was used by many college teams during the early 1970s, but almost never in professional football.

The essence of the wishbone is the triple-option series. The quarterback can hand off to his halfback, pitch to the trailing fullback, or keep the ball himself (and either run with it or throw).

Pro football coaches were reluctant to use the wishbone because it requires the quarterback to be a runner. And to coaches, running implies injuries.

Wojciechowicz, Alex

Hall of Fame, 1968.

During his football days at Fordham College, Alex Wojciechowicz once consulted coach Jim Crowley about changing his name. He wanted to make it Wojack.

"Don't do that," said Crowley. "Keep your name the way it is. No one will ever forget you."

Crowley's advice may have been well meaning but, actually, it wouldn't have made any difference. Alex's accomplishments were such that people still remember him. He could have called himself anything he wanted to.

At Fordham, Wojciechowicz was one of the legendary Seven Blocks of Granite. A center, he had a guard named Vince Lombardi slotted on one side of him.

The No. 1 draft choice of the Detroit Lions in 1938, Wojciechowicz had the misfortune of playing on some of the worst teams in Lion history. In 1942, they failed to win a single game. In 1943 they improved, winning three.

Wojciechowicz

335

Wojciechowicz escaped from the Lions in 1946, landing with the Philadelphia Eagles. There he enjoyed far greater success.

Earle (Greasy) Neale, who was to coach the Eagles to NFL titles in 1947 and 1948, employed a 7–4 defense at the time, using a pair of linebackers to "chug" the ends, that is, impede their downfield progress at the line of scrimmage.

Wojciechowicz became a master chugger. He was once described as "a thousand elbows put together without a plan." Not only were his chugs creative, they had authority. Wojciechowicz, you see, weighed 240 pounds.

There may have been better centers than Wojciechowicz, and there may have been a few linebackers that were more skilled. But as a chugger, Wojciechowicz has had no equals.

World Bowl

The World Football League's championship game. In World Bowl I, played in December, 1974, the Birmingham Americans defeated the Florida Blazers, 22–21.

World Football League

World Football League

A professional football league that would involve the entire world. It sounded ambitious. But founder and Commissioner Gary Davidson was confident. "We will have problems," he said. "But it will work and I will make it work."

Davidson had to be listened to. After all, he was one of the founders of the American Basketball Association and World Hockey Association, and both were not unsuccessful operations.

Davidson announced the WFL to be in existence as of October 2, 1973, and then he quickly lined up 12 franchises. League competition was to begin in July, 1974. Exciting new rule changes were announced, among them:

A touchdown was to be worth seven points. The placekick for an extra point following a touchdown was to be eliminated. Instead, there was to be an "action point," that is, an attempt for an additional point by running or passing the ball over the goal line from the $2^{1}/_{2}$-yard line.

Following touchdowns, field goals, and at the start of each half, the ball was to be kicked off from the 30-yard line, thus ensuring more runbacks.

The goalposts were to be moved to the end line.

Pass receivers would be required to have only one foot in bounds for a completion.

Fair catches were not to be permitted on punts.

In the case of ties, there would be 15 minutes of additional playing time.

In the case of a missed field goal, the ball would be spotted at the line of scrimmage (except when the attempt was from inside the 20-yard line).

When many of the changes were adopted by the National Football League for the season of 1974, the WFL earned a good deal of stature. But what really got people enthusiastic was the league's ability to sign NFL stars. Late in March, 1974, when it was announced that Larry Csonka, Paul Warfield, and Jim Kiick of the champion Miami Dolphins were switching over to the WFL, it sent shock waves through the pro-football world. In quick succession other signings were announced: the Raiders' Ken Stabler by the Birmingham Americans, the Bengals' Bill Bergey by the Florida Blazers, and the Cowboys' Calvin Hill by the Honolulu Hawaiians. These and scores of other NFL stars were to begin playing WFL football in 1975.

The WFL held a college draft and signed a television contract that guaranteed a nationally tele-

337

vised "Game of the Week." Plans were announced for the league's championship game, to be called the World Bowl.

Training camps opened. Competition began. WFL GLEEFUL OVER OPENING CROWDS declared a headline in *The Sporting News*.

The glee lasted about a week. Tales of financial woe began to be heard, and by midseason the problems were of terrifying size.

For instance, before a night game in New York City between the New York Stars and Detroit Wheels, the Wheels announced they had filed for bankruptcy. At the game's conclusion, the Stars announced they were fleeing to Charlotte, North Carolina, where they became the Hornets. Not long after their arrival, sheriff's deputies confiscated a set of uniforms because of the team's failure to pay a laundry bill.

The Chicago Fire owner, Tom Origer, who reportedly lost $800,000, called off his team's final game, ending its chances to play in the World Bowl. Origer said the team wasn't good enough to compete in the playoffs.

In all but a handful of cases, teams ran behind in their payrolls. Some players went months without being paid. "We just want to get back in the NFL," said one player. "The money doesn't matter any more." Tax liens proliferated.

By the season's end, two clubs had folded, four had been taken over by the league. Gary Davidson had been ousted. Philadelphia, Memphis, and Honolulu were said to be the only solid franchises.

A survey by the Associated Press estimated the league's losses to be about $20 million for its first year of operation. If true, it would constitute the biggest financial failure in the history of American sports.

The league did manage to complete the season, with the Birmingham Americans defeating the Florida Blazers in the World Bowl. Quarterback George Mira of the Americans was named the game's Most Valuable Player.

Not long after the World Bowl, a WFL spokesman described the outlook of the owners as being one of ''cautious optimism.'' *Very* cautious.

WR

See wide receiver.

WS

See weak-side safety.

yardage

Distance gained or lost by the offensive team on a play from scrimmage.

yard line

Any of the lines marked at five-yard intervals across the field of play between the two goal lines.

zig-in

A pass route in which the receiver breaks straight downfield, slants over the middle, cuts back to the outside and, last, veers straight across the field, again over the middle; also called a Z-in.

zig-out

A pass pattern in which the receiver breaks straight downfield, slants to the outside, cuts back inside, then, in his final break, darts toward the sideline; also called a Z-out.

zig in

zone

An area of coverage assigned to a linebacker or member of the defensive secondary.

zig out

zone defense

A type of pass defense in which each of the three linebackers and four deep backs is assigned to cover a specific area of the field. Zone defense contrasts with man-to-man defense in which each one of the defensive players covers a particular receiver.

Teams use many different methods for covering the zones. *See* rotating zone, double-double, prevent zone.